THE MADNESS ESTABLISHMENT

Also Available:

RALPH NADER CONGRESS PROJECT

THE MADNESS ESTABLISHMENT

Ralph Nader's Study Group Report on
the National Institute of Mental Health

Franklin D. Chu and
Sharland Trotter

Grossman Publishers   New York   1974

All royalties from the sale of this book will be given to The Center for
Study of Responsive Law, the organization established by Ralph Nader
to conduct research into abuses of the public interest by business and
governmental groups. Contributions to further this work are tax deduct-
ible and may be sent to the Center at P.O.B. 19367, Washington, D.C.
20036.

Task Force

Franklin D. Chu, *Project Director and Co-author*
   Harvard College, A.B. 1971, student at the Yale Law
   School
Sharland Trotter, *Co-author*
   Goucher College, B.A. 1965,
   Associate Editor, APA *Monitor*,
   American Psychological Association
Gottlieb Simon, Ph.D., *Consultant*
   Assistant Administrative Officer for Professional Affairs,
   American Psychological Association
Sidney M. Wolfe, M.D., *Consultant*
   Director, the Health Research Group, Washington, D.C.

"*By the very nature of what we do, no 'Nader's Raider' type is ever likely to challenge our performance—the customer has only the seller—therapist, teacher, consultant—to look to for the promise of the excellence of the product. The possibility is always there that this may work to the detriment of the customer.*"
—*Charles Cleeland, Ph.D.*
President's Message to the
Wisconsin Psychological Association
October, 1971

INTRODUCTION BY RALPH NADER

It was not easy to assemble and analyze information about the federal government's decade-long program of community mental health centers, as this volume has done. For one thing, the very definition of the consumer class that was supposed to benefit from these services was ambiguous, broad, and the subject of controversy among professionals, policy-makers, administrators, and the public. For another, the idea of a consumer evaluation of the program was considered a novel affront—a lay intrusion into the world of specialists and experts. Difficult as it was to elicit public candor from people involved with community mental health centers in Washington and throughout the nation, Franklin Chu and Sharland Trotter persevered to piece together a thoughtfully pertinent study of this highly touted but failing social innovation.

A principal reason for the deficiencies of this program is the absence of consumer information and participation at all levels of decision-making. Since by definition the consumer of mental health care is considered "mentally ill," it is not surprising that the citizen-participation provision of the federal law has been readily avoided. The community mental health centers became the domain of the psychiatrists, who brought to their newest realm their business acumen, upper-middle-class bias, and professional hubris to burden this massive federal subsidy. They also brought confusion about their role and the kinds of people they are equipped to help.

Professor of psychiatry Willard Gaylin, in discussing ideas of mental illness over the years, has stated:

> From [the] original point of departure at the turn of the century, definitions of mental illness have expanded to include progressively milder disorders; in that process, inevitably, the number of people that can be termed "mentally ill" has increased. Confusion was bound to follow.

> For example, if unusual behavior can indicate mental illness, then so too can the absence of normal behavior, and one of the early additions to the list of mental malfunctions was the concept of nonfunctioning or inhibitions. But this development implied a standard of normality in the field of mental activity and emotions, indeed, in the field of behavior. It suggested that there are things that a person ought to feel or do, and that if he can't, it is the job of the therapist to help him develop the capacity. But the whole idea of normality is subject to serious question in the area of mental health. It is one thing to establish 98.6 degrees Fahrenheit as a normal body temperature; it is quite another to establish a "normal" standard of integrated behavior; biases are automatically introduced and objective standards seem particularly corruptible by personal values. . . .

> The unfortunate result of all this is that psychiatry itself is not at a stage where it is capable of defining mental illness.

Though there is confusion over the definition of mental illness, there is no doubt that the "jurisdiction" of psychiatrists has been broadened—by psychiatrists themselves, by medicine in general, and finally by government. In a more authoritarian society, this trend could have spelled serious trouble for all people who deviated from established or imposed norms in their personal behavior, values, or causes espoused. In this country, it has spelled waste, lost opportunity, and discrimination against those citizens who wished to be helped.

The community mental health centers have been neither accountable backward to the National Institute of Mental Health, which established them, nor forward to the consumers and citizens in the community they allegedly serve. They have often become regular windfalls for psychiatrists who have systematically ignored the program's directives to serve the poor and the program's purposes in reaching blue-collar workers. The indiscriminate overlap of patients with objective mental diseases (such as brain damage) and citizens who have been exposed to socioeconomic stresses (such as inhuman working conditions, racial discrimination, sexism, domestic pressures, and traumatic but nonrecurring experiences, as in a disfiguring or disabling auto crash) has distorted priorities and stretched psychiatry beyond the effective limits of its present competence.

It should be clear by now that the gap between life stresses and life skills is increasing for millions of people. Restoration of what is called mental health requires a restoration of relatedness between individuals and various supportive units (family, neighborhood, union, church, courts, voluntary groups, etc.) and a restoration of personal self-confidence. If community mental health centers are to play any role here, it is an initiatory one, as intelligent and compassionate catalysts for other social forces to interact successfully with individual self-rehabilitative attributes. For the consumer of mental health services, false application of the medical model and institutional introversion can be worse than mere neglect, because the stigma and isolation that accompany treatment may undermine any of its beneficial effects.

One of the declared goals of the community mental health centers program—beyond reaching more people in need at the community level—was to reduce the number of admissions to state mental hospitals. For years, investigative reporters and other writers have depicted the horrible conditions in these "human warehouses." For years, the public was temporarily shocked—before it looked the other way. With few exceptions, the community mental health centers program has not been traceably responsible for reducing the number of these hapless inmates. This grievous failure reflects in turn the failure to involve the concerned portions of the community and generate citizen participation and accountability. For to appreciate what the community mental health centers could have done would have been to recognize what has to be done about the state mental institutions.

Contemporary psychiatry and its government-university infrastructure has more than an economic class bias in its offer of services. Its most fundamental theoretical and practical prejudice and insensitivity relate to the pathology of institutional structures. The literature on this subject is as slim as is the funding for research therein. What about the institutional pathologies of corporations whose products seriously abuse consumers; factories and mines that subject workers to intolerable working conditions and hazards; unions that ignore rank-and-file grievances; government agencies that do not serve their citizens in need; police, merchants, and landlords who rule the slums with the heaviest of hands; courts that distribute injustice to defenseless people; liquor and drug industries that make consumers into addicts; juvenile detention homes; and, not the least, state mental institutions? Why is there such a paucity of literature on institutional insanity and its victims?

The answers to these questions are many. One of them is that psychiatry has not chosen to diagnose institutions that can both resist observation or access and retaliate to the detriment of psychiatry's funding and status. Moreover, like so many other professions, psychiatry waits for clients to come to it, and institutions rarely desire such examination for themselves. For General Motors to admit that it is mentally ill due to its obdurate posture against safer and less-polluting vehicles would be too excessive a boon to psychiatry's potential and broader institutional concerns. But this is clearly the direction in which psychiatry must move if it is not to be empirically starved of critical factors that condition the mental health of human beings in a highly organized society. For example, if an institution can be said to be "mentally ill" or "sociopathic," what is the effect of that illness upon its customers and employees? The problems of workers on automobile assembly lines, discussed in these pages, reveal that institutional insanity can have disastrous impact on individuals. These effects clearly merit attention by psychiatrists and especially by community mental health centers.

Such an expanded focus should also nourish a healthier utility to psychiatric theory and a mutually enriching exchange between psychiatry and social-science disciplines. When distinctions between disciplines become less analytically useful, the boundless search for the ways to improve the workings of programs designed to help people will be freer of the trappings of past doctrines and dogmas and present totems and tabus.

Ralph Nader
Washington, D.C.
April, 1973

PREFACE

The idea that Ralph Nader should investigate the National Institute of Mental Health (NIMH) and its community mental health centers program grew out of a consumer conference sponsored by the Citizen Participation Branch of NIMH in the fall of 1969. Attending this conference were some mental health professionals and a few academics, a number of NIMH officials, a group of welfare mothers, other groups representing blacks, chicanos, and Puerto Ricans, and a representative from Ralph Nader's office. The conference, as might have been expected, was heated. There were accusations from some of the consumer groups that mental health services and facilities were not only discriminatory, but also inadequate, ineffective, and irrelevant; there were some passionate disclaimers and some equally passionate *mea culpas* heard from the professionals present. The upshot was a recommendation from the steering committee appointed by those in attendance that some outside group study NIMH and the responsiveness of its programs to the public. After exploring various possibilities, the steering committee recommended that the Center for Study of Responsive Law undertake the project, which NIMH graciously offered to fund.

At this early point, the Center for Study of Responsive Law was only mildly interested in NIMH and problems of mental health. Although we did not have much experience in the field, we did tentatively agree to take on a project. As the proposal of its own steering committee to fund a Nader study group worked its way up the NIMH organization, however, it made somebody nervous. Subsequently, the proposal was quashed. Whereupon the Center grew decidedly more interested: NIMH's response suggested that the Institute probably had something to hide, and any agency that had something to hide might very well be worth investigating. A ten-thousand-dollar grant was obtained independently by the Center from the New World Foundation, and the study began in the summer of 1970.

During the course of the project, NIMH officials were for the most part extremely cooperative and courteous in responding to our requests for interviews and information. Though their interpretations of the Freedom of Information Act denied several important sources of documentation to us, they always acted in good faith and as dedicated public servants.

We released a preliminary version of this report in July, 1972, to elicit the reactions and criticisms of experienced people in the field. Their responses have been very useful in reformulating certain sections of the report. But their responses also indicated a misunderstanding of the purpose of our report and our role as advocates for the public interest.

One of the objectives of the Center for Study of Responsive Law is to open up the administrative and regulatory policy-making process to all legitimate interests that are affected. Thus, many of our reports call for public hearings, written rationales for agency decisions, the right to appeal decisions, increased citizen participation, and making hitherto-confidential documents public information. All of this attempts to establish greater procedural democracy, to create new opportunities for wider public participation in the spirit of legitimate confrontation and challenge. And in this confrontation we are concerned not so much with the numbers of people involved as with the diversity of interests represented and the kinds of issues raised.

Therein lies our second objective, which is to ask fundamental questions that will require agencies, corporations, and professional groups to bare before public scrutiny their policies, their ideology, and the data base on which their decisions are made. Throughout our report, for example, appear such questions as "What can psychiatrists do that no one else can do?" and "How do they know that what they do does anyone any good?" Admittedly, these questions are enormously difficult to answer, but they do raise issues that have been too long ignored by psychiatry. Furthermore, the very lack of response we have received to these questions indicates that many psychiatric claims to "expertise" are based on *imputed* knowledge and *assumed* effectiveness rather than on factual evidence.

The way we proceeded to research and write our report follows from our evaluative role. Our report is *not* a scientifically controlled study. Its methodology is more akin to that of investigative journalism, with the aim of presenting and analyzing certain facts, theories, and policies for public scrutiny. Our approach was essentially to utilize the knowledge available to all educated people in analyzing available data on community mental health centers.

A number of people have asked us what criteria we used to judge NIMH and the community mental health centers program. We used NIMH's criteria. We studied the legislative history of the program and the NIMH regulations, read volumes of congressional testimony, and decided that if community mental health centers lived up to the rhetoric, they would be doing a very good job indeed. Only later, when the facts indicated that there was a significant gap between the rhetoric and the reality, did we go back to examine the underlying assumptions and internal contradictions of the Community Mental Health Centers Act and the federal regulations designed to implement it. And in turn this led us to question the appropriateness of psychiatric treatment for the estimated millions of "mentally ill" and concepts such as the medical model and prevention.

Our preliminary report has been criticized by some for its

failure to include examples of "good" centers. We did try to find the "good" centers. Lacking extensive resources of time, manpower, and money, we asked numerous NIMH officials to give us the names of its most successfully operating centers, and we thoroughly studied the reports of the Joint Information Service based on "model centers." We included a case study of the South Central Community Mental Health Center in Atlanta after reading a rather glowing article about it in *Science* magazine. A closer look revealed that even the most highly touted centers have serious problems; and, to the extent that they are "good," centers are forced to ignore at least some of the federal guidelines. In fact, the most innovative and responsive community programs we learned about during the course of our research had studiously avoided taking federal money. The fundamental point is that our report is primarily concerned with analyzing the *structure* of the federal program. We did not arbitrarily choose a handful of community mental health centers to study and then draw sweeping conclusions from them. The seven centers described in Part II are not meant to be representative of all currently operating centers in the nation; they do, however, highlight some of the critical problems of the centers program on the local level and exemplify various power configurations which counteract meaningful community involvement and inhibit local accountability. In each of the seven centers here discussed, control has remained solidly with the providers of services, and the degree to which consumers or potential consumers are allowed to participate in policy or program decisions is determined by professionals—in conjunction with, in one case, a city government, in another a prominent medical school, in another a state hospital, and so on.

The point of the case studies is not how poorly or how well these centers are implementing NIMH guidelines and regulations. The point is that in the present system of nonaccountability, it doesn't matter: most have continued to receive federal funds regardless of their effectiveness or ineffectiveness.

Our critique of the mental health professions in the following pages should not be construed as a blanket condemnation of psychiatry. We are, however, concerned about the increasing vulnerability of American psychiatry to political and institutional manipulation, and its propensity for extending itself into ever-widening spheres of interest. Lest our words regarding the inappropriate use of the "disease" or "medical" model for the vast majority of individuals suffering from "mental illness" be considered merely gratuitous criticism, it should be remembered that Freud himself was emphatically outside the medical fraternity. The revolutionary movement begun by Freud has, in America, become increasingly conservative, its bureaucratic and hierarchical aspects at odds with the spirit that created it. Freud distrusted American psychiatry precisely because it was narrowly concerned with the medical applications of his ideas, and because it rejected his proposal to utilize "lay analysts." It should be noted that some of the most creative and distinguished individuals in the mental health field have not had medical training—Bruno Bettelheim, Erik Erikson, Anna Freud, Erich Fromm, Ernst Kris, Abraham Maslow, Rollo May, Theodor Reik, and Carl Rogers, among others.

The following pages do not contain any short-cut answers to the many and complex questions concerning public policy in mental health. We do, however, express *a point of view*, which growing numbers of mental health professionals share, that we must establish priorities to care for the most severely disabled in the light of our limited resources in mental health; that the providers of "mental health care" must be broadened to include a wide variety of paid staff and volunteers; that the great majority of those individuals labeled "mentally ill" are in no way sick; and that deception and delusion—whether of self, or of citizens by their government, or of "patients" by their "therapists"—are ultimately destructive. We feel that the expression of this consumer point of view is entirely legitimate.

And in this regard, the director of the National Institute of Mental Health concurs. In a speech delivered shortly after our first summer at NIMH, Dr. Bertram Brown told his audience:

> I would like to say that in the opinion of the NIMH staff, Nader's Raiders represent a positive social force, and their interviews relate to legitimate public issues which can be debated in the public interest. . . .

Rightly or wrongly, health professionals have the reputation of being touchy and tender, when consumers question our work. Because we, too, as citizens are consumers of the health services we provide, and we might just as well learn to be mentally healthy about consumer health.

Franklin D. Chu
Sharland Trotter
April, 1973

CONTENTS

xxiii

Part One
COUCH AND
COMMUNITY

1

*We must be aware of the dangers which lie in
our most generous wishes. Some paradox of
our nature leads us, when once we have made
our fellow men the objects of our enlightened
interest, to go on to make them the objects
of our pity, then of our wisdom—ultimately
of our coercion.*

—Lionel Trilling
The Liberal Imagination

The Bold, New Approach

The Community Mental Health Centers Act, passed by Congress in 1963, marked an unprecedented public commitment to provide comprehensive mental health services to all Americans without regard to race, creed, or ability to pay. Borrowing a phrase from President John F. Kennedy's February, 1963, address on mental health, the legislators proclaimed the program a "bold, new approach" to mental health care and placed it under the administrative authority of the National Institute of Mental Health (NIMH) within the Department of Health, Education, and Welfare (HEW).

Since that time a good deal of rhetoric has come to surround the program, some of it suggesting that community mental health centers will usher in the millennium for mental health services. Critical and sometimes cynical discussion of the program has not been lacking either. Some of the more cogent criticism is

3

leveled at the lack of adequate evaluation of the program's effectiveness. Another body of criticism has focused on the problems of implementation, particularly the social and political
realities that impede the establishment of a new set of treatment
institutions. The extreme right has tended to see community
mental health centers as another wasteful welfare program.
The far left has attacked the centers for attempting to mesmerize
citizens into an acceptance of their exploited situation. And
radicals from both left and right, along with civil libertarians,
share the fear that a centralized system of psychiatric institutions
may endanger individual rights and pave the way for pervasive
social control. Private practitioners see the program as a threat
to the fee-for-service system of medical (and psychiatric) care;
proponents of socialized medicine claim the centers are not
treating the poor. In a similar way, many doctors have criticized
the program for not tying in more directly with the regular
medical care system, while nonmedical professionals contend
it is too closely linked with general hospitals. An offbeat religious
group, the Church of Scientology, has attacked the centers program as part of its broader questioning of the general worth of
psychiatry.

Perhaps at the root of all these divergent views of the centers
program lies the inherent vagueness of what is meant by "mental health" in general and "community mental health" in particular. Unlike many medical diseases that have scientifically
verifiable etiologies and prescribed methods of treatment, most
of the "mental illnesses" have neither scientifically established
causes nor treatments of proven efficacy. One point of view with
a growing number of adherents is expressed by psychiatrist
Thomas Szasz, who contends that "mental illness" is a myth.[1]
Inevitably, the community mental health ideology, which draws
its ideas primarily from medicine, but also from public health,
behavioral science, sociology, and even strategies of social action and political lobbying, is open to a dizzying variety of
interpretations.

There is less confusion, however, when the community mental health centers program is viewed in the context of a broad
social program administered by a government agency. That is
the primary perspective adopted herein. Insofar as possible, we

have focused our discussion on the goals that NIMH specified for the centers program, its criteria for achievement, its program regulations, and its successes and failures as substantially evidenced by its own internal documentation. To a lesser extent, we have appraised community mental health centers in relation to psychiatry, the dominant profession in the mental health field.

There are now some four hundred community mental health centers, partially funded by the federal government and supposedly adhering to certain minimum standards of care, operating throughout the nation. Supporters of the program estimate that these centers treated as many as one million patients in 1972 in an unprecedented effort to bring decent, community-oriented mental health care to every citizen who needs or wants it. Viewed from a historical perspective, the community mental health centers program promised a dramatic reversal in public policy: instead of "protecting the community" by locking up the so-called mentally ill in distant institutions, the "ill" were to be protected and cared for in their own communities. More than this, it called for massive financial participation by the federal government in an area that had long been the domain of the states, for the purpose of making mental health services available to anyone who might need them—not merely to special target populations. "The federal mental health program," observes mental health historian Jeanne Brand, "develop[ed] not from a broad interest in the over-all problem, but through federal responsibility for several special activities which related to mental illness."[2]

Early federal involvement with problems of mental illness focused not on those people who were necessarily in greatest need of psychiatric care, but on those who were the most visibly troublesome and potentially disruptive of American society— aliens, drug addicts, and prison inmates. In 1904 Dr. Thomas W. Salmon, one of the pioneers of American psychiatry, began to direct mental examinations of immigrants at the Ellis Island Immigration Station.[3] From the work of Salmon and his successors came the development of intelligence and performance tests. In the late 1920s, as the American public clamored over the increasing crime rate attributed to drug addicts, Congress established two federal narcotic "farms" for the confinement and treatment of persons addicted to the use of habit-forming drugs —and for other purposes."[4] To administer the farms a Narcotics Division was created within the Public Health Service. A further congressional directive to provide psychiatric care for prisoners in federal penal and correctional institutions led the Public Health Service in 1930 to rename its Narcotics Division the Division of Mental Hygiene. It was this division that later became the National Institute of Mental Health.

Created by an act of Congress in 1946 and beginning operation in 1949, the existence of NIMH was justified in congressional hearings on the twin bases of the scandalous conditions in state mental hospitals, which Congress hoped NIMH could improve, and the astounding number of men—more than one million—rejected as mentally unfit for military duty during World War II. Nevertheless, the thrust of the 1946 National Mental Health Act was neither on improving treatment facilities nor on providing care. Flushed with the success of war-related research, which produced such measurable results as the atom bomb and radar, the federal government believed that research would also yield solutions to domestic problems, among them mental illness. Not surprisingly, the 1946 National Mental Health Act focused on:

> the improvement of the mental health of the people of the United States through the conducting of researches, investigations, experiments, and demonstrations relating to the cause, diagnosis, and treatment of psychiatric disorders; assisting and fostering such research activities by public and private agencies, and promoting the coordination of all such researches and activities and the useful application of their results.[5]

Consistent with the thrust of the Mental Health Act, Congress placed NIMH within the National Institutes of Health (NIH), the research arm of the Public Health Service. The new institute quickly embraced the program direction of its parent agency, whose faith rested with the researcher engaged in his individual pursuit of scientific truth, and the bulk of whose dollars, in the form of research and training grants, went to investigators in prestigious universities and medical schools. Until the second half of the 1960s, NIMH flourished in the garden of biomedical research. Aided by the tremendous political popularity of improving health through research, by doting congressmen in positions of great influence, by advantages in legislation, and perhaps most of all by a highly efficient, well-funded health lobby, NIMH appropriations grew at a geometric rate. From a budget of $18 million in 1956, NIMH's appropriations soared to $315 million in 1967, an increase of almost 1800 percent!

Although NIMH soon became the largest and fastest-growing component institute in NIH, it was never completely content within the NIH fold. In part, its discontent reflected the independent leadership of Dr. Robert Felix, director of NIMH from 1949 to 1964, who was not always willing to follow the policy decisions set forth by the NIH director. But more than the conflict of personalities, NIMH's uneasiness within NIH reflected psychiatry's precarious position within the medical fraternity during the late forties and early fifties. Due to a number of factors (among them, the lack of a scientific basis of knowledge, the poor reputation of state hospitals, and the low social status of most mental patients) psychiatry had long been viewed as the "Cinderella" department of medical schools. In a similar way NIMH felt something like a second-class citizen within NIH. Perhaps fearful that psychiatry would receive short shrift within any medical agency and convinced that the rest of the medical community would not mightily promote a mental health institute, NIMH always seemed to try harder than the other institutes of health and incessantly strove to increase its own power within NIH, even after the prestige of psychiatric medicine became great.

The combination of continually increasing budgets and the vague mandate of improving "mental health" gained visibility for NIMH and aided the expansion of its professional domain. Two of the Institute's science advisers explain:

> The professional focus of NIMH . . . expanded from the comparatively narrow study of mental illness to the broader subject matter of mental health. The Institute began to support not only clinical psychologists but all psychologists and soon became the largest supporter, next to the Department of Defense, of behavioral science in the United States. Its area of concern broadened to include basic biological research, sociology,

psychology, and even urban studies—all, of course, related in some way to a mental health context.[6]

By the early sixties, NIMH had come to support programs in crime and violence, suicide prevention, child and family development, alcoholism, and drug abuse. (For the last NIMH cultivates its own marijuana field.) Later on the Institute participated in the Ford Foundation's Mobilization for Youth Program, the President's Committee on Juvenile Delinquency, and the Surgeon General's study of television violence. The expansion of NIMH's programs mirrored a growing trend in society to extend the definition of mental illness to include a kaleidoscope of disorders from organic and functional psychoses to neurotic disorders, alcoholism, drug addiction, school learning difficulties, juvenile delinquency, employment and marital problems, and even political dissent. By the late sixties some individuals, including a number of psychiatrists, began to see the entire nation as mentally ill and brought into vogue the epithet "the sick society."

The jewel of all these new programs and the most visible proof of NIMH's arrival in the heady world of big-money politics was the community mental health centers program, which made NIMH the only institute within NIH to control a nationwide network of service centers. NIMH's entrance into the service business, its quest for visibility, personal antagonism between top NIMH and NIH officials, and active lobbying by the American Psychiatric Association, among other things, brought about its split from NIH in 1967, giving it independent agency status within HEW. A year later, in a reorganization of the Public Health Service, NIMH was placed within the Health Services and Mental Health Administration, the service arm of the PHS.

Community mental health centers, of course, represented much more than an opportunity for bureaucratic expansion on the part of NIMH officials. Except in its support of research, the federal government is a newcomer to mental health treatment—which has been the primary responsibility of state governments since the middle of the nineteenth century. Whereas colonial America made no formal arrangements for the mentally ill, finding it cheaper to let "lunatics" wander through the sparsely populated countryside, the increasingly urbanized and more structured society of the nineteenth century prompted strident public demands that such individuals be locked up. During this latter period, state legislatures created huge state mental hospitals, some with as many as fifteen thousand beds. Treatment and rehabilitation were the hopes of the reformers who helped to establish these institutions; incarceration of society's castoffs was the unacknowledged societal intent. Over the years lack of sufficient staff and funds, society's disdain for the mentally ill, political and economic dictates, and professional and bureaucratic self-interests eroded all efforts at treatment, and mere custodial care soon became the raison d'être of state mental hospitals.

Then, following World War II, researchers began to see the state hospital as a "total institution"[7] that isolated mental patients in distant warehouses, imposed arbitrary and rigid rules governing every aspect of hospital life (including dress, meals, and recreation), and encouraged a kind of social deterioration far beyond what might have been expected to result from the medical diagnosis that had led to hospitalization in the first place. Sociologist Erving Goffman puts it thus:

> In response to his stigmatization and to the sensed deprivation that occurs when he enters the hospital, the inmate frequently develops some alienation from civil society. . . . This alienation can develop regardless of the type of disorder for which the patient was committed, constituting a side effect of hospitalization that frequently has more significance for the patient and his personal circle than do his original difficulties.[8]

The community mental health movement was a response to this situation, emphasizing instead an early return of the patient to his community and the provision of alternatives to long-term hospitalization.

Community mental health centers must also be viewed in the context of liberal social programs of the 1960s—the hunger program, neighborhood health centers, Model Cities, and the Elementary and Secondary Education Act of 1965, to name but a few. All of these programs, the centers program included, were clumsily implemented and collided with hard political realities. Good intentions prompted the development of such programs, though their current disarray is painfully obvious. In an effort to explain what happened, Washington columnist Elizabeth Drew has singled out three major themes that repeat themselves in the histories of Great Society social programs. First, many of them were designed by or in cooperation with the very groups that provided the services—psychiatrists, nurses, college administrators, teachers—and a major impetus in perpetuating the programs was the interest of these groups in protecting their existing domains. Second, the planners of the programs oversimplified the problems to be solved and approached them with a kind of easy optimism; at the same time, few evaluative efforts were initiated to see if the programs were truly effective. Third, in the interest of ensuring that the money was spent for intended purposes, the power to make an infinite number of detailed decisions was vested in a remote bureaucracy in Washington.[9]

In assessing the successes and failures of community mental health centers, one must take measure of still other factors. Although no one knows for certain to what extent the centers have been effective in treating mental illness or promoting mental health, no doubt more of the mentally ill are being treated or at least given humane attention; in some communities centers do provide an alternative to state hospitals. The question, of course, is whether the gains have been worth the cost, though it seems to be a truism that any substantial government program will involve some waste and inefficiency.

The community mental health centers program is presently in danger. For one thing, as the following pages will show, the deficiencies of the program are now too glaring to be brushed aside, despite some successes. For another, the political climate in the country is clearly antagonistic to the tactic of "throwing dollars at problems" and to vague open-ended approaches that promise to provide all things to all people. Furthermore, NIMH is no longer an agency sustained by unquestioning congressional largesse and insulated from interests other than those of academics in universities and medical schools. The Nixon Administration is exercising stringent control over the NIMH budget and its funding priorities, and, in something of a historical *déjà vu,* favors efforts once more aimed at those "special" populations (drug addicts, alcoholics, and criminals) which it perceives as the most threatening to American society.

In its present budget presentation to Congress, the Administration recommended that legislation for the community mental health centers program (which expired July 1, 1973) not be renewed. The President's budget allows no more money to start new centers and provides no additional funds for existing centers once current grants run out. Although mental health lobbyists managed to salvage the community mental health centers program for a while by persuading Congress to extend the act for one year, it is impossible to foresee at this time what the long-term result will be. The outcome will furthermore be influenced by what coverage for mental illness is provided for under a national health insurance plan, some form of which seems destined shortly to be enacted into law. But whatever happens—whether the program is allowed to lapse into desuetude, extended without changes, or financed by national health insurance—the problems that community mental health centers were supposedly designed to rectify will largely remain. In this sense, the community mental health centers program has been a very expensive experiment in service delivery, and we might do well to learn from its successes and failures before another "bold, new approach" is envisioned.

2

Psychiatric Evangelism

The community mental health ideology, combining medical progressiveness with a touch of social responsibility, has been embraced by many mental health professionals. During the decade of the 1960s, it became both fashionable and highly profitable to attach the "community" label to various professional disciplines—fashionable because it seemed to answer the popular demand for "relevance," profitable because the federal government held out irresistible financial incentives to those who would solve such "community" problems as crime, poverty, and mental illness. The federal community mental health centers program was proclaimed as the "third psychiatric revolution" by its sponsoring agency, the National Institute of Mental Health.

Ironically, the aim of this third psychiatric revolution was to supplant what the "first psychiatric revolution" had wrought: the establishment of the state mental hospital system. The concentration-camp-like conditions in state mental institutions, the mainstay of mental health care in the United States since the mid-nineteenth century, have been described in grisly detail by a cavalcade of American writers for nearly seventy years; shortly after World War II their efforts erupted in a volley of publicity. Among the most respected of these writers is Albert Deutsch, who wrote a chilling account—called *Shame of the States*— of his visits to more than two dozen mental institutions during 1946 and 1947. He witnessed:

> scenes that rivaled the horrors of the Nazi concentration camps—hundreds of naked mental patients herded into huge, barn-like, filth-infested wards, in all degrees of deterioration, untended and untreated, stripped of every vestige of human decency, many in stages of semi-starvation.[1]

Community mental health centers were to replace what Deutsch and others branded as "snake pits," "human warehouses," and "houses of horror." This was an awesome task. By the mid-fifties, the resident patient population in state hospitals had reached a peak of 558,022—more than the population of Denver—with about two out of every five hospital beds in the entire country located in state and county mental hospitals. To sustain these institutions, states apportioned well over $600 million in 1955 alone. By 1963 this figure had climbed to over a billion dollars simply to cover maintenance costs.[2]

Yet the well-intentioned supporters of the community mental health centers program outlined even more ambitious goals. Born amid the optimism of the early sixties, the Community Mental Health Centers Act, passed in October, 1963, marked a public commitment to provide coverage not just for the hundreds of thousands of severely disabled, poor, black, aged, or unwanted individuals in state hospitals, but for the millions upon millions of people NIMH estimated to be suffering from some degree of emotional impairment. (In an appearance before Congress, NIMH director Bertram Brown estimated that forty million Americans may need "psychiatric care."[3])

The Community Mental Health Centers Act also underscored federal recognition of a long-cherished hope of preventing mental disorders. John F. Kennedy, himself one of the most fervent supporters of the act, stressed the notion of early detection and prevention. In the first presidential message ever devoted entirely to mental health, Kennedy asserted in February, 1963:

> We must seek out the causes of mental illness and of mental retardation and eradicate them. . . . For prevention is far more desirable for all concerned. It is far more economical and it is far more likely to be successful. Prevention will require both selected specific programs directed especially at known causes, and the general strengthening of our fundamental community, social welfare, and educational programs which can do much to eliminate or correct the harsh environmental conditions which often are associated with mental illness.[4]

Though pregnant with revolutionary implications for the United States, the combined ideas of community care and prevention on which the program was based were not entirely new. More than fifty years ago Adolf Meyer wrote: "Communities have to learn what they *produce* in the way of mental problems and waste of human opportunities, and with such knowledge they will rise from mere charity and mere mending, or hasty propaganda, to well-balanced, early care, prevention, and general gain of health." In 1931 Harry Stack Sullivan expressed a similar point of view:

> Either you believe that mental disorders are acts of God, predestined, inexorably fixed, arising from a constitutional or some other irremediable substratum, the victims of which are to be helped through an innocuous life to a more or less euthanasic exit . . . *or* you believe that mental disorder is largely preventable and somewhat remediable by control of psycho-sociological factors.[5]

The first major study to emphasize increased community treatment of the mentally ill was conducted by the World Health Organization (WHO) in 1955. Its report stressed the need for community information services and the development of community facilities—such as outpatient clinics, day hospitals, and halfway houses—that would reduce the need for admission to (and thus the number of patients in) mental hospitals. Following the WHO report, many American psychiatrists journeyed abroad to study the pioneering programs of community-based treatment being developed in England, France, Holland, and Canada.

Gradually a new mental health ideology developed around the concept of community care. In his study *Mental Health and Social Policy* David Mechanic, chairman of the Department of Sociology at the University of Wisconsin, summarizes the main tenets of this ideology:

> The community care ideology developed from the growing realization that the mental hospital as it existed did much to isolate the patient from his community, to retard his skills and, in general, to induce a level of disability above and beyond that resulting from the patient's condition. . . . The new emphasis is on outpatient care and short periods of hospitalization when necessary. Moreover, new alternatives were urged which fell somewhere between total separation characterized by the mental hospital in isolation from the community and outpatient care. If some form of institutional care is necessary, less radical alternatives than full-time hospitalization can be implemented—day hospitals, night hospitals, halfway houses, hostels, and so on. Moreover, an understanding of the importance of maintaining patients' skills and sense of activity led to added emphasis on vocational services, sheltered workshops, continuing employment while . . . in the hospital, and the like. Finally, great emphasis has been given to the idea that patients should be kept in their home surroundings and that the necessary services should be provided to them and their families so that they can cope with the problems that arise.[6]

Mechanic is quick to point out, however, that while the community care ideology may be coherent, it has been neither widely implemented nor proven effective and feasible for every community. He observes, "the operation of mental health programs has proceeded more on an ideological thrust than on any empirically supported ideas concerning the feasibility and the effectiveness of particular alternatives."[7]

By the mid-fifties, discontent with treatment programs for the mentally ill in the United States, particularly those in state hospitals, was widespread. Despite post-World War II advances in mental health research and innovations in treatment—especially the use of tranquilizing drugs—most states had neither the facilities nor the money to implement new ideas. This led a concerned Congress to establish, in 1955, the Joint Commission on

Mental Illness and Health to study the problems of mental illness in America and to make recommendations for a national mental health program.

The Joint Commission completed its work in 1960, and in 1961 published its report, *Action for Mental Health*, which was widely hailed as a landmark document. It urged an expanded program of services and long-term research by doubling mental health expenditures in five years, and tripling them in ten years. It attacked large state hospitals and proposed that these be converted into smaller, regional intensive-care centers of no more than a thousand beds. It argued for the development of community mental health centers, suggesting that one would be appropriate for every fifty thousand persons. It recommended emergency psychiatric services in the community for both chronically and acutely ill patients as a means of reducing the need for prolonged or repeated hospitalization. In addition, the report envisioned a broad range of rehabilitative services to be made available to the mentally ill both before and after hospitalization. The Joint Commission's central focus, however, was on the state hospital system; its final report was largely hospital-oriented, the bulk of its recommendations having to do with enlarging and improving state mental health programs. Comparatively little emphasis was placed on the development of programs aimed at the prevention of mental illness.

The Joint Commission proposed massive financial participation by the federal government in the care of mental patients who had been the major responsibility of the states. It outlined the principle of matching grants to facilitate federal involvement, and it also recommended "that the grants should be awarded according to *criteria of merit and incentive* to be formulated by an expert advisory committee appointed by the National Institute of Mental Health."[8] [Emphasis in original.] This last recommendation of the Joint Commission had potentially the most far-reaching policy implications, for it suggested that the federal government establish and maintain standards for the quality of care of the mentally ill. With the release of *Action for Mental Health* the stage was set for federal action. The executive branch grasped the initiative, and the Community Mental Health Centers Act began to take shape.

Legislative Background and the Politics of Passage

President Kennedy, upon receiving *Action for Mental Health*, appointed a cabinet-level task force headed by Anthony Cele- brezze, then Secretary of Health, Education, and Welfare, to study the numerous recommendations and make specific pro- posals for implementation of a national program. The Cele- brezze committee recruited its members from various agencies, including the Department of Labor, HEW, the Veterans Admin- istration, the Bureau of the Budget, and the Council of Economic Advisers. Serving as staff to the committee were officials of NIMH, headed by Dr. Robert Felix and Dr. Stanley Yolles, then director and deputy director, respectively.

Action for Mental Health, although its specific recommenda- tions were focused on the reform of the state hospital system and the treatment of mental *illness*, was largely an ideological document; as such, it was sufficiently ambiguous to allow vari- ous interest groups to read what they would into its 338 pages. Consequently, a vigorous political battle ensued in Washington between those psychiatrists and their supporters with a public health point of view, who stressed a far broader conception of mental *health*, and those psychiatrists and their supporters, within the more traditional medical approach, who felt that the state mental hospital system should be improved with federal support. The former group had more influence with President Kennedy, and constituted a majority on the Celebrezze com- mittee.

From its beginning, the Celebrezze committee favored a radi- cal break with the past and the creation of an alternative service system, for the most part independent of the mental hospital system. Disregarding those recommendations of the Joint Com- mission that suggested improving state hospitals, the committee pressed for the translation of the community care ideology into practice: a nationwide network of centers to be located close to patients' homes, eventually eliminating the need for state hos- pitals altogether.

The report of the Celebrezze committee, delivered to the President in December, 1962, greatly influenced the legislation passed by Congress. While the legislation was taking final draft form, top NIMH officials and other lobbyists for mental health rallied political allies and attempted to blunt the opposition. Strong support came from the White House, but Congress was by no means unanimously enthusiastic, and the American Medical Association, along with a number of state hospital directors, was outright antagonistic. The AMA feared that the program, which envisioned small intensive treatment centers in and near poverty areas requiring salaried professionals, would amount to socialized intervention in medicine. According to George Albee, former president of the American Psychological Association, "virtually every member of Congress had a call from his personal physician asking him not to vote for the community mental health centers act."[9]

Supporters of the program fared somewhat better with the newly established National Association of State Mental Health Program Directors. Dr. Stanley Yolles, NIMH director from 1964 to 1970, explains that "State hospital program directors thought community mental health centers would be located mostly in state hospitals. When they realized that they would not get the funds, they started screaming bloody murder."[10] A slightly different view is given by Mike Gorman, chairman of the National Committee Against Mental Illness and a long-time health lobbyist. He says the state hospital directors believed that community mental health centers were simply another fad. Many attempts had been made in the past to close down state hospitals; they thought they could ride out the community mental health movement, too.[11]

Both views are disputed by Harry Schnibbe, executive director of the National Association of State Mental Health Program Directors. Schnibbe contends emphatically that most of his association's members supported the community mental health centers program. "It's an extension of what we were doing," asserts Schnibbe, adding that similar "community programs" in mental health had already started in some states. While Schnibbe is correct that a few states had initiated community programs in the 1950s, the fact is that the great majority had not. And in the political jockeying that took place before the passage of the act, state mental health program directors vigorously tried to gain state control over federal funds to local centers.

As Schnibbe states, "the thing we got hung up on in the battle with Yolles was in direct federal [staffing grant] funding of centers, which bypassed the state capitals."[12]

However ambiguously the program was presented to opposition groups, the justification federal officials presented to Congress was explicit: the prime goal was to supplant the state hospital system. At the 1963 hearings before the House Committee on Interstate and Foreign Commerce, Boisfeuillet Jones, special assistant for health and medical affairs of the Department of Health, Education, and Welfare, testified:

> What is contemplated in the mental health program is an effort to transfer care of the mentally ill from custodial institutions operated almost exclusively by the state, to community facilities and services whereby those who have mental and emotional problems can be served in their communities in a way comparable to the services provided for those who are physically ill. . . . *This bill, then, is designed to provide a stimulus to the states to give special attention to the need for psychiatric facilities, to move the care of the mentally ill into the community and out of these large mental institutions.*[13] [Emphasis added.]

During the same hearings, Anthony Celebrezze testified:

> It is clear that huge custodial institutions are not suited for the treatment of mental illness. . . . Therefore, the national program for mental health is centered on a wholly new emphasis and approach—care and treatment of most mentally ill persons in their home communities.[14]

Implicit was the necessity for local involvement, both financial and otherwise. Additional goals were also proposed in the hearings. Foremost among them was the provision of services to underprivileged areas which had few, if any, services, and to underprivileged persons in any area. "Continuity of care" was to be provided through a "coordinated" system of "comprehensive services" to treat individuals from early diagnosis through treatment and back into the community.

But perhaps most important for the enactment of the legislation was the unqualified support of President Kennedy. Kennedy praised the "bold, new approach" outlined in the Celebrezze committee report that would "return the care of the mentally ill to the mainstream of American medicine."

Draft bills submitted to Congress provided federal matching funds for both the construction and staffing of community mental health centers. The Senate passed the bill without hesitation, but the House gave it more critical scrutiny. Major concern focused on the staffing provision, which was vigorously attacked by the AMA. Robert H. Connery and a team of investigators point out in *The Politics of Mental Health* that the House hearings revealed two conflicting views within the AMA on the matter. One view favored federal staffing funds *if* they were strictly limited in duration. The other view vehemently opposed any federal staffing assistance whatever. "Apparently," notes Connery, "opposition within the AMA to federal funds for initial staffing was founded on the twin bases of professional concern over the medical importance of the program's community emphasis and political concern over governmental centralization."[15]

The no-staffing faction won the first round; the House committee cut out the staffing provisions by a vote of fifteen to twelve, and the bill Congress finally passed sustained the committee's action. The 1963 legislation authorized $200 million in federal matching grants for construction over a four-year period. (Of this sum, only $180 million was actually appropriated by Congress.) The federal money was to cover from 45 to 75 percent of the construction costs of community mental health centers.

One member of the House committee later said:

A political decision . . . resulted in the AMA's opposition to this provision. This body [the House of Representatives] should not fail to note that the competent professionals, the experts on mental health within the AMA, recommended otherwise.

It is unfortunate that the majority of the Committee on Interstate and Foreign Commerce chose to follow the political views of the AMA leadership rather than the professional views of the AMA's own expert body in this field.[16]

(Indeed, not until 1965, shortly after Lyndon Johnson had won an overwhelming victory in the presidential election, did the political climate permit the act to be amended to include grants for staffing. These grants, to be matched by state and local funds, operated on a formula basis of declining federal support over a period of fifty-one months: federal funds could cover up to 75 percent of staffing costs for the first fifteen months, 60 percent for the first year thereafter; 45 percent for the second year thereafter; and 30 percent for the third year thereafter. By then, it was expected, the centers would have enough local support to operate without federal help.)

Even with House opposition in 1963, the commitment of the President and the zeal of mental health lobbyists was such that the community mental health centers program was adopted by Congress in an amazingly short period of time. In retrospect, it is perhaps unfortunate that Congress moved so quickly. Between the community mental health centers concept and its implementation looms the social reality of narrow institutional and professional interests and the economic reality of deeply embedded priorities that are not amenable to change. In their haste to win legislative approval and then to get the centers going, NIMH officials overlooked the program's inherent contradictions. Many now recognize that the centers were based on a set of unproven assumptions which augured ill for realization of the program's goals.

Building in Program Failure

Two prominent psychiatrists, Leonard J. Duhl and Robert L. Leopold, point out, "the community mental health centers established under this Act reflected the expansion of the mental health world's system-conception to include non-mental-illness concerns, but continued to rely upon psychiatry as the ruling discipline for the centers."[17] Psychiatric domination of the program meant that centers would inevitably regard the problems and needs of clients from the narrow perspective of a sickness requiring medical attention from medical personnel. Nowhere is this perspective more evident than in the program's outlook toward state hospitals. The framers of the centers program assumed that state mental hospitals were primarily treatment institutions; that the individuals residing in or sent to state hospitals suffered from "mental illness"; that mental health professionals and psychiatrists in particular were the most appropriate personnel to help these individuals; and that psychiatric intervention was truly effective in dealing with such problems. Without questioning these assumptions, which the following pages will show to be largely erroneous, the program's originators simply proceeded to design another system of psychiatric treatment institutions. They believed that constructing more buildings and hiring more mental health professionals was the appropriate and effective strategy for meeting the needs of state hospital inmates.

Another crucial assumption of the legislation was that federal grants would constitute "seed money" which would stimulate state and local agencies to assume ultimate financial support of the centers. Not only Congress but the White House, HEW, and NIMH concurred that long-range federal subsidies for operating the centers were neither necessary nor desirable. It appears that no one made a realistic appraisal of how state and local communities were to finance a program of this magnitude, or determined if they even wanted to finance it. If any NIMH official did recognize that long-term federal support would be needed to bail many centers out of insolvency, they concealed the fact, since it would have been politically unfeasible to suggest that the federal government foot the bill for the centers indefinitely.

The seed-money concept received its first jolt when Congress's bad timing made a shambles of the initial attempts at federal, state, and local planning coordination. While the legislation was still being debated in the late spring of 1963, Congress separately authorized $8.4 million to finance statewide mental health planning over a two-year period. States that fulfilled satisfactory requirements were given money to identify the mental health needs of their citizens, to determine the available resources, to establish priorities among different areas, and to recommend specific plans and programs. Less than four months later Congress passed the legislation providing construction funds—to become available in mid-1964—for community mental health centers. Thus, it became necessary for the states to attempt to develop specific plans for their centers at a time when they had barely begun comprehensive statewide planning efforts.

It has been suggested by Dr. Jon Bjornson in *New Physician* that, in view of the subsequent congressional action on mental health,

> the statewide planning provisions were mainly meant to initiate closer relations between interested parties because of their need for future cooperation. . . . This [community mental health center] legislation defined what the plans should say regardless of ("local") planning groups. Any possibility that innovative problem-solving ideas might result at the grass roots level was greatly diminished.[18]

In any case, the timing of the two pieces of legislation created mass confusion by requiring that the two planning efforts be carried out simultaneously. Because federal funds for the centers had to be parceled out within a year, that plan took on a kind of urgency which undermined efforts at coordinating health and welfare planning. In their hurry to obligate funds, NIMH officials often ignored local and state mental health planning as well. Moreover, the state planning requirement for epidemiological and demographic surveys, along with the urgency to develop construction plans, produced critical shortages of manpower for service delivery. Bjornson observes that with some 43,000 professional and lay people involved in statewide mental health planning, the time actually spent caring for patients was diminished.[19] Some states gave the planning tasks to their division of mental health. To meet the new paperwork demands, these states substantially increased the staff of their mental health bureaucracies, leading to a further decrease in care-giving hours.

The rush to fund centers also revealed a basic defect in the relationship between the legislative branch and federal agencies dependent upon it for appropriations. To return a portion of obligated funds to Congress because it could not spend them was politically unthinkable for NIMH, since such an act would have brought both the Institute and the need for community mental health centers into grave doubt. This would also, it was felt, have influenced Congress to appropriate smaller amounts in the future. NIMH was in a dilemma typical of government agencies: it was under pressure to launch a nationwide program as quickly as possible with no clear idea of how it should be implemented or how effective it would be. Instead of first setting up a few pilot projects and evaluating them intensively, NIMH rushed headlong into the business of establishing a national program.*

Institute officials also ignored the major problem—that few individuals on the state and local levels had any training or experience in the relatively new community mental health field. The program was, therefore, thrust into a leadership void. This is a problem that has not been resolved in subsequent years, for the Institute has fostered few new programs in community mental health in professional schools, nor has it set up many training programs for volunteers and citizens in local communities.

Dr. Saul Feldman, the highest ranking NIMH official in charge of the centers program,† told us in March, 1972, that even if he had the opportunity to do it over again, he would *not* choose to set up a few experimental centers, evaluate them, and then go ahead with the rest of the program. "I wasn't there at the beginning of the program," said Feldman, "but even if I had control then, I would not have chosen to set up a pilot program. Evaluation takes too long," he explained, "and besides I am not convinced that the results of even ten years of experimentation would have been very helpful. The decision was to go ahead and make changes along the way."[20] As the following pages will show, exceedingly few changes have been made along the way.

But the major reason Feldman gave for not setting up and evaluating a small group of experimental centers was "political expediency." He maintained that "the timing was the critical factor. . . . I would imagine that the forces were right in 1963 for the passage of the Act. If we had done experimentation and waited until now to start the program, I imagine that the present Administration would never have let us build community mental health centers."[21]

---

* This is not to say that pilot programs cannot be used as a "stalling tactic" to halt or prevent the implementation of a program. However, one must distinguish between a pilot program's potential for political manipulation (which can happen to any governmental action) and its value for providing hard information on which to base future decisions.
† Feldman's official title is associate director for community mental health services in the Division of Mental Health Service Programs.

So the building of centers was the important thing. The need to get them going while money was available naturally favored those areas with existing resources (hospitals, manpower, money) that could most expeditiously complete the complex application forms and meet the federal regulations for funding. Thus, ironically, the neediest areas as defined by the states were discriminated against from the program's inception. Moreover, no provisions were made to ensure that an applicant would be responsive to the entire community. The road was left open to financial or political opportunism by local professional power blocs, whose actions were to mirror what had already occurred on the national level.

Congressional preference for construction money over staffing money is not difficult to understand. Buildings provide tangible evidence to constituents that their congressman is doing something, while staffing and program money produce less visible results. Congressmen, and perhaps citizens, tend to suffer from an "edifice complex," which prompts us, whenever there is a problem, to build around it—hospitals, drug addiction centers, prisons—in the belief that buildings and bureaucracy will offer appropriate solutions. Thus, instead of concentrating on the development of social support systems and service networks, the preferred first step is to provide for structures. But mental health care does not need impressive-looking buildings; in particular it does not need the kinds of large, imposing buildings we normally think of as hospitals. Psychiatrists and other mental health workers need little of the technical paraphernalia and equipment required by medical doctors, and mental patients need a host of other things before new buildings. In Europe, as psychologist Martin Gittleman notes, construction of new facilities for mental health is de-emphasized. According to Gittleman, who has extensively studied mental health service delivery in western Europe, Europeans have generally found that old buildings in the community, remodeled to accommodate new services, are more effective, more economical, and more acceptable to the community.[22]

In light of the piddling overall federal expenditure for mental health, Congress's preference for bricks and mortar over service programs seems particularly unfortunate. In the first five years of the program's operation, well over half of all funds provided for community mental health centers went to construction. For the first six years, the total amount appropriated for construction and staffing grants was $477 million—less than the amount of money the New York State Department of Mental Hygiene spends in one year. In 1970 alone, the states spent over $3 billion for mental health and mental retardation programs.

Interpretation of the Dream: The Federal Regulations

To transform the sweeping concepts of the community mental health centers legislation into operational realities, authority was given to NIMH, through the Secretary of HEW, to write specific regulations and to administer the program. Taken in large part from the regulations pertaining to the Hill-Burton hospital construction program, the mental health centers regulations were first issued in May, 1964.

Perhaps the most striking aspect of the regulations is what they omit. They prescribe no plans, mechanisms, nor procedures to guide centers in determining their relationship to state hospitals; no methods to divert potential state hospital admissions to community mental health centers; and no procedures whereby patients released from state hospitals could be rehabilitated and assisted back into the community. Indeed, the regulations contain not a single reference to the goal of supplanting state hospitals! Devised by a small number of officials in Washington with little input from the local groups that were to operate the centers, the regulations embodied little of the rhetoric about a genuine alternative.

The regulations simply required a center to serve a geographic area (which NIMH has termed a "catchment area") with a population of no fewer than 75,000 and no more than 200,000 people. To qualify for federal funds it must provide "five essential services": inpatient services, outpatient services, partial hospitalization services (such as day care, night care, and weekend care), emergency services available twenty-four hours a day, and consultation and education services. These five services plus an additional five (diagnostic services, rehabilitative services, precare and aftercare services, training, and research and evaluation) define a "comprehensive community mental health center."

The distinction between "comprehensive" and "noncomprehensive" centers is an important one. No program meets the federal definition of "comprehensive" unless it provides all ten services, but only the first five are necessary to qualify for federal funds. Although many centers call themselves "comprehensive," very few actually provide all ten services.

In contrast to the strict regulations specifying essential services and catchment-area population limits are vaguer regulations requiring a community mental health center to provide "a reasonable volume of services to the indigent"; to assure "continuity of care for each patient"; to effect "maximum coordination" with other public and private agencies that concern themselves with mental health or human services; and to develop "adequate community involvement."* But it is precisely the vagueness of these regulations that opens them up to conflicting interpretations and has rendered them meaningless in center after center.

In mid-June, 1972, NIMH official Ralph Kennedy stated that there were 325 community mental health centers then operating nationwide. Only a few months before, Bertram Brown had told Congress that there would be 389 fully operational centers (out of a total of 529 funded) by the end of June.† "The goal of, say, 1,500 to 1,600 centers (by 1980)," continued Brown, "which would be the amount that you would need to have to provide services to the whole country is realistic based on our

* The original regulations included no provision for community involvement. A provision requiring some "assurance" that citizens were to participate in the planning of programs and formulation of policy was added in February, 1972, nine years after the original legislation was passed.
† We include two estimates of fully operating centers because there is considerable discrepancy among different sources within and outside NIMH even about the numbers of community mental health centers. It should be noted that Ralph Kennedy gave his estimate of 325 operating centers on June 12, which is only eighteen days before the end of fiscal year 1972, a date by which NIMH director Bertram Brown promised Congress there would be 389 fully operating centers. Furthermore, according to Mike Gorman, chairman of the National Committee Against Mental Illness, as of late June, 1972, there were 265 operating centers. Asked to explain the discrepancy between his figures and those of NIMH, Gorman told us, "my figures are hard, NIMH double counts all over the place. . . . The Institute relies on fiction." Over the entire two-year period we have been studying community mental health centers, not once did different Institute officials agree on their estimates of the number of operating or funded centers.

experience of the past eight years."[23] Numbers alone, however, are poor indicators of success. This is particularly true of the centers program, whose broad social goals do not readily lend themselves to simple measurement.

Moreover, formidable obstacles stand in the path of the program's far-reaching goals. Given a need for cooperation among different levels of government, professional groups, and related community services, the political problems alone are labyrinthine. Enormous complexities arise as centers attempt to deal with conflicting demands from community groups, levels of government, and agencies—universities, hospitals, clinics, county or city health departments—through which local programs are administered.

There remain unresolved issues regarding the distinction between legal applicants for federal grants and the providers of service; the definition of community and who represents it; the nature and scope of citizen involvement; the use of paraprofessional workers; the impact of interagency relations on the functioning of a center; and the crucial question of who is accountable to whom and for what. These issues are intensified by the necessity for multiple-source funding required by the federal program and by the politics of intergovernmental relations. It is these difficult issues, however, that must be open to wide public debate, or some day the NIMH goal "of, say, 1,500 or 1,600 centers" may have been reached without necessarily contributing much to the nation's mental health.

3

Supplanting State Hospitals: The Numbers Game

In 1969, three years after the first centers started operation, then-NIMH director Stanley Yolles told Congress:

> This program has really gone across with the people of the United States and its results are impressive. . . . Largely because of the impetus of community mental health centers we have seen a startling reduction of patients in mental hospitals in the United States. We are predicting now that instead of having reduced the population of mental hospitals as, in the 10-year period 1963 to 1973, by one-half, we will reduce it by two-thirds because of the services thus provided.[1]

In subsequent congressional testimony, press releases, speeches of its top officials, and almost every public announcement about its centers program, NIMH has claimed that community mental health centers are largely responsible for the reduction in the resident patient population of state hospitals. In his March, 1972, congressional appearance, current NIMH director Bertram Brown iterated: "We had 557,000 in mental hospitals in 1957. We are down to 308,000 in 1971. That is the kind of progress that you can see [regarding the centers]."[2]

The extent to which community mental health centers are responsible for reducing the state hospital resident population is important, because NIMH's claim that this is true has been a major justification for the continued funding of the centers program in its present form. An October, 1970, memo of the National Association of State Mental Health Program Directors contends that the centers program has not reduced hospital population. Entitled "Who's Confusing Congress?" and written by the association's executive director, the memo observes, "It is a very curious circumstance that in both House and Senate Appropriations committees we constantly run into the kind of 'non sequitur argument' [that centers are responsible for reducing the state hospital resident population]." The memo continues:

> Someone in H.E.W. is deliberately confusing the Congress and I think it is time that we had a confrontation with H.E.W. officials to *stop it*.
>   (OR . . . it may very well be that H.E.W. *itself* is "confused" and needs an *education* session!)[3] [Emphasis in original.]

The fact no one disputes is that the state hospital resident patient population has declined from a peak of 558,922 in 1955 to 308,024 in 1971. The steady decline in resident patient population started, however, in 1956, a full decade before the first federally funded centers began operation. Thus NIMH's claim that community mental health centers were in any possible way responsible for the decline from 1955 to 1966 (when the resident population dipped to 452,089) is therefore patently absurd.[4]

Many other factors explain the decline in resident population during this period as well as much of the decline following 1966. First of all, the mid-fifties ushered in the widespread introduction of psychotropic (tranquilizing) drugs in state hospitals. Although there exists great potential for the abuse of these drugs and although they never "cure" anyone of "mental illness," they have been properly used in many instances to alleviate some symptoms of mental impairment. The "tranquilizer breakthrough" made possible the earlier release of many patients, even the severely disturbed, and their treatment under drug therapy as outpatients. Furthermore, the late fifties and sixties witnessed changes in social attitudes toward the mentally ill—reflected in concerted efforts by local groups to get patients out of state hospitals—and the corresponding increase in admissions to the psychiatric services of general hospitals and other medical facilities.

Another reason for the decrease is the policy adopted by many states to cut summarily the number of resident patients in order to curtail the rising costs of their continued hospitalization. In addition, there has been a growth of alternate-care facilities, including nursing or foster-care homes for the aged, which have proliferated over the last decade. As Dr. Morton Kramer, chief of NIMH's Biometry Branch, observed in 1967, "the decrease in the age group 65 years and over in the state and county mental hospitals has been accompanied by an increase in the numbers of aged mentally ill persons in nursing homes and related facilities for the aged." Moreover, writes Kramer, "As a result of the increase in the number of nursing homes since 1963, and the continued decrease in the number of aged mentally ill in state and county mental hospitals, the number of our elderly mentally ill citizens [in nursing homes] probably now exceeds that in the mental hospitals."*[5]

* The "aged mentally ill" represent two distinct categories of people. According to research psychiatrist and practicing gerontologist Robert Butler: "The first group comprises the chronically mentally ill, such as chronic schizophrenic and manic-depressive patients. They constitute one-third of state hospital populations. They have grown old in the mental hospitals and, in effect, are the treatment failures of psychiatry. . . .

"The second group is composed of old people who have developed psychiatric disorders for the first time in old age. They account for one-fourth of all mental hospital admissions annually. Disorders may be organic, principally so-called senile brain disease and cerebral arteriosclerosis. These are distinct mental diseases. It is inaccurate to say, as some psychiatrists and others have, that the old mental patient is 'senile and not suffering from a mental disorder.' On the other hand, 'senile' is a wastebasket . . . appellation and along with cerebral arteriosclerosis often is misapplied to the depressed, the anxious-confused, or paranoid old patient."[6]

The establishment of community mental health centers is thus only one of many interrelated factors that have together contributed to the decline in state hospital resident populations. In fact, evidence indicates that centers have played a relatively minor role in this decline. And, although scattered centers across the country have managed to decrease the number of individuals going to state hospitals from their catchment areas, documentation reveals that many other centers have contributed to the state hospital problem rather than alleviated it.

For example, in 1969 (the same year Stanley Yolles told Congress about the "impressive results" of the centers in bringing about a "startling reduction of patients") two studies of the Joint Information Service of the American Psychiatric Association and National Association for Mental Health found that community mental health centers had apparently lost sight of their congressional mandate. The Joint Information Service found instead that some centers consciously discriminated against poor and chronically ill patients who came to them for help:

> In one center to require inpatient care and be unable to pay for it was tantamount to being shipped off to the state hospital, regardless of diagnosis or history; this program in the year preceding our visit had provided inpatient treatment to only two persons unable to pay, and even these had been paid for by the welfare department. At other centers . . . certain categories of patients and patients with certain histories of previous treatment were quite casually transferred to the state hospital.[7]

The authors further reported that "Everywhere we went we found the state hospital being relied upon as the principal facility for long-term patients, including some who were labeled 'chronic' merely because they had had a previous hospitalization."[8] And they observed:

> At three facilities we visited there were more, or at least as many, patients from the catchment area going to the state hospital as there were before the mental health center began operating. At the same time, about half of the beds on the inpatient service of the mental health center were empty. *If there is anything to the idea that the mental health center will*

supplant the state hospital as the locus of treatment, perhaps the centers should not be sending just as many patients to the state hospital when half of their own beds are empty.[9] [Emphasis added.]

By the summer of 1970, NIMH itself had seemingly forgotten the program's original goal. In an internal document listing the objectives for the centers program, there is no mention of state hospitals until one gets to the fine print. "Process objective" Number 12 states that "Mental health centers shall insure the proper utilization of state mental hospitals and their services for residents of their catchment area."[10] What does "proper utilization" mean? That is left to the discretion of each center, despite the evidence that state hospitals continue to be used as dumping grounds for the poor and chronically ill. Thus, the expressed intent of Congress for creating community mental health centers was diluted to a minor process objective that allows individual centers to "utilize" state hospitals in whatever way they see fit.

The Amarillo Community Mental Health Center in Amarillo, Texas, has come up with an interesting method for discouraging the use of the state hospital. The officials of this center send only a few patients to state hospitals, primarily because they operate a mini state hospital themselves with an NIMH staffing grant. Built with Hill-Burton funds, this "community mental health center" is a traditional one-hundred-bed psychiatric hospital. According to four separate NIMH regional office site-visit resports,[11] when this center began operating, 90 percent of the inpatients were given electroshock treatments! In a separate September 22–23, 1971, site-visit report written by NIMH central-office official Lucy Ozarin and marked "For the Record," Dr. Ozarin states:

The second floor [of the center] houses three inpatient units which lead into each other. Each 33-bed unit has a large central dayroom and is ringed by bedrooms. Each ward also has a prison-like corridor behind the main unit along which there are seclusion rooms. There are a total of 9 seclusion rooms and they are used. Beds in the seclusion rooms have heavy leather straps attached to them. We saw several patients in the seclusion rooms. . . . I would question the need for so many seclusion rooms. . . .

About 15 patients were receiving shock treatment the week of the visit. We were told this is less shock therapy than in previous years. Except for the adolescent and young adult group programs, there does not appear to be a therapeutic community program that I can identify.[12]

Ozarin further noted: "The program of the center is unbalanced in that most of the effort and the largest part of the staffing grant is being spent on inpatients. During the past year more than twice as many inpatients were treated than outpatients."

We asked Dr. Ozarin what action she took to rectify the glaring deficiencies of this center. She stated that her only action was to "file my report with the regional office. I go on the site visit as a consultant to the regional office," she explained. "What they do with the report is their responsibility."[13] Katharyn Fritz, head of NIMH's Dallas regional office, which is responsible for the Amarillo center, told us that her staff was well aware of the problems of the Amarillo center. At least once a month, she said, a member of her staff contacted the Amarillo center officials to persuade them to cut down the number of patients receiving electroshock treatments. "It's rather sad," she said, "all those seclusion rooms."[14]

Looking solely at the decline in resident patient population, one might think that the days of seclusion rooms and state hospitals were numbered. While these selected statistics are accurate, they present an inaccurate picture of what is really going on in state hospitals. Among the other facts (which NIMH has never presented to Congress) is that admission and readmission rates to state hospitals have soared above any increase in the country's population. What this means is that more Americans than ever before are going to state hospitals, though they are going for shorter periods of time. According to the National Association of State Mental Health Program Directors, the total number of patients treated in state hospitals rose from 802,216 in 1966, when the first community mental health centers started operating, to 836,326 in 1971.[15] This is an *increase* of 34,110 since the establishment of the centers program. Corresponding to this greater use of state hospitals has been a sharp rise in state expenditures for mental hospitals. Maintenance costs alone rose from $1.3 billion in 1966 to over $2 billion in 1971, a climb of 54 percent.[16]

The striking increase in state hospital admissions vitiates whatever impact community mental health centers may have had in decreasing the resident population itself. Consider that hospital populations can be decreased primarily by a decrease in admissions and/or an increase in releases. (Such factors as average length of stay and transfers are reflected in these rates.) Since community mental health centers were designed as alternatives to hospitalization and since very few of them have extensive rehabilitation and aftercare programs, it is logical to expect that they would primarily affect admissions rates—that is, they would treat people who otherwise would have gone to state hospitals. But this is precisely what has *not* happened. Resident populations have gone down primarily because net releases from state hospitals have more than made up for the increase in admissions.* (See Chart 1.)

The sharp drop in state hospital resident populations raises a crucial question: Where have all these former patients gone? For many patients, state hospitals, as bad as they are, provide their only "home." Many are without families and friends; others are no longer wanted back into their homes. Many who have been patients for years are so molded by the institutional environment that they would find it difficult, if not impossible, to adjust to the perhaps harsher environment of what we like to call our "communities." Unfortunately, the community care ideology developed far faster than actual services and facilities. Most communities lack the social support programs and transitional facilities necessary to properly sustain former state hospital patients in the community. It is therefore important that these people be assured of help in returning to noninstitutional life.

By using the number of resident patients as its primary measure of success or failure in supplanting state hospitals, NIMH has avoided the necessity of assuming responsibility for

* It is likely that another NIMH program, the Hospital Improvement Program (HIP), has had a greater impact on reducing state hospital resident populations than the centers program. The HIP program provides direct grants to state hospitals for innovative approaches to hospital services and care. Individual grants, however, cannot exceed $100,000, a relatively small amount considering the multimillion-dollar budgets of most state hospitals. Furthermore, NIMH's HIP program has always been fairly limited in scope; its annual appropriations have never exceeded $11 million and its current funding level is down to $6.9 million (about 1 percent of NIMH's total budget).

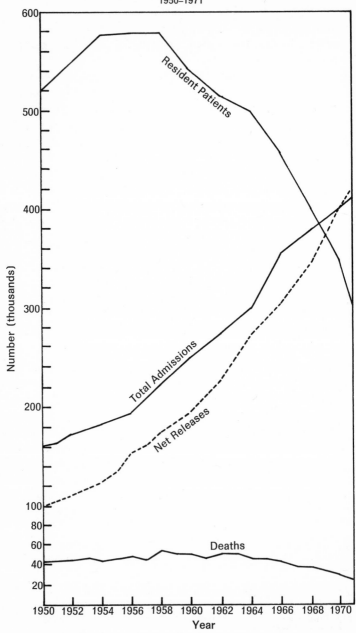

Chart 1.
NUMBER OF RESIDENT PATIENTS, TOTAL ADMISSIONS,
NET RELEASES IN U.S. STATE AND COUNTY MENTAL HOSPITALS,
1950–1971

Number (thousands)

Resident Patients

Total Admissions

Net Releases

Deaths

Year

Source: NIMH Biometry Branch.

providing care to discharged patients. As psychologist Martin Gittleman explained to the New York state legislature in 1970:

> It is clear that we have to begin to rethink our concepts of success in treatment. Success can no longer be measured in terms of reduction of beds set aside for mental patients or in discharge rates. Untreated and poorly treated patients can be hidden in the community as well as in the back wards. . . . We must be aware that institutionalism, with its debilitating effects on the mentally ill, can occur outside the hospital as well as inside. The former mental patient who is relocated into dozens of hotels throughout the state, supported by the Department of Welfare, is not immune to the effects of institutionalism. He has merely been removed from a hospital where he has been cared for in some fashion by a professional team, to a setting where he is not treated.[17]

While much evidence shows that the thousands of chronically impaired individuals who leave the back wards of state hospitals *can* live productive lives in the community, such patients can do so only if social supports are readily available. And these would have to include halfway houses, sheltered workshops, and job training. Some of these facilities and services are included in the federal definition of a "comprehensive" community mental health center—which means that they are optional, not essential. Overall, the emphasis on rehabilitation and maintenance services in the implementation of the community mental health centers program has been minimal.

The low priority attached to such services is attributable in large part to the lack of incentives offered to centers to care for chronic patients. According to Dr. H. G. Whittington, "The state keeps most of the money to run the state hospital. The community programs are left with what NIMH hands out, which isn't enough to do anything significant for the bulk of the chronic schizophrenic population. The public morality says it's a fine idea; the private morality of money doesn't work that way."[18] Moreover, as NIMH official Dr. James Beck points out, many people simply cannot tolerate working with chronic schizophrenics. "Doctors and nurses," Beck states, "don't like to treat patients who don't get well." He continues:

> It's oversimplifying . . . to say that chronic patients are sent away only because the state hospitals are "there." There are

powerful forces within the professional community which prevent the development of alternative kinds of treatment for these people.[19]

Just as community mental health centers tend to refer "chronic" cases to state hospitals, they do *not* make it their daily business to assume responsibility for such people once they are discharged from state hospitals. Harry Schnibbe calls the lack of follow-up on former patients "a disaster situation." "Follow-up service is our number one headache," he says. Schnibbe explained to us that a number of his association's mental health program directors have lamented, "This is criminal. We're sending people to even worse places, to rat holes."[20]

Although there is no comprehensive documentation on what happens to formerly institutionalized mental patients, available evidence strongly suggests that a number of patients are being transferred *en bloc* to nursing or so-called "foster" homes, where conditions are frequently worse than in state hospitals.

An example of this occurred recently in Washington, D.C., where both the state hospital involved and the Area D Community Mental Health Center, located within the state hospital, are under the direct administrative control of NIMH. In the summer of 1967, NIMH took responsibility for the administration of St. Elizabeths Hospital, which was created by an act of Congress in 1852 as the "state mental hospital" for the nation's capitol. Consisting of more than 120 buildings spread over some 300 acres, St. Elizabeths currently maintains about 4,000 inpatient beds. Upon assuming control of St. Elizabeths, which over the years has been shifted from one federal agency to another, NIMH declared that it would make the hospital a "national model" which would eventually be transferred to the District of Columbia government. Judged by the reduction in the resident patient population, NIMH has scored a considerable achievement; at the end of October, 1971, St. Elizabeths had 3,342 resident patients, about 2,000 fewer than when NIMH took over.[21] But where have these former patients gone?

According to the *Washington Post*, more than six hundred of these patients were transferred between June, 1969, and June, 1970, to foster homes as part of the hospital's com-

munity placement program.[22] This occurred despite an internal
memo dated August 19, 1969, warning the hospital administration of the numerous problems in many of the homes. The
memo, written by C. Richard Treadway and George Doebler, a
psychiatrist and chaplain, respectively, at St. Elizabeths, to the
chief of the foster-care section, said in part:

> Of 148 foster homes housing more than 400 active St. Eliza-
> beths Hospital patients, 141 of the homes (95%) are segre-
> gated. . . .
>
> A second problem has been the finding of several cases of
> undernourishment and inadequate nutrition in foster care
> patients. Three patients . . . have stated that they were having
> to spend some of their very limited weekly allowances for
> food since they were not getting enough to eat at their foster
> homes. Another patient . . . said that the patients in his home
> were receiving for lunch only a small bowl of soup, two soda
> crackers, and a cup of cold punch. . . .
>
> [Another] problem is the inadequate protection of the patients
> from violence in their community. Several incidents of assaults
> on foster care patients were not reported to the police or to
> the hospital. [One patient] was beaten with a board by a
> young man at the corner of 5th and Mellon, S.E. [The victim]
> notified his foster sponsor . . . who did not notify the police or
> the patient's therapist. Another patient from the Gershing
> home was robbed and beaten. Neither police nor therapist was
> notified. . . . [He] told his therapy group that he was the errand
> boy in the foster home because the others were too afraid to
> go to the store due to the frequent robberies. He talked of
> wanting to return to the hospital to live since the foster home
> was so unsafe. . . .
>
> [A] less tangible problem is the presence of fear in the homes
> of some foster sponsors. Some patients are fearful to raise
> problems in their foster homes and one patient . . . reported
> that she was taking only one of her two prescribed tablets a
> day because she was afraid to ask the foster sponsor for the
> other.
>
> [Another] problem is that in some homes patients are restricted
> to their rooms for most of the day while the use of a recreation
> or living room is limited only to the use of the foster care
> sponsor and his family.[23]

This memo was buried by hospital administrators, but rumblings of the disturbing conditions in some foster homes reached the District of Columbia Advisory Committee on Aging, which began an intensive investigation of the situation in early 1970. News of the foster care homes also reached the *Washington Post*, which ran a number of stories, and Jim Michie, an investigative reporter for the Washington affiliate of CBS television, took a film crew into one of the foster care homes. Following these public exposés, the chairman of the advisory committee, Dr. Robert N. Butler, escorted Philip Rutledge, then director of the District of Columbia Department of Human Resources, on a visit to some foster care homes. In a letter to Rutledge, Butler described the effect the visit had on him:

> Dear Phil:
> I couldn't sleep Friday night.
> I believe you too were deeply affected by the visit to so-called foster homes.
> The list of deficiencies is long—no one of responsibility present—no fire evacuation procedure or drills—untrained sponsors—no medical, dietary, social services, etc.
> There was the stench. There was the man who could only remember his name yet had bottles of Stelazine [a tranquilizer] and Dilantin [for epilepsy] in his own keeping. There were forlorn patients who answered the doors.
> This is not outplacement care. It is no *care*.[24] [Emphasis in original.]

Testifying in late 1971 before the Special Committee on Aging of the U.S. Senate, Butler stated:

> There is no virtue to playing a game called "moving patients" where there is no change in services but only a change in the scene. Indeed, people may be moved from one inadequate facility for the elderly—St. Elizabeths—to other even more inadequate facilities—called foster care homes.[25]

In its hearings and investigations on nursing and foster care homes, the Senate Special Committee on Aging found evidence of states indiscriminately dumping elderly patients into what were called "mini snake-pits." Dr. Murray C. Brown, Commissioner of Health of the City of Chicago, told the Senate Committee that "far in excess of 50%" of the seven thousand patients discharged by Illinois state hospitals in 1970 and the first three months of 1971 were "sent to nursing and residential care homes" in Chicago without adequate provisions that they would receive decent care. Brown also stated, "We have further learned that such former patients were discharged not only into licensed facilities, but into rooming houses and converted low-class hotels, some of which the Chicago Board of Health has never been able to identify or locate."[26]

NIMH statistical reports show that from 1966, the year the first centers began operating, to 1970, the total state hospital resident population declined by 114,472 individuals. Of this total, 35,623 persons were aged sixty-five and over and 31,881 were from the ages of fifty-five to sixty-four. Thus, individuals fifty-five and over made up 67,504, or almost 60 percent, of the total decline in the state hospital resident population from 1966 to 1970.[27] Despite these statistics, "No more than five percent of those served in community mental health centers are old despite their higher representation in the population and the heavy incidence and prevalence of emotional problems," Dr. Robert Butler observes.[28] Indeed, in its November 8, 1971, report, the Senate Special Committee on Aging declared that the "entire nation" must face up to the fact that:

> Community mental health centers, authorized by legislation 8 years ago, are failing to meet the needs of the elderly, and thus are increasing the pressure for institutionalization even when the institutions are less capable of meeting those pressures.[29]

Although most states have been eager to lower their costs by decreasing the inpatient populations of state mental hospitals, they have not seized many opportunities to actually close down state hospitals. In fact, the number of state-supported hospitals has increased from 307 in 1967 to 321 in 1971.[30] The resistance to shutting down state hospitals, according to Harry Schnibbe, comes primarily from state legislatures. He asserts that the resistance of state legislatures is greatest in the eastern and midwestern states where the state hospital systems have been entrenched since the Civil War. In these states the loss of property, jobs, and money, the principle dilemmas of shutting down a state hospital, have yet to be resolved. "Telling these states to close down state hospitals," observes Schnibbe, "is like going down South and telling them they can't play Dixie anymore."[31]

California seems to be the only state in the nation where there has been a concerted effort to eliminate state hospitals. California's most important pieces of mental health legislation are the Short-Doyle Act of 1957 and its subsequent amendments and the Lanterman-Petris-Short Act, which went into effect in 1969. In brief, the Short-Doyle Act contributes state funds on a matching basis to counties, or in some cases cities, to provide mental health services. The Lanterman-Petris-Short Act discourages involuntary commitment by requiring that all patients be screened at a local facility before being admitted to a state hospital. It also guarantees patients certain rights when hospitalized such as keeping all records confidential to the hospital.

These two acts should be viewed in combination. At the same time that the Lanterman-Petris-Short Act cuts down on admissions to state hospitals, the amended Short-Doyle Act provides state funds to pay for 90 percent of the cost of local mental health services. The amended Short-Doyle Act also requires that counties pay 10 percent of the cost of keeping their residents in state hospitals. (Before this amendment was made, the state bore the entire cost of all county residents in state hospitals.) Thus, because of the high cost of inpatient care at state hospitals, counties have a clear economic incentive to favor community programs.

This legislation has made a striking impact on the number of state hospital patients released. From 1969 to 1972, the number of patients in California state hospitals decreased from 15,700 to 7,200; the number of state hospitals dropped from nine to six. Yet here, as in Washington, D.C., and other parts of the country, there is a growing body of evidence showing that many patients have been unceremoniously dumped from state hospitals *without provisions for alternative care*. Instead, some of these patients have gone to run-down transient hotels where they pay twelve to fifteen dollars a week for a single room; some have gone to "board and care" homes, located typically in poor, crime-ridden areas.[32] The supervision of former patients in these homes is often minimal, since the only license needed to operate a six-bed board-and-care home in any county in California is a ten-dollar business license. Other patients have gone to premature deaths. The California State Employees' Association, which represents employees of the state Department of Mental Hygiene, estimates that the death rate among transferred patients is from 5 to 10 percent higher than among patients who have remained in state hospitals.[33] However exemplary the mental health legislation of California looks on paper, the state has clearly failed to devote sufficient attention to the provision of quality alternative care for released patients.

In general, admissions to state mental hospitals come from a large "residual population" made up of the poor, the aged, the abandoned, the members of minority groups, and others who are brought for psychiatric treatment not because they have been diagnosed according to any medical or psychological criteria but because they have disturbed, bothered, or shocked the sensibilities of someone or some group. Why "mental patients" end up in state hospitals instead of in jails or nursing homes or on the welfare roles or on park benches is often a matter of chance and circumstances. Thus it is not too surprising that one of the most salient characteristics of the great majority of patients now in state hospitals is that they should not have been admitted in the first place. Each year individuals who are diagnosed by the state hospital as "without mental disorders" become inmates. This mysterious group, which numbered more than two thousand in 1968, is apparently hospitalized though the individuals have nothing seriously wrong mentally.[34]

A recent experiment by D. L. Rosenhan, professor of psychology and law at Stanford University, is illuminating. For Rosenhan's study, eight eminently normal people gained secret admission to different psychiatric hospitals across the nation. The object was to see if "sanity" would be detected amid "insanity." It was not. Although the pseudopatients behaved on the wards just as they did ordinarily, none of them was discovered. (Eventually, they got out for good behavior: each was discharged with a diagnosis of schizophrenia "in remission.") All the pseudopatients took extensive notes, often publicly; but even this did not arouse any suspicion of sanity. On the contrary, nursing records for three patients, reports Rosenhan, indicate that the writing was seen as an aspect of pathological behavior. "Patient engages in writing behavior" was the daily nursing comment on one patient.[35] Once a diagnosis of pathology is made, the study shows, everything flows from that.

Psychiatric diagnoses, concludes Rosenhan, may tell us far more about the diagnosticians than about the patients or their problems. George Albee, former president of the American Psychological Association, takes a similar tack. He argues that as few as 10 percent of present first admissions need to be incarcerated in a protective environment. He writes:

> Elderly senile people, alcoholics, and others lumped together as persons with personality disorders or psychoneurosis, who together constitute nearly three-quarters of all first admissions to mental hospitals simply don't belong there! The remaining quarter is really the smaller pool from which might be drawn the limited number of persons society must lock up. But what percentage of functionally psychotic people are truly dangerous? If you will agree that not more than half are dangerous, we are down to close to 10% of present first admissions. And, if you agree that many of these people would not be dangerous if properly controlled by intensive care programs, we arrive at a point at which we have practically eliminated the need for the state hospital for first admissions altogether.[36]

Number studies support Albee's position. In an analysis of decisions concerning psychiatric hospitalization, Werner M. Mendell, professor of psychiatry at the University of Southern California Medical School, discovered that 84 percent of patients who were hospitalized would not have required it if more adequate family and community resources had been available.[37] In a study of the inpatient population at St. Elizabeths Hospital, two NIMH officials, psychiatrist A. S. Abraham and sociologist Kathleen Bueker, found that "sixty-eight percent of the patient population have no behavior problems which would limit outplacement." According to Abraham and Bueker, their findings match those of studies of other public mental hospitals across the country.[38]

That long-term hospitalization actually harms patients more than it helps them has become one of the best documented findings in psychiatric research. The most popularized version of this research is sociologist Erving Goffman's book, *Asylums*.[39] Goffman describes in detail the destructive and inhuman characteristics of the "total institution" where sleep, play, and work proceed in monotonous regularity in the same place, at the same time, with the same fellow inmates, and under the same relentless and unyielding authority. Ernest Gruenberg, one of the most distinguished researchers in this area, has coined the term "social breakdown syndrome" (S.B.D.) to account for the deterioration in social functioning that is not the direct consequence of mental disorder but due to the characteristics of social systems and the attitudes of the community and hospital toward the mentally ill and their treatment. Gruenberg laments, "It is a pity that this body of experience has not become incorporated into our writings on the psychoses and into our training programs."[40]

Why has this experience not influenced the treatment of so-called mental patients? Why are so many individuals admitted to state hospitals only to get worse during their hospitalization? In large part, the answers to these questions are found in the fundamental, if unpublicized, role state hospitals play in our society.

Historically, state hospitals have served more as an extra-legal force, by containing people who could not be labeled "criminal," than as treatment facilities. They were first constructed in the mid-nineteenth century, partially as the result of the efforts of reformer Dorothea Dix, who advocated care and not punishment for mentally ill paupers, but primarily because the economic and social conditions of the day dictated a need for such institutions. Sociologist David Mechanic explains that the industrial revolution in America, accompanied by urbanization and immigration, led to increasing intolerance for bizarre and disruptive behavior and a decreasing ability to contain deviant behavior within the social structure.[41] Life in the new urban environment was particularly harsh for unskilled immigrants, who not only had to adjust to a completely different culture, but experienced the misery that was the daily life of the industrial working class in the nineteenth century. It was often such persons who exhibited the behavior that American society at that time thought so bizarre and disorganized. Such behavior only added to the general disdain that American so-

ciety held for its immigrants, and led to strident demands that
the mentally ill be removed from the community and placed in
mental hospitals.[42]

The crush of immigrants on existing state hospitals fundamentally changed the character of treatment. For example,
Worcester State Hospital, established in 1830 as the first state
hospital in Massachusetts, had practiced "moral therapy" for
the first decade and a half of its operation. This approach is
based on the simple assumption that a mentally ill person will
improve if he is treated in a considerate and friendly fashion,
if he has the opportunity to discuss his troubles, if his interest
is stimulated, and if he is kept actively involved in life. But as
Massachusetts society required that the hospital accommodate
increasingly large numbers of Irish immigrants, moral therapy
was abandoned and patient regimentation and custodial procedures adopted.[43]

The custodial nature of the hospital soon became its *raison
d'être*. In terms of long-term incarceration of unwanted individuals, state hospitals have done far better than prisons. Table
1 compares the lengths of stay of 2,349 patients resident at
St. Elizabeths Hospital on May 31, 1970, with the jail terms of
the 20,150 prisoners in all federal prisons in 1965.

These considerations call into question whether the most ap-

TABLE 1.
Comparison Between Lengths of Hospitalization
at St. Elizabeths Hospital and
Jail Terms in Federal Prisons

Time in hospital or prison	Percent of patients at St. Elizabeths	Percent of prisoners in federal prisons
5 years or less	34	94
5 to 10 years	13	5
10 to 19 years	16	t
20 to 39 years	29	o
40 years or more	8	t \} 1
		a
		l

Source: the statistics for St. Elizabeths Hospital are taken from "Preliminary Findings for the Psychiatric Inventory of Saint Elizabeths Hospital" prepared as of May 31, 1970, by the hospital staff (mimeographed).
The statistics for the federal prisons are taken from an unpublished report of the Office of Information, Bureau of Prisons, Department of
Justice.

propriate help for former state hospital patients or potential patients is to provide them with another set of medical treatment institutions. As the recent research of Professor Harvey Brenner of Johns Hopkins suggests, economic conditions are far more crucial determinants of mental hospitalization than psychiatric intervention. In an extensive study of mental hospitalization in New York State from 1841 to 1967,* Brenner finds that admissions to mental hospitals bear a striking inverse relationship to economic change. In other words, mental hospitalization increases during economic downturns and decreases during economic upturns. Chart 2 portrays this relationship for the years 1915–1967 for New York State. No matter how one cuts the patient population pie—by sex, age, marital status, ethnic background, level of educational attainment, or diagnostic category—the inverse relationship still holds. Thus, it is not only the traditional "poor" but members of *any* socioeconomic group who can become the psychiatric victims of economic stresses. It is also evident that the inverse relationship is a very long-term phenomenon, holding for the entire 127-year period for which data are available. Furthermore, not only first admissions to psychiatric hospitals (both public and private), but readmissions, emergency admissions, and admissions to hospitals for the criminally insane are highly inversely related to economic downturns.

Perhaps more significant is the fact that this inverse relationship has become even stronger in the last thirty years. In other words, the impact of economic change on mental hospitalization has become greater since the end of World War II. Brenner calculates that a relatively minor increase in unemployment (of, say, 3 to 5 percent) may result in an increase in mental hospital admissions that is equal to or even greater than the increased admissions that occurred during the Depression of the 1930s.[44] The significance of this recent trend is far greater when one realizes that exactly the opposite might be expected to have occurred, given the advances in mental health research and treatment techniques since World War II. But, according to Brenner's

* Now unavailable, this unpublished study was complete under NIMH contract #PH-43-68-996. In revised form it was published by the Harvard University Press in 1973 as *Mental Illness and the Economy*.

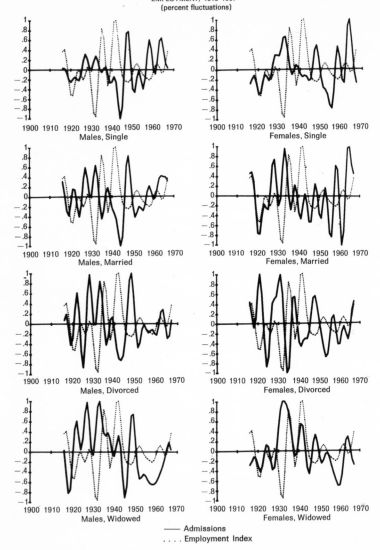

Chart 2.
RELATIONSHIP BETWEEN THE NUMBER OF FIRST ADMISSIONS
TO NEW YORK STATE CIVIL STATE HOSPITALS AND CHANGES
IN THE NEW YORK STATE INDEX OF MANUFACTURING
EMPLOYMENT, 1915–1967*
(percent fluctuations)

——— Admissions
. . . . Employment Index

* Fourier Transformations (Smoothing) of Annual Changes so as to Represent 2–4 Year Changes.

Source: M. Harvey Brenner, *Mental Illness and the Economy* (Cambridge: Harvard University Press, 1973).

data, all these advances do not seem to
ence—recent economic downturns have res
admissions to mental hospitals.

Brenner's findings indicate that employment o
adequate housing, and the widespread provision of so
ices may be a far more rational way of coping with large-
mental health problems in the United States than any form o
segregated mental hospitalization—whether in state hospitals,
psychiatric wards of general hospitals, or community mental
health centers. At best, the centers represent a Band-Aid approach to a number of social sores that will continue to fester
regardless of the amount of first aid. And, although many
existing centers have done little to reduce the number of
patients in state hospitals, the community mental health ideology
may have contributed to the dumping of former patients, already
debilitated by long hospitalization, into a society that has provided no means to care for them.

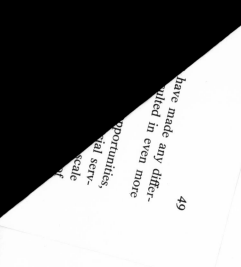

have made any differ-
...ulted in even more
...pportunities,
...ial serv-
...scale
...f

49

The Holy Five

Instead of emphasizing social support programs for released
state hospital patients or allowing communities to decide their
own most appropriate alternatives to hospitalization, NIMH
formulated its community approach to mental health care
around "five essential services." According to NIMH regulations, a center must provide inpatient services, outpatient services, partial hospitalization, emergency services available twenty-
four hours a day, and consultation and education services
in order to receive federal funds. The Institute maintains
that these five services plus an additional five (diagnostic
services, rehabilitative services, precare and aftercare services,
training, and research and evaluation) represent a "comprehensive" approach to community mental health care. But does
comprehensiveness defined as a range of professional service
components mean comprehensive care in terms of the various
interlocking problems that people have? William Ryan, chair-

man of the Department of Psychology at Boston College, suggests that in measuring comprehensiveness by the number of service components

> we tie ourselves in large measure to the past, in that we are able to include only those kinds of practices and procedures that have attained a name and an established status. In this sense, comprehensiveness means only that all of the different kinds of services that have so far been devised by psychiatric practitioners should be included in any new program. Unfortunately such a definition often leads to a situation where "maximum" and "minimum" are defined in precisely the same way. That is, we are constrained to provide the five basic services but often are at the same time constrained not to provide very much else.[1]

There is little evidence that the five basic services prescribed by NIMH are essential for every community in the country; on the contrary, some of the Institute's own officials admit that adhering to the five-essential-services formula is actually detrimental in many communities. Abel Ossorio, director of NIMH's regional office in Denver, says bluntly:

> We made a mistake about the five essential services. Communities provide what is required by the regulations rather than what is needed by the community. The regulations call for inpatient services, but in my book if you can design a center which does not need an inpatient facility, you should not be penalized but get a big, fat plus.[2]

Furthermore, the five-essential-services regulation goes against the findings of some of the landmark research completed at the time of the passage of the Community Mental Health Centers Act. The Boston Mental Health Survey, a widely praised study of mental health needs and services in Boston completed in the spring of 1962, concluded that:

> There are compelling reasons to suggest that mental health services for persons with complex patterns of social and emotional pathology—and this necessarily implies most services for persons of low socioeconomic status—may very appropriately be removed from the province of accepted psychiatric responsibility. Not only are many of these persons not well adapted to the standard psychotherapeutic procedures, but the intertwined strands of social and psychological disorder

can rarely be solved by the skill of the mental health professional alone.[3]

Earlier, the New York State Department of Mental Hygiene had pointed out in its 1959 *Guide to Communities in the Establishment and Operation of Psychiatric Clinics*:

> A psychiatric clinic . . . is by no means the invariable solution to community needs. . . . Many circumstances can produce disturbed behavior . . . and it is sometimes just as important for all immediate purposes to insure a stable home by making it possible for a deserted mother to stay with her children or help a depressed, unemployed father find a job or see that a school child is placed in the grade he needs to be in . . . as it is to resolve emotional conflicts and relieve the inner tensions of the past.[4]

Some of NIMH's own supported research similarly rejects the essential need for inpatient clinical care. In 1961 the Institute funded a two-and-a-half-year study by B. Pasamanick, F. Scarpitti, and S. Dinitz, which showed that chronic schizophrenic patients could be successfully maintained at home with the help of drugs and public-health nursing care.[5] In a recent follow-up to this study the same researchers elaborate that "chronic schizophrenics, in order to remain successfully in the community, must have continuous supervision and medication. They and their families must receive social services and psychological support to alleviate the all too familiar patterns of personal and family disorganizations." They conclude:

> If clinics are to play a major role in providing community care for schizophrenic patients, the *laissez-faire* model and its assumptions will have to be replaced by an aggressive delivery system designed to deal with chronic, marginal patients, like the psychotics in this study and those who comprise the bulk of state hospital populations. . . .

> The unique contribution of this research may be in calling attention to the absolute necessity of continued mental health surveillance and community treatment of former hospital patients.[6] [Emphasis in original.]

But NIMH's five prescribed services have nothing to do with follow-up care or the provision of social support services.

With the exception of consultation and education, NIMH's

essential services are part and parcel of the "disease" or "medical" model on which psychiatric treatment has been based since the nineteenth century. There is some controversy among different observers over what is meant by the disease or medical model, but as it is usually described in the literature the model conceptualizes a wide range of "mental disorders" as if they were "diseases," locates the cause of the "disease" within the individual, and prescribes the proper intervention techniques as medical "treatments" in hospitals, clinics, and similar facilities staffed by doctors, nurses, and other attendant personnel. A growing number of authorities, among them some prominent psychiatrists, are seriously questioning the validity of the disease model for "mental disorders."* This debate focuses on what

* See, for example, J. Elkes, "Word Fallout: Or, On the Hazards of Explanation" (presidential address, American Psychopathological Association), in *The Psychopathology of Adolesence*, ed. Joseph Zubin and Alfred Freedman (New York: Grune & Stratton, 1970), p. 118; Ronald Leifer, *In the Name of Mental Health* (New York: Science House, 1969), pp. 196–198; Karl Menninger, "Toward a Unitary Concept of Mental Health," in *A Psychiatrist's World: The Selected Papers of Karl Menninger*, ed. Bernard H. Hall (New York: Viking Press, 1959), p. 670; M. Roth, "Seeking Common Ground in Contemporary Psychiatry" (presidential address, Section of Psychiatry), in *Proceedings of the Royal Society of Medicine*, Vol. 62 (1969), p. 765; Mervyn Susser, *Community Psychiatry: Epidemiological and Social Themes* (New York: Random House, 1968), pp. 10–20; Thomas Szasz, *The Myth of Mental Illness* (New York: Harper and Row, 1961).

The medical model of mental illness has been questioned even more by behavioral scientists outside psychiatry. See, for example, G. Albee, "Models, Myths, and Manpower," in *Mental Hygiene*, April, 1968, pp. 168–180; G. Albee, "The Uncertain Future of Clinical Psychology," (presidential address, American Psychological Association), in *American Psychologist*, Vol. 25 (1970), p. 1071; William Schofield, *Psychotherapy: The Purchase of Friendship* (Englewood Cliffs, N.J.: Prentice-Hall, 1964); E. Wolf, "Learning Theory and Psychoanalysis," *British Journal of Medical Psychology*, Vol. 39 (1969), p. 525 (paper and critical evaluations); William Ryan, *Distress in the City: Essays on the Design and Administration of Urban Mental Health Services* (Cleveland: Press of Case Western Reserve University, 1969); S. P. Spitzer and N. K. Denzin, eds., *The Mental Patient: Studies in the Sociology of Deviance* (New York: McGraw-Hill, 1968).

For four critical views of the medical model by lawyers, see *United States v. Brawner*, 153 U.S. App. D.C. 1 (1972) (see opinion of Bazelon, C.J., at p. 42); J. Ziskin, *Coping with Psychiatric and Psychological Testimony* (1970); Nicholas Kittrie, *The Right to Be Different: Deviance and Enforced Therapy* (Baltimore: Johns Hopkins University Press, 1971); and Bruce Ennis, *Prisoners of Psychiatry* (New York: Harcourt Brace Jovanovich, 1972).

kinds of problems can be appropriately viewed as diseases and over what areas the psychiatric profession should maintain jurisdiction and control. Within the psychiatric profession, there are differences in emphasis between practitioners with an "organic" approach to mental disorder and those with a "functional" one. But by and large, both approaches have tended to uphold the legitimacy of the medical model.

There is, of course, a small core of definable disease entities that afflict a small minority of the millions of individuals who are said to suffer from mental illness. According to William Ryan, these include brain diseases, some severe psychosomatic disorders, and a quantitatively minor set of metabolic and toxic disorders that produce deviant behavior.[7] A second group of patients in mental institutions suffer, in addition to whatever mental disturbances they may or may not have, from quite real medical disorders such as tuberculosis, diabetes, vitamin deficiencies, cerebral arterial sclerosis, and so forth. Few would disagree that both groups of disorders should be treated primarily by medical personnel within a medical setting.*

In addition to mental illnesses that are unequivocally organic disorders, the disease model is applicable to some extent for schizophrenia and manic-depressive psychosis. There is mounting evidence that biochemical or genetic components may characterize both these disorders; furthermore, there is clear evidence that appropriate medication can abort most episodes of these disorders and to some extent prevent their recurrence—

---

* The recognition, treatment, and prevention of even obviously medical diseases, however, does not always fall entirely within the control of medical doctors. "Black lung disease" which occurs frequently among miners and only rarely in the rest of the population is an obvious case. A major thrust in dealing with this problem involves forcing mining companies to upgrade working conditions in their mines. This requires the social action of many diverse groups, not the leadership and control of the medical profession. In determining the logical extent of medical control and intervention for any health or mental health problem, according to the eminent medical sociologist Eliot Freidson, the task is "to discriminate between the fatty tissue and the solid heart of medical work and to press for influence in trimming off medical jurisdiction over the fatty tissue. Much of what is called patient management, as distinct from the identification of illness, its cause, and its treatment, is not sustained or chosen by any systematic scientific knowledge, but rather by personal preference and experience and by occupational custom and folklore."[8]

as in the case of manic-depressive psychosis, which can sometimes be averted by treatment with lithium. This does not imply that schizophrenia or manic-depressive psychosis are solely biological, but simply acknowledges that psychiatry can make an important contribution in these areas.

The largest category of patients with so-called "functional" psychoses, however, falls outside the realm of any scientifically verified disease categories. For these people the concept of "mental illness" (as defined by the disease model) serves primarily as a *metaphor*. And it is here that the use of the disease analogy results in far-reaching social consequences which suggest that it is not only a bad metaphor, but a dangerous one. First of all, the reference to nondiseased people in medical terminology (i.e., "symptoms," "diagnosis," "treatment," "therapy," "patient," "therapist," "prognosis," "nursing," "hospital," and many others) labels the individual seeking help as being "sick." Once labeled as "sick" or "psychotic" or "schizophrenic," an individual meets persistent discrimination and intolerance among family, friends, and employers. Karl Menninger, one of the most prominent American psychiatrists, has written extensively about the social stigma attached to such terms. He comments:

> Psychiatrists talk in public as if we all agreed about basic principles and about the meaning of our pompous fraternity jargon. Of course, we don't. I think we ought to discard all of our obscurantist, pejorative designations, just as cultured people have discarded words that once had a specific meaning but which now connote an attitude rather than merely describing a fact. It used to be proper, at least in some circles, to refer to some of our fellow citizens as "niggers." And it used to be proper to refer to some individuals as "psychotics" and "schizophrenics." All such name calling should be stopped.[9]

Inappropriate labeling also renders highly questionable epidemiological studies which attempt to count population groups with certain disorders. Because so-called personality and character disorders remain ill-defined and depend as much on the person doing the labeling as on the ones so labeled, collecting precise epidemiological information on the incidence and prevalence of such disorders seems highly improbable. In fact, the subjective, value-laden nature of "mental health problems" in general strongly suggests that they are not susceptible to epidemiological methods at all except through a feat of metaphorical gymnastics.

Perhaps the most damaging consequence of the disease analogy is that it seriously impedes alternative and innovative service programs. The federal requirement for inpatient beds has meant that well over half of the centers receiving federal construction funds have been built as part of a medical facility (most frequently a private, voluntary hospital, sometimes as part of a university medical school complex).[10] In general, community mental health centers focus on the usual medical inpatient/outpatient service core to the exclusion of alternatives to hospitalization and transitional facilities. Even the one center under the direct administration of NIMH, the Area D Community Mental Health Center in Washington, D.C., is overwhelmingly traditional in its approach to the mental health problems of its predominantly black and poor community. (See Chapter 8.) According to Katharyn Fritz, director of NIMH's regional office in Dallas, one of the largest problems in her region is the resistance of the medical community to the development of partial (day care or night care) hospitalization. This resistance, she explains, is due to the fact that partial hospitalization "is a mode of treatment that is not medically-oriented enough. Many professionals are not familiar with it."[11]

The projection of tradition-bound services into the community has also meant that people who have traditionally been spurned by psychiatrists continue to have limited access to community mental health centers—notably, drug addicts, alcoholics, old people, children, ethnic and racial minority groups, and the poor in general. The obvious exclusion of such groups from community-based care led to a 1968 amendment to the Community Mental Health Centers Act authorizing additional facilities and grants for the construction and staffing of community facilities and services for alcoholics and narcotics addicts. When the act was amended again in 1970, a new grant program was established to support the development of services for children. A suggested future amendment is a categorical grant for the construction and staffing of facilities for the elderly. But with an already clear mandate to provide the necessary services for "all residents living within the catchment area" one must ask: *Who are the people that community mental health centers have been serving?*

Part of the answer is the professional community. A 1971 General Accounting Office (GAO) study found that in some cases the number of beds in a center was determined simply on the basis of the amount of space desired by the applicant. In one case, according to the GAO, after construction had begun on an eight-story addition to its hospital, the applicant decided to capitalize on the availability of NIMH funds and convert two floors of the addition into a community mental health center. The hospital administrator told the GAO that "the size of the inpatient unit in one center was determined primarily by the size of the space to be converted into the center."[12]

The ethics of men who deliberately seek to use public monies for their own purposes speak for themselves. According to Lawrence S. Kubie, a professor of psychiatry at the Johns Hopkins University School of Medicine, such ethics are not uncommon in medical schools. In a recent article in the *Archives of General Psychiatry* Kubie writes:

> Several department heads have stated frankly that they are glad to take federal money (or any other money that comes their way) in order to build the facilities . . . they need. They admit that in today's climate, if they are to get this money, they are forced to call their new facilities "community mental health centers." They do not hesitate to add that within a dozen years the words will have dropped into innocuous desuetude, leaving the department in possession of the additional space it needs.[13]

Kubie, however, finds nothing wrong with such ethics, for he concludes, "there is no reason to object to such benevolent profiteering on the current fad."[14]

Another example of the misuse of the disease analogy can be found in the architecture of mental hospitals and community mental health centers where, as William Ryan observes,

> features appropriate to a general medical and surgical institution are transferred and applied thoughtlessly—and very ex-

pensively—not because of any particular need but because the
medical analogy bears down on the imaginations of the architect
and the builders and the planners of the building. Oxygen out-
lets in every room of a mental health center are an outright
absurdity.[15]

Clinging to the disease model furthermore impedes rational
thinking about the need for increased manpower. The logic is
that, if emotional disorder is a disease, the nation must have
hundreds of thousands of doctors and nurses and medically
trained attendant personnel to cope with it. Based on the
assumption that emotional disorder is a disease, NIMH has
projected that the country needs from three to eight times the
current number of 88,000 mental health professionals. But as
psychiatrist Robert L. Taylor, a former official in NIMH's training division and currently director of mental health for Marin
County, California, observes:

> NIMH manpower projections are subject to gross distortions.
> These distortions stem from the very subjective nature of what
> are "mental health" problems and how long and by whom they
> should be treated. Seldom do these projections question the
> traditional assumption of the four core mental health pro-
> fessions. At NIMH the idea is that mental health treatment
> can only be delivered by the four professions—psychiatrists,
> psychologists, social workers, and nurses.[16]

By concentrating on the supposed need for ever more
mental health professionals, NIMH obscures the serious problems that beset the deployment of existing mental health professionals. Nowhere are these problems more striking than in
the psychiatric profession. A psychiatrist is a doctor who has
undergone four years of medical school, three years of residency
in an accredited psychiatric hospital, and often a year of
internship sandwiched between the two. During this time he is
drilled in chemistry, anatomy, pathology, bacteriology, internal medicine, surgery, pharmacology, psychiatric nosology,
psychopathology, special diagnostic procedures and medical
therapies, and principles of psychotherapy. What does a psychiatrist do with all this impressive medical training?

The Joint Information Service of the American Psychiatric

Association and National Association for Mental Health study on mental health center staffing found that psychiatrists in the eight centers they visited spent almost one-quarter of their time in staff meetings. Moreover, the time spent in meetings together with the time spent in planning, administration, telephone calls, and supervision accounted for nearly one-third of the time of psychiatrists at the centers. Added to this is the necessity for grant-writing, fund-raising, and related activities which inevitably fall to senior staff. Surely this is not an optimal use of the most highly trained professional group—particularly since more than half the psychiatrists in this survey were working only part-time in the centers. The Joint Information Service further found that psychiatrists spend less time in activities related directly to patient care than any other group of workers in the centers—professional or nonprofessional. In fact, the data supplied by the Joint Information Service indicate that the more highly trained a staff member, the less time he spends treating patients and the more time he spends in the bureaucratic maintenance of the center.[17]

In general, the Joint Information Service found that center professionals, the great majority of whom lack any special training or experience in community mental health,* were hard put to define for or among themselves their programs' purposes and were uncertain about their roles in this "new" type of facility. The staffs of all eight centers suffered, in varying degrees, from confusion over goals, poor leadership, rivalry and mistrust among professionals of different disciplines, and serious communication problems. The resulting pressures led most of them to fall back on the traditional approaches and methods for which their training had prepared them. The authors point out, for example, that all of the top administrators had been trained as clinicians and none of them as administrators.

* Since there is no professional consensus about what community mental health means, or what centers are supposed to do, there is a good deal of controversy over what kind of specialized training, if any, is needed. Fairly well established programs in community psychiatry are offered at a few large universities—most notably Columbia and Harvard. Recently a number of other universities have added training programs in community mental health, usually as a subspecialty of psychiatry.

Robert Taylor commented on this lack of administrative training in an NIMH memo:

> Practicing without adequate training is the rule in the area of mental health administration. Despite the fact that psychiatrists, psychologists, social workers, and nurses carry out *55%* of the general administrative activities within the CMHC's, the basic educational programs for these mental health professionals fail to include formal administrative training. The absence of such training is reflected in a general administrative ineffectiveness.[18] [Emphasis in original.]

Taylor concludes that: "Although an understanding of human behavior is essential to any effective administrator, it is not sufficient. Mental health professionals forced to administer mental health facilities solely on the basis of their clinical training are severely handicapped."[19]

But it is not only the fact that psychiatrists spend so much of their time maintaining the mental health bureaucracy that makes the present utilization of manpower so inefficient. The problem also lies with the kinds of patients psychiatrists see. According to the latest statistics of the American Psychiatric Association, compiled by Dr. J. Frank Whiting, psychiatrists spend approximately 43 percent of their time in direct patient contact with private patients and 19 percent in direct contract with all other patients.[20] Thus the time that psychiatrists spend treating patients in private settings is *more than double* the time they devote to treating patients in public settings.

Who are these private patients toward whom psychiatric care is now so clearly directed? A 1967 American Psychoanalytic Association study of private patients revealed that 98 percent of the patients were white and 78 percent had at least a college education.[21] William Ryan's survey of metropolitan Boston found that two-thirds of the private patients are female; half are between twenty-two and thirty-six years of age; and four out of five have gone to college or are now college students. Ryan reports, "about one-quarter of all Bostonians who are private patients are young women in their twenties and early thirties who live within an area of less than 100 blocks."[22] The area he refers to is one of the most fashionable in the city.

Common to these private patients is what psychologist William Schofield has labeled the YAVIS syndrome—youthful, attractive, verbal, intelligent, and successful.[23] According to psychiatrist E. Fuller Torrey, special assistant to NIMH director Bertram Brown, they also tend to be "good patients" or "those who share your values and vocabulary, never call you at home, never cancel appointments, pay their bills on time, and never question the ground rules you set down."[24]

It should be noted that NIMH has spent over $300 million in the last decade to support psychiatric residency training programs, half of whose graduates turn exclusively or primarily to private practice. In this sense, tax money has been used to subsidize psychiatric care for the wealthy.

In contrast to treating YAVIS-type patients, psychiatrists rarely treat patients who suffer from brain dysfunction, severe psychosomatic disorder, metabolic deviance, perinatal trauma, and other disorders that require primarily medical attention. Neither do most psychiatrists treat individuals suffering from schizophrenia or manic-depressive psychosis. Such individuals make up the "hard core" of the mentally ill and the only mental health facility in which they appear in substantial numbers is the state mental hospital. The average psychiatrist, however, is not drawn to this type of patient. (According to one expert on mental health manpower, there are now fewer total psychiatrists working in public mental hospitals than there were twenty years ago when the membership of the American Psychiatric Association was only one-fourth its present size.)[25] The average psychiatrist prefers to deal with nondiseased persons whose problems can just as easily (and often more appropriately) be viewed in social, psychological, semantic, or learning terms. Perhaps the supreme irony of the psychiatric profession is that psychiatrists, who are trained as doctors, are treating people who are in no way "sick" and who do not require medical attention.

If in recent years the medical model has been disparaged *as a conceptual model*, nonetheless, in terms of a power structure it is more prevalent than ever. Psychiatrists occupy the most prestigious positions and hold the reins of power in the mental health field. They are the only ones who can prescribe medica-

tion or authorize hospitalization, and in most mental health
facilities it is they who make all the important decisions,
whether or not those decisions have to do with medical issues.
Most current medical financing mechanisms (e.g., health insurance) reinforce medical dominance by covering the services
of psychiatrists and other physicians but not psychologists,
social workers, nurses, or paraprofessionals. Such dominance,
according to sociologist Eliot Freidson, "permits the medical
profession to reinforce and protect itself from outside influence
and to claim and maintain jurisdiction and control over many
more areas than logic or evidence justifies."[26]

This situation does not engender much optimism for the
development of the role of paraprofessional workers within
the present structure of medical practice. Although there exists
a "multiplicity of evidence derived from a great variety of different sources, stemming from different investigator biases,
using diverse methods and indices . . . that paraprofessionals
play an important role as treatment agents and contribute to
the improved mental health of clients and patients in highly
significant, often unique ways,"[27] the implications of this evidence have been resisted by most professionals. Until May,
1971, NIMH had no organized program devoted to the training
of paraprofessionals. Much of the slim Institute support in the
area had been given by NIMH's Experimental and Special
Training Branch, whose demonstration grants are typically for
small amounts and limited in duration. Even in 1972 the total
budget of NIMH's New Careers Training Branch (established
in 1971) was restricted to $1.5 million.

Most NIMH officials we interviewed were apologetic for the
Institute's delay in supporting paraprofessional training and
cited the difficulties of red tape and bureaucracy. One official,
who asked not to be identified, spoke more frankly: "Basically,
the New Careers Program is the house nigger. Right now it's
politically advantageous for the Institute to give the program
a little money—to do a little window dressing. Also the evidence [of its effectiveness] was getting so overwhelming. The
Institute could no longer ignore it. They had already ignored
it as long as they could."

The new-careers concept was first introduce in 1965 by

Arthur Pearl and Frank Reissman in their book *New Careers for the Poor: The Nonprofessional in Human Service.*[28] They outlined a very general concept of providing poor people with training that would lead not only to decent jobs but to opportunities for moving up the career ladder in the area of human services. In practice, however, most new-careers programs provide neither adequate training nor decent jobs nor opportunities for advancement. As early as 1969, Arthur Pearl had this to say about the implementation of the new-careers concept:

> I have a lot of concerns about this phony program called new careers. It has nothing to do with what I had in mind when I wrote a book, which really talked about changing the nature and quality of life. It had nothing to do with conning poor people into doing some lousy jobs.[29]

The major difficulty in the development of paraprofessional careers is that they must be implemented within a hierarchical structure of services dominated by the medical profession. And within the present framework no effective and widespread program using such workers is possible without the active cooperation of the dominant profession. If psychiatrists do not trust paraprofessionals, or fear and resist them, patients will not be referred to them, nor will psychiatrists readily accept patients from them. Furthermore, it is improbable that without the active encouragement of physicians, laymen will utilize the services of paraprofessional workers.

Prevention

Under the banner of "consultation and education" falls the major preventive thrust of the centers program and its single most innovative service element. Of the five essential services, this is the only nonmedical service required of a community mental health center. Consultation has to do less with individual *case consultation* than with a more broadly focused *program consultation* provided by mental health center personnel to a variety of community agencies, such as schools, courts, welfare departments, police, clergy, even employers. Education involves both increasing the visibility of the center in the community and, according to NIMH guidelines, promoting mental health and preventing emotional disturbance through the dissemination of "relevant mental health knowledge."[30]

Notions of prevention have developed from an increasing recognition of the large role played by the environment in emotional disturbance and the realization that an individual's inner conflicts cannot be understood apart from social and political realities. In addition, the tendency of the mental health professions to view a large range of human behavior along a "health-sickness" continuum led eventually to the introduction of public health concepts, most explicitly in the field of community mental health. The public health-epidemiologic model focuses on "target conditions" and "high-risk populations" rather than on individuals, and embodies the idea that changing the environment to prevent "disease" from occurring in the first place is more effective than diagnosis or treatment. Thus the concerns of a community mental health center are supposed to include "primary" as well as "secondary" and "tertiary" prevention. Gerald Caplan, a professor of psychiatry at Harvard and one of the early leaders of the community mental health movement, defines these terms as follows:

> Primary prevention is the reduction of the incidence of mental disorders of all types in a community. Secondary prevention is reduction of the duration of a significant number of those disorders that do occur. Tertiary prevention is the reduction of the impairment which may result from these disorders.[31]

The provision, as a required element of service, of a mechanism by which mental health workers can reach out to other agencies and "care givers," help them to identify and deal with mental health problems, and thereby to prevent their further development, can be viewed as a hopeful and even exciting notion. For one thing, it seeks to widen the impact of mental health insights by extending services to larger groups than could be seen individually at the mental health center, or who might never reach the center at all. For another, it alleviates the shortage of mental health manpower by enabling non-mental-health personnel to deal more effectively with certain emotional or behavioral problems of the people with whom they are in frequent or daily contact. By going to the places where people live, work, or seek help, it is thought, mental health specialists can most efficiently help to alter stressful conditions and thus prevent mental disorder.

There are, however, a number of problems with this concept as it tends to operate in community mental health centers based on the NIMH model. To begin with, of all the essential services, consultation and education seem to be the least practiced and the most poorly understood. Interviews with center directors, other mental health center personnel, and NIMH regional-office staff indicate either a lack of interest in consultation or uncertainty about what it is meant to accomplish. According to Joseph Perpich, a former staff psychiatrist at the Area D Community Mental Health Center in Washington, D.C., it is also seen by some staff members as a way to avoid direct treatment. "It's much easier," said Dr. Perpich, "to sit around sipping coffee with the neighborhood cop than to deal directly with the messy, difficult cases. Everybody would rather run around offering consultation to the schools."[32] In the centers they visited, the Joint Information Service found indifference to consultation as a means of prevention and also found that persons from agencies, particularly the schools and the courts, preferred direct treatment services over any form of consultation. A staff member of the NIMH regional office in Philadelphia told this Task Force that consultation has a low priority for the staffs of the centers he is familiar with. "Most of them don't provide it at all," he said.

More basic than the question whether preventive services are being implemented, however, is the question whether prevention can actually be accomplished. And the answer to this rests in turn upon a still more fundamental question: What are mental health specialists trying to prevent? If it is that small core of definable disease entities, or what are recognized as the "major psychoses," brain disease, etc., one should note that there is little conclusive evidence on which to base preventive work. Very little is known about the etiology of the most debilitating "mental illnesses"; for example, conflicting studies abound on the nature and origin of schizophrenia. Some claim that it is genetic, others contend that it is chemical, still others maintain that its roots are to be found deep within the structure of the family. Advocates of primary prevention within a community mental health context appear to favor the notion that environmental manipulation is the most effective way of preventing "mental illness."

It is a commonplace observation that harsh, dehumanizing environments are unlikely to promote healthy characteristics— either physical, social, or mental. Nevertheless, there is no conclusive research to indicate that "emotional disturbance" is in fact preventable. Direct cause-and-effect relationships between environmental deprivation and disabling psychological conditions have never been established. According to Frederick C. Redlich, one of the pioneers in research relating social class and mental illness:

> One gathers the impression that we have definitive knowledge that poverty produces behavior disorders. Actually such knowledge does not exist yet. We do not know that extreme poverty or extreme affluence increases the risk to develop certain behavior disorders, although this is quite likely. *We only know that poverty excludes efficient help or makes such help inefficient because of overwhelming socioeconomic stress.* At present, we do not possess reliable incidence studies of different behavior disorders, and we have not established correlation between different types of socioeconomic deprivation.[33] [Emphasis added.]

When so-called preventive efforts focus on changing family patterns, housing conditions, occupational practices, and the educational system and eliminating social, racial, and economic injustices, far more is involved than mere questions of health. As former NIMH official Franklyn N. Arnhoff puts it:

> To the extent that the target conditions are rather vaguely stated, involve moral and legal issues of good and bad, are imbedded in social values, race, politics, history, and national economic trends the health aspects are minimal, if not at times altogether irrelevant. In this regard it is essential to recognize that much mental health concern and practice involve not scientific and/or medical findings but, rather, essentially "norm" management or manipulation.[34]

While challenging economic inequalities and changing social priorities are important battles, they are *political* battles. Placing these problems in a mental health or medical context serves to mask the real issues. For example, Gerald Caplan sees social action as a proper professional role for psychiatry. But in practice, Caplan's social action program is nothing more than political lobbying. He writes:

> The mental health specialist offers consultation to legislators and administrators and collaborates with other citizens in influencing governmental agencies to change laws and regulations. Social action includes efforts to modify general attitudes and behavior of community members by communication through the educational system, the mass media, and through interaction between the professional and lay committees.[35]

Caplan goes even further by suggesting that mental health specialists become arbiters of morality and matrimony by convincing unwed mothers to marry.

> In some states, the regulation of these grants [Aid to Dependent Children] in the case of children of unmarried mothers is currently being modified to dissuade the mothers from further illegitimate pregnancies. Mental health specialists are being consulted to help legislators and welfare authorities improve the moral atmosphere in the homes where children are being brought up and to influence their mothers to marry and provide them with stable fathers.[36]

And here is another psychiatric contribution proposed by Leonard Duhl:

> One fact psychiatrists have learned is that in times of social crisis people are susceptible to help. We also know it is at such moments that they are willing to change. If we can reach the mayors and the people concerned about the cities in their crises with assistance in the acute problems they are facing, they will begin to use us and we can help bring about change. I suggest that we begin to take them on as clients. We cannot wait for them to request our services, because they are not going to ask us. We must begin right now to fill in and be of assistance to them with the issues they are facing.[37]

Such exhortations probably result as much from good intentions as they do from any heady sense of psychiatric manifest destiny. But if psychiatry and the other mental health professions can genuinely contribute anything to broad social change, they should realize that they have as much to learn about communities, social institutions, and politics as they have to teach about individual personality or psychopathology. In this sense, consultation must essentially be a collaborative venture— not a matter of experts offering their wisdom or a magical pill. For professionals who desire to take on responsibility for any institutional change, their efforts would seem more logically, more appropriately, and more effectively directed at their own institutions. They should actively seek the reform of the mental health establishment itself, which is one of the most inefficient, outdated, and discriminatory of our social/medical systems. Here, if anywhere, they are most likely to have an impact on the enrichment and expansion of training programs, the sharing of decision-making power, and the growth of more relevant and responsive institutions. For even if mental health professionals had sufficient expertise to change society at large and sufficient wisdom to create new social structures more conducive to positive mental health, they do not have the necessary power. To put it bluntly, it is highly unlikely that society will alter its priorities because mental health professionals point out that present priorities may not be good for the mental health of millions.

All of our case studies bear out in one way or another the difficulty of real prevention. A particularly illuminating example is the North Oakland Community Mental Health Center located in a suburb of Detroit (Chapter 12). Although there is a wealth of evidence that modern auto plants have become breeding grounds for narcotics addiction, alcoholism, and other forms of severely alienated and destructive behavior, there is not a great deal that the community mental health center can do about it. The North Oakland Center has by no means taken an aggressive role in this area, but there is little reason to believe that even the most enlightened and committed mental health professionals could persuade General Motors to change its production policies.

Despite the confidence of Howard P. Rome, one of American psychiatry's most prominent spokesmen, that "actually, no less than the entire world is a proper catchment area for present-day psychiatry, and psychiatry need not be appalled by the magnitude of this task,"[38] it seems clear that the "prevention" of human suffering or the promotion of "mental health" in our society (let alone the entire world) will never come from mental health systems. As Stanley J. Matek, executive director of the Mental Health Planning Committee of Milwaukee County points out, "It will come from our educational systems, our family developments, our recreational patterns, our employment practices, and our mass media communications."[39]

In the meantime, the mental health professions must determine what they can and cannot do, where their particular skills are likely to make a difference and where they will probably not matter. This is not to suggest that psychiatrists and other professionals should not, as individuals, be involved in social change. Nor do we mean to suggest that community mental health programs cannot contribute to improved public understanding of human behavior and mental impairment. Programs aimed at genuine alternatives to the customary labeling and segregation of people with emotional disturbances or other problems that inhibit an individual's self-sufficiency are to be encouraged. Similarly, the efforts of mental health professionals to help their individual patients gain greater self-control over their own lives are commendable. But all this should be clearly aimed at helping individuals, not at expanding the domain of professional dominance.

5

Community, Coordination, and Citizen Involvement

The well-intentioned architects of the Great Society, out of concern for the poor, the black, and other groups of disenfranchised citizens, attempted to redirect resources and services to these groups. In *Regulating the Poor*, Frances Fox Piven and Richard A. Cloward argue that Great Society programs dealt with the political problems of this new and unstable constituency, "not simply by responding to its expressed interests, but by shaping and directing its political future."[1] Whether its aims were altruistic, political, or both, the Great Society's managerial programs carried a new trademark: a direct relationship between the federal government and "community groups," with lessened involvement on the part of state and municipal agencies which had hitherto controlled services and disbursed federal funds.

But the relationships among government levels and various agencies were never clearly spelled out, an omission that did much to undermine local responsibility and citizen involvement from the outset. This was particularly the case for the community mental health centers program, whose basic tenet was the transfer of care for the emotionally disturbed from the distinctly separate or distant state institutions to the community.

A good part of the problem, of course, lay with the ambiguity of the word "community," whose various interpretations led to markedly different consequences. "Community" has at least two obvious and distinct meanings, one geographical, the other social. The community emphasis might mean, therefore, simply making mental health institutions more accessible by locating them physically closer to where people live. Or it might mean, as is often implied, making them an integral part of an existing social community, responsive to community needs and accountable to community residents for the quality of the services offered. We have already seen that the regulations specifying the essential services of a center clearly supported professional domination of services. Other regulations, relating to service responsibility, coordination, and citizen involvement, were to favor the professional community as well.

Catchment Area

"Catchment area" is the term coined by NIMH to designate community in the sense of geographic accessibility. Every center funded by NIMH must serve a "catchment area" with a population of no fewer than 75,000 and no more than 200,000. For any one applicant to be eligible for NIMH funds, the entire state must first be divided into catchment areas based solely on these population units. Once it possesses a construction or staffing grant, a community mental health center assumes responsibility for making mental health services available to everyone residing within the catchment area, or "community."[2]

While increasing the geographic accessibility of mental health services is a worthy goal, apparently no one in Washington seriously questioned the validity of the catchment-area definition. In rural areas where people are scattered and distances are great, and in congested metropolitan areas where the vagaries of public transportation may not provide easy access to facilities, natural ecological boundaries make far more sense. In a great many communities, travel time is a major factor in determining whether a center is "near and accessible," as the regulations stipulate. Moreover, the arbitrary population limits mean that catchment-area boundaries rarely coincide with existing political or service boundaries, such as police precincts, welfare stations, health agencies, and school districts. Thus, there are significant but unnecessary obstacles to meaningful coordination with related health and welfare agencies and organizations.* This situation is particularly acute in large metropolitan areas, as Robert Connery et al. point out in The Politics of Mental Health:

> The realities of big-city living in the mid-twentieth century suggest that rigidity of approach to the community idea, whether thought of in catchment area or local involvement terms, will hamper the development of an effective program. The catchment area concept, given the population standards of the regulations, will require in many instances that variations from one residential area to another be ignored, variations that may lie at the heart of community identity.[3]

According to Saul Feldman, NIMH's top official for community mental health centers, "The important thing about catchment areas is the idea of geographic responsibility." When reminded that the regulations specify population limits and not specific geographic boundaries, Feldman replied, "What I'm saying is that it may not be very critical how you draw the lines." He added, "We do not see it as our responsibility to define to the country what is a community."[4]

The regulations, however, do define "what is a community." The Code of Federal Regulations provides the following definitions:

> "Area" means the geographic territory which includes one or more communities served or to be served by existing or proposed community mental health facilities. . . .

---

* It should be pointed out that this is a problem that bedevils city, county, and state governmental boundaries throughout the United States. NIMH is obviously not solely to blame for this problem. On the other hand, adding yet another conflicting jurisdiction does not alleviate it.

"Community" means an area or that portion of an area served or to be served by a program providing at least the essential elements of comprehensive mental health services. . . .[5]

As Connery *et al.* point out, the above is a neat tautology: a community mental health center is a facility that offers a comprehensive mental health services to persons residing in a particular community, and a community is a geographic area in which is offered comprehensive mental health services by a community mental health center.[6] In other words, the federal regulations, which disregard place of work, transportation and communication patterns, and other governmental boundaries, have defined "community" simply as the "catchment area" of the mental health center.

It is somewhat mystifying that the program should be committed to the population stipulation, since the 75,000–200,000 limits appear to rest on no sound basis. Dr. Walter Barton, medical director of the American Psychiatric Association and a key figure in setting the center regulations, told us, "There was no real reason behind the limits . . . 50,000 seemed too small and 300,000 too big. We felt that 75,000 to 200,000 was about right."[7] Thus, what was originally a "right feeling" among the regulation writers has become one of the most disrupting requirements of the entire program.

Stanley J. Matek, executive director of the Mental Health Planning Committee of Milwaukee County (which has a reputation for being one of the best mental health planning operations in the country) calls the catchment guidelines "absurd" in terms of metropolitan reality. He cites as an example what he calls the federal "Balkanization" of Milwaukee. Milwaukee had to divide its 1.2 million residents into six catchment areas of 200,000, with a separate facility for each. Matek comments:

It is a given in Milwaukee's political ecology that programs paid in any part by county government will service the entire county population. It is also an economic fact that six-fold duplication of facilities is out of the question. So, the county proposed to build one center, out of which six teams under one administration would serve the entire population. This was irrefutably sensible at the local level.[8]

According to Matek, NIMH vetoed the idea. "The logic of the federal plan required that the center buildings be *in* the area to be served.* So the locally feasible catchments were scrapped." (Emphasis in original.) The resulting federal catchment scheme Matek sees as being "meaningless in terms of how the community lives. . . . It is destroying normal communion, rigidifying attitudes, limiting options, fictionalizing freedom, and marring the mental health of staff, politicians, taxpayers, and clients alike."[9]

Philadelphia is another area for which the catchment guidelines make no sense, writes Jon Bjornson in *New Physician*:

> The city has eight school districts, ten public health districts, twelve mental health center catchment areas, over three hundred city planning areas, six Congressional wards, nine county public assistance districts, approximately fifty data collection districts used for "employment density" and "land use projection" surveys, etc. Now what is so magical about 75,000 to 200,000?[10]

Across the country a 1971 GAO study of the community mental health centers program revealed that Los Angeles County officials also found the federal catchment guidelines inappropriate. County officials pointed out that the federal plan would result in segregated mental health services. Moreover, county and state officials complained that NIMH ignored advance planning by the county. In a letter addressed to the GAO dated September 11, 1970, Harry R. Brickman, M.D., director of the Department of Mental Health, County of Los Angeles, wrote:

> We have been complaining about being left out of the planning and reviewing processes but at the same time must point out that patients, potential patients, and concerned citizens in general are totally left out of the planning in the federal program. Whereas both the regional medical program legislation and comprehensive health planning legislation have included de-

---

* This "logic" seems to operate according to federal whimsy. For example, in Washington, D.C., most inpatient and emergency services are centrally located—which means that they are miles outside two of the city's four catchment areas; in Pontiac, Michigan, the whole operation is located outside its catchment area; in Atlanta, Georgia, inpatient and emergency services are also located outside the catchment boundaries. (See chapters 8, 10, and 12.)

vices to assure citizen participation in planning, the mental health program has not.

. . . We are saying that local mental health planning needs to be custom tailored to the needs of the local and not imposed by formula.[11]

In Washington, D.C., most services, including night and weekend emergency services, for the entire city (which is divided into four catchment areas) are located either on the grounds of the city-run D.C. General Hospital or at St. Elizabeths, the "state" mental hospital operated by NIMH. And even though one hospital might be closer than another for many people, catchment boundaries are rigidly enforced. This had tragic consequences not long ago, when a young black woman, having wandered around in the middle of the night for several hours, actively hallucinating and with her two small children in tow, finally made her way to St. Elizabeths. Because she did not belong in the catchment area assigned to that hospital, she was refused admission and told to go across town to D.C. General. She was killed by a car on the highway outside St. Elizabeths, with her children the only witnesses.[12] Here, as in other places, the original legislative intent of "community based" centers has been perverted. When the catchment area concept is viewed more as a means of excluding those who live outside than as a mandate to provide services, checking "membership" too often takes precedence over responding humanely to people's needs.*

Living within catchment boundaries does not necessarily guarantee accessibility to treatment either. Time and again, community mental health center personnel have explained to members of this Task Force and to others, that they are reluctant to publicize themselves for fear of being "swamped" with patients. Obviously a community mental health center cannot be effective if large sections of the catchment area have never even heard of it. Despite the NIMH rhetoric about "accessibility," a number of centers are not only physically invisible in the community, but remain culturally, economically, or psycho-

---

* In some places, such as the North Oakland Community Mental Health Center in Pontiac, Michigan, catchment boundaries are drawn with seeming deliberateness to *exclude* the neediest segments of the population (see Chapter 12).

logically inaccessible. The North Oakland Center in Pontiac, Michigan, for example, is situated within and is physically indistinguishable from the state mental hospital; moreover, investigation has shown that substantial segments of the population (local social service agencies, the media, and the citizenry) are unaware of the center's existence, location, or functions.

At the mid-Missouri Mental Health Center in Columbia, admission to the children's outpatient service is "preceded, except in dire emergency, by the completion of an eleven page, ninety-five question application form and at least a three-hour face-to-face intake procedure," according to an April, 1972, NIMH regional site-visit report. The report notes that "most applicants manage to return the questionnaire in one or two weeks." In addition, the site-visit report observed that "at the time of our review there were sixty-two applicants for outpatient service with a waiting time of approximately three months. . . . The intake procedure is so unresponsive to public needs that some clients, those in the Columbia-Boone County area, have learned the most effective way to get service is by aggressive demands on a walk-in emergency basis."[13]

Significantly, it was not until February, 1972, nine years after the passage of the Community Mental Health Centers Act, when NIMH issued revised regulations, that community mental health centers were officially required to publicize their services and programs so as to be "generally known to the population of the catchment area" and to be "so located as to be readily accessible to the general population of the catchment area." It was evidently assumed, up to that time, that community mental health centers would automatically take pains to broadcast their services to the public. There is no indication in the regulations, however, as to how these two new requirements are to be enforced, and one can only suspect that they, like other vaguely worded regulations, will be ignored or so loosely interpreted as to nullify their intent.

Coordination and Continuity

The catchment-area concept is bad enough when it perverts the geographical and social meanings of "community" and excludes people from the centers; worse, NIMH's catchment stipulations have in many cases lowered the quality of care given to consumers. Because the federal program funds only one grantee within any given catchment area, service monopolies are created. As Dr. H. G. Whittington, director of the Comprehensive Community Mental Health Center of Denver General Hospital, explains:

> As the catchment area concept tends to work out . . . it really turns out to be just a franchising operation. The arrangement operates in constraint of competition, and some of the franchises have gone to facilities that are not up to scratch.[14]

Not that lack of competition is unique to community mental health centers; on the contrary, it is one of the prime structural characteristics of health and social service agencies in general. In place of open competition these agencies have "specialized," dividing the social service "market" among themselves in a cartel-like arrangement (some deal with children, some with alcoholics, some with unwed mothers, some with Catholics, some with Jews, and so on). Because of their monopoly over professional and financial resources, these agencies have little incentive to be responsive to the needs of individual clients; instead they are responsive only to those needs recognized by professionals and administrators. This insensitivity to clients is enhanced by the pervasive ideology dictating that the providers of service are better judges of what is needed than are the consumers of their services, an attitude particularly common in mental health services, since mental patients are not supposed to know what they need or want.

The community mental health centers legislation, providing funds, and the NIMH regulations, providing operational guidelines, in no way altered the noncompetitive status quo. Instead of attempting to build competition into the system, the designers of the program did just the opposite. The watchword was "coordination." The rationale behind the concept of coordination was largely an attempt to redress the so-called manpower crisis in mental health. Since NIMH believed that even a doubling of professional resources would not be enough to provide for the needs of all the millions said to be suffering from emotional distress and behavior disorders, a more efficient use of existing resources was called for. Essentially this would mean greater collaboration between mental health services and other public and private agencies and institutions in the community.

Thus, prior to receiving federal grant funds, applicants had to draft plans showing how they would "coordinate" their services with other pertinent human services in the catchment area according to a "comprehensive plan." "Coordination" meant that representatives of various agencies had to agree to provide mental health services; "comprehensive plans" meant that they would also agree to a federally supervised scheme for delivering those services to the community. Theoretically community mental health centers stand at the center of an easily accessible "network" of services. The very general nature of these notions of coordination and planning, however, offered little assurance of improved efficiency, accessibility, or care.

In a bureaucratic and political world, the instinct to retain one's corporate identity is strong. A hospital might agree to set aside some inpatient bed for "center" patients; a child guidance clinic might agree to provide some outpatient services; the psychiatry department of a local medical school might operate a crisis clinic. But the problem, as one National Association for Mental Health official observed, is that "everyone wants to coordinate and nobody wants to be coordinated."*[15]

Federal money is the lure held out by the 1963 legislation as an incentive for specialized local agencies to work together. But the prospect of federal dollars is at least as likely to encourage professional opportunism at the local level as it is to encourage the hoped-for institutional reforms. In this respect, the community mental health centers program is little different from

* The lack of coordination among related federal agencies provides an illuminating counterpoint. In Atlanta, three federal agencies—NIMH, the Department of Housing and Urban Development (Model Cities), and the Office of Economic Opportunity—all devoted to the concept of coordination among social agencies on the local level—have created overlapping "target" areas. The planning that went into the three federal programs was, it would seem, entirely unrelated; all three have different catchment boundaries, different regulations, different financing mechanisms. Thus, in the process of trying to effect local coordination, they have helped to heighten local fragmentation (see Chapter 10).

other Great Society programs. Piven and Cloward make the point:

> What some critics see as incredibly intricate networks of Great Society agencies held together by multitudes of subcontracting arrangements that bring tears of frustration to the eyes of auditors were merely the structural reflections of the politics of implementation, which required that many interested parties —municipal agencies, private social agencies, universities, new ghetto organizations, private corporations, etc.—be co-opted into the programs. Professionals helped to justify these arrangements. . . . Social problems were seen as "multifaceted," thus requiring "comprehensive" and "coordinated" solutions: to all appearances, the laws of science were dictating the politics of implementation. As for the professionals . . . if they were politically useful, they were glad to be so, for federal intervention . . . provided funds and authority for the expansion of professional interests as well.[16]

Dr. Robert Felix, director of NIMH when the centers legislation was passed and one of the chief architects of the program, states that specific organizational criteria to guide "maximum coordination" was deliberately omitted. He writes:

> We had some idea as to how these centers should be organized, but we purposely refrained from incorporating these into the law and regulations. We knew each center would be different. Most important, we wanted the communities to feel they were their centers—not the Federal Government's—and one way of furthering this was to encourage them to develop organizational systems adapted to the communities' needs and interests.[17]

This seems evasive at best, particularly since the original regulations made no mention whatever of how the "communities" in question were to participate in the planning of "their" centers. Instead, the regulations virtually guaranteed that community mental health centers would be designed and controlled by mental health professionals, whose territorial claims, as psychologist Anthony M. Graziano has observed, "are seldom challenged, despite what might be a history of failure, irrelevance, or ignorance."[18] Furthermore NIMH's insistence upon the primacy of clinical services made it inevitable that instead of the nature and

scope of the defining problems of a given area to define the
organizational structure, the structure of the professions and
agencies has defined the nature and scope of the services and
the organizational form of community mental health centers.

And this has everything to do with how well another key
concept, that of "continuity of care," is understood, and how
effectively it can be implemented. Broadly defined, "continuity
of care" is the delivery of consistent and coherent services to an
individual as he moves through various phases of treatment—
admissions screening, inpatient and outpatient care, rehabilitation, and so on. As such, it is the acid test of coordination in a
community mental health center.

It should be noted that while the phrase itself has become a
shibboleth of the centers program, there is not a single agreed-
upon operational definition of the term. The Joint Information
Service noted that:

> Some persons feel that care cannot be considered to have
> continuity unless the patient is treated by the same therapists
> throughout his illness. Others maintain that continuity of care
> is preserved as long as the facility continues to accept responsi-
> bility for the patient and to see to it that at any given time
> some element of service is responsible for him. It might thus
> be useful to introduce two differentiating terms, "continuity
> of therapist" and "continuity of responsibility."[19]

NIMH, while its regulations stipulate that centers must "assure continuity of care for patients," has offered no useful
definition. According to the regulations, continuity of care is
considered to be accomplished when the following criteria are
met:

> (i) That any person eligible for treatment within any one ele-
> ment can and will also be eligible for treatment within any
> other element of service;
> (ii) That any person within any one element can and will be
> transferred without delay to any other element (provided space
> is available) whenever such a transfer is indicated by the
> patient's clinical needs;
> (iii) That clinical information concerning a patient which was
> obtained within one element be made available to those respon-
> sible for that patient's treatment within any other element;

(iv) That those responsible for a patient's care within one element *can, when practicable and when not clinically contraindicated,* continue to care for that patient within any of the other elements.[20] [Emphasis added.]

Thus, while NIMH might see some advantage to the idea of continuity of therapist, the regulations by no means require it. Indeed, the above criteria suggest that NIMH is more concerned with the efficiency of the system of information flow and patient movement than with the effectiveness and continuity of any given treatment plan for any given patient. And a community mental health center often turns out not to be a "place" where one can go to get help with what might be a multitude of different problems, but only a somewhat more efficient referral system through a confusing maze of "services." It is a familiar irony that the point of view of planners, administrators, and providers is stressed, while the point of view of the person receiving "comprehensive treatment" is virtually ignored. One can question whether continuity of care means anything at all unless that person perceives his own experience as having meaning and continuity, regardless of how systematically he may be transferred from one "element" to another.

Some community mental health centers have adopted the notion of "continuity of responsibility"—primarily because staff are assigned to separate services rather than to specific clients. Thus there is much talk about the need for swift and effective exchange of information; this is not always accomplished, however, even when all the elements of service are under one roof. In a field that is notorious for multiple points of view, and in which professionals for the most part seem disinclined to treat one another's "diagnoses" with reverence, open sharing of information does not have much historical precedent. Few centers have yet managed to establish efficient data systems or procedures for the exchange of clinical records and other information, although some are now beginning to develop computerized information systems. One of the centers most praised for its innovation in this regard is the Westside Community Mental Health Center, Inc., of San Francisco, a consortium of sixteen separate autonomous agencies. The Westside Center has insti-

tuted the "transaction reporting system," a computerized central
information system providing chronological listings (containing
no clinical information) of admissions, transfers, referrals, and
discharges of all center patients. This system, costing an estimated $18,000 a year to operate, is one answer to "continuity
of care" and is likely to become a model of the future for those
centers that can afford it. No doubt such a system is helpful to
administrators and providers, but how helpful it is to an individual seeking help is another question.

The larger issue concerns the appropriateness of the referral
model itself—regardless of how efficient and sophisticated it
is—for problems that involve emotional disturbances. The way
people are identified and referred is, again, based on the medical
model, which assumes an individual is "sick," and that the
only problem is getting that individual speedily to a doctor or
other medical personnel skilled in "curing" his or her particular
disease. For large numbers of people, whose problems are many
and inseparable from a complex of social problems, the referral
system is illogical and dysfunctional. The following case from
psychologist William Ryan's study of metropolitan Boston
provides a superb example:

> Consider the case of a depressed and defeated working-class
> housewife turning to someone for help with a multitude of
> problems that are overwhelming her: an alcoholic husband
> who disappears for days at a time; the piling up of pressing
> debts; an eviction notice from the landlord; two children in
> diapers and a third who is enuretic; a sickly daughter and a ne-
> glected oldest son whose school work is worsening daily; head-
> aches and stomach aches; increasing trouble with her neighbors
> as she becomes more and more short-tempered; and a growing
> sense of guilt as she finds that she herself is turning more and
> more to liquor for consolation.[21]

As Ryan goes on to suggest, to diagnose this woman as suffering
from depression and refer her for psychotherapy would probably be futile, since she is neither verbal nor introspective and,
more to the point, she would no doubt tend to view psychiatric
treatment as a totally inadequate method for helping her with
her problems. Her depression is not "curable" in isolation, since
it is a natural response to what is happening to her. "To call

her situation a marital problem," asserts Ryan, "seems, not only to her but to most people, a rather glaring understatement."[22]

In summary, "coordination," "comprehensiveness," and "continuity of care" as they are presently understood and implemented in most community mental health centers have meaning only for the providers of services: they in fact tend to contribute to the fragmentation of individuals into as many pieces as there are agencies to deal with "special" problems or populations. Unless and until they refer to the way in which human beings, as complex totalities, receive help, they will remain irrelevant in human terms.

Community Involvement

By the late sixties, it had become clear that agency coordination alone, even where it was operative, was not a sufficient means of reallocating local services. Belatedly, NIMH began to urge "citizen participation" in the planning, decision-making, and priority-setting of community mental health programs. But while the Institute now encourages increased community involvement, community boards are neither required by federal law nor defined by federal regulations. Consequently, most of the centers now operating, and particularly those that were funded early in the program, have no formal mechanisms for citizen participation. By and large, community advisory boards have been added after the fact, few of them with any real fiscal control, policy-making power, or program responsibility.

As a result, the concept of citizen participation is open to any number of interpretations by various individuals and interest groups. In general, the degree to which citizens are involved, how they are involved, and in what they are involved are left entirely to the discretion of the professionals in charge of the center. All of our case studies illustrate this phenomenon. In only two centers (the South Central Community Mental Health Center in Atlanta, Georgia, and the Area D Community Mental Health Center in Washington, D.C.) is citizen participation taken at all seriously, and in only one (Atlanta) were citizens involved at the outset. In *none* of the centers do community advisory boards have any legal authority or responsibility.

The Metropolitan Community Mental Health Center in Minneapolis offers an example of how the professional community
determines the limits of citizen involvement. In 1969, the center
submitted to NIMH a proposal for developing consultation and
education services, including the creation of a long-overdue
community advisory board. By March, 1970, the Metropolitan
Center claimed that a "Community Advisory Committee" was
meeting monthly to assist in the planning of consultation and
education services, and identified a local Indian as its chairman.
A subsequent check by two NIMH central headquarters officials revealed that the Indian was never aware that he had been
made chairman. On the contrary, he had attended only "one or
two meetings of the group because it was clear they didn't want
to do anything."[23] Nevertheless, the center proceeded to outline further plans for "citizen involvement" in what should become a classic in how not to relate to the community:

> A committee has been set up to develop the Community
> Advisory Board; the consensus of staff is to wait until the
> community leaders identify themselves by criticism of the
> program and then to invite them to be on the committee.[24]

A recent NIMH-contracted evaluation study, conducted under
the auspices of Tufts University, focused on six poverty-area
centers and found that three of them had "elitist" boards of
prominent citizens and few, if any, consumers; one had a board
composed of potential consumers, but with a very narrow
advisory function and no real power; one embodied the point
of view that having community residents on the staff constituted
citizen participation; and one was in the process of developing
a "consortium" of consumer representatives and agency representatives.[25] The authors of this study pointed out that all but
one (participation-through-staff) reflect middle-class patterns of
citizen involvement, with historical roots in charity-minded
boards of housewives, businessmen, lawyers, and ministers,
whose main function is to raise money and who do not question
the domination of professional interests over consumer interests.

In the 1970s, debate over the issue of citizen participation—
in community mental health centers as in other local institutions—has grown heated; in many places the issue is no longer

citizen participation but community control. Clearly community representatives must have a major voice in planning and decision-making, for the determination of the goals of service and the ways they are to be reached should not and must not be left solely to mental health professionals. To move toward this goal, the federal guidelines should require that the official grantee be a governing community board, selected in some systematic democratic manner, which would exercise control over the dispersion of funds and be permitted to contract with various professional groups to provide specific services. Of course, the powers of this governing board should be balanced by holding its actions accountable to the community and by federal guidelines and standards for the disbursing of federal funds, the protection of minority and individual rights, and the maintenance and upgrading of quality of service. Furthermore, since community representatives are not always cognizant of the needs of patients or devoted to the protection of their rights, a governing board should include among its members past and present patients and their relatives.

6

Perpetuating the
Two-Class System of Care

In no other medical discipline is there such marked disparity
between the care available to those who can afford the high
cost of services and those who cannot. An important goal of
the community mental health centers program was to abolish
the prevailing two-class system of care, first by giving priority
in funding to those areas with few existing services, then by
making the services of a center equally available to all residents
of a catchment area without regard to age, sex, race, creed,
color, diagnostic category, or ability to pay. NIMH hoped to
provide services of high enough quality to attract the middle
classes *and* to make those same services accessible to those
who could not afford to pay for them. "The care of the indigent is a major concern to us at NIMH," Dr. Alan Levine, then

chief of NIMH's Continuing Development Section, told a 1967 conference on community mental health centers. "We feel it is one of the major threats to the centers program. If after a few years we still see two standards of care, with the poor going one place and the rich another, this could do in the centers program."[1] The concern was not, however, translated into the legislation or regulations. Instead, the funding mechanisms, the catchment-area concept, and the essential-services regulation have raised enormous barriers to providing quality services for the poor.

Despite the intention of giving funding priority to needy areas, the requirement for matching funds has made the establishment of community mental health centers in such areas extremely difficult. Each state is required to submit a statewide plan ranking its catchment areas on the basis of "the extent of mental illness and emotional disturbance" and "the existence of low per capita income, chronic unemployment, and substandard housing." But priorities for funding have actually been based on two other criteria: "the comprehensiveness of the services to be provided in the proposed center" and "the association of the center with a general hospital."[2] Thus, the very lack of existing services, including general hospitals, and the inability to come up with matching funds have served to work against poverty areas from the outset. The result is that poor communities that need services most get the least.

Irving Chase, president of the National Association for Mental Health, contends that "no state plan for construction of community mental health centers . . . has not given priority to centers in rural and urban poverty areas."[3] NIMH does not require, however, that construction or staffing grants be awarded in the same order as these priorities. Because affluent areas are more likely to generate the matching funds required, they are far more likely to be funded—which in effect renders the priority rankings meaningless.

A 1971 GAO study found that many of the areas highest on their state's priority list had not been funded, while lower-priority areas had been. For example, California's state plan assigns priority positions to 148 catchment areas. The range of priority positions for the 23 construction projects which had been approved as of April, 1969, can be seen in Table 2:

TABLE 2.
Constructed CMHCs in California

Catchment area priority positions	Number approved
1 to 25	6
26 to 50	1
51 to 75	3
76 to 100	–
101 to 125	4
126 to 148	9
Total	23

Source: The Community Mental Health Centers Program—Improvements Needed in Management, Report to the Congress by the Comptroller General of the United States (Washington, D.C., July 8, 1971).

The table shows that of the twenty-three projects approved, only six were among the twenty-five neediest catchment areas. At the same time, nine were approved among the catchment areas ranked at the bottom of the list, between places 126 to 148; four were approved between 101 and 125. In other words, thirteen of the twenty-three projects approved in California were for the areas of least need.

The GAO found a similar situation in Florida, where only one of the five neediest areas had been funded. Table 3 shows

TABLE 3.
Constructed Community Mental Health Centers in Florida

Priority positions	Number approved
1 to 5	1
6 to 10	4
11 to 15	2
16 to 20	1
21 to 25	2
26 to 30	2
31 to 43	–
Total	12

the range of priority positions among Florida's forty-three catchment areas for the twelve construction projects funded as of April 1, 1969. For those centers that have been constructed in poverty areas, the declining formula for staffing grants leaves them in an extremely vulnerable financial situation.* Moreover,

* The Community Mental Health Centers Act was amended in 1970 to increase the level and duration of financial support for poverty-area centers. This will be discussed more fully later in this chapter.

the fact that a center is situated in a designated poverty area does not guarantee that services will be provided to those unable to pay for them. The catchment-area concept can too easily be perverted—particularly since the mandated "responsibility" of the centers remains largely ignored and unenforced. As Dr. H. G. Whittington, director of the Comprehensive Community Mental Health Center in Denver, has noted:

> We have set up fiefdoms so that various people have their respective pieces of real estate to which they're supposed to provide services. What are the social regulatory mechanisms that are going to control this? What's going to keep them from operating, as some of the Hill-Burton hospitals do, entirely in the private sector? How are they going to stay public? I see evidence that many of them are going to be private facilities.[4]

In fact, far too many community mental health centers supported with public money do operate largely as private facilities. According to Ralph Kennedy, chief of NIMH's Community Mental Health Centers Support Branch, well over half the centers now functioning are operated under private auspices.[5] While this does not in itself mean that they are exclusively private, the odds are good that many of them will go in that direction if they can—for financial reasons, if for no other. The experience of the Kern View Community Mental Health Center, a poverty-area center in Bakersfield, California, illustrates the lack of social regulatory mechanisms to protect the public interest where community mental health centers are concerned (see Chapter 9). Relying perhaps too much on the professional integrity of those who run the centers, neither NIMH nor Congress has felt it necessary to build in any safeguards against professional abuse of public funds.

Interviews with NIMH officials and practicing professionals, as well as contacts with citizens in various parts of the country, indicate that the undue emphasis placed by the regulations on hospital-based care has been interpreted in many instances as an open invitation to psychiatrists to expand their private practices. Commented Martin Keeley of the NIMH regional office in Chicago, "It is a rule of thumb that whenever you see a general hospital associated with a community mental health center, you immediately look to see if the inpatient facility has been co-opted by private psychiatrists."[6] Joseph E. Coon of the regional office in Atlanta made similar observations. He estimates that in at least twelve of the one hundred centers in his region, private psychiatrists use the inpatient unit primarily for their private patients. Universities, says Coon, are often no better than hospitals in using center funds for their own purposes. "They say they have community programs, but they don't have anything to do with the community."[7] According to the director of NIMH's Dallas regional office, Katharyn Fritz, the psychiatric community has posed major problems in that region as well. For example, the Touro Infirmary Community Mental Health Center in New Orleans was, she said, "set up as a doctors' workshop." Most of the patients are private, while indigent patients are sent either to state or charity hospitals. These charity hospitals, Fritz explained, are state-operated facilities that Louisiana has set up especially for the indigent.[8] "Louisiana has a two-track system in mental health, one public and one private and never the twain shall meet," elaborated Glen Rollins, a mental health consultant for the Dallas regional office. Rollins explained that he was "puzzled why a place like this got into the community mental health centers program in the first place." He answered his own question by saying, "it was mostly the construction grant. They run a minimally acceptable program and get by with it, and in the meanwhile they will get a valuable facility for their own use."[9]

This state of affairs is hardly surprising. The most important regulation regarding treatment of the indigent in community mental health centers is among the vaguest. The regulation stipulates that a "reasonable" amount of care be provided to indigent patients. Specifically, the original regulations stated that grantees for community mental health center construction and/or staffing grants must assure that:

> The facility will furnish below cost or without charge a reasonable volume of services to persons unable to pay therefor. As used in this paragraph, "persons unable to pay therefor" includes persons who are otherwise self-supporting but are unable to pay the full cost of needed services. Such services may be paid for wholly or partly out of public funds or contributions of individuals and private and charitable organizations such

as community chest or may be contributed at the expense of the facility itself. In determining what constitutes a reasonable volume of services to persons unable to pay therefor, there shall be considered conditions in the area to be served by the applicant, including the amount of such services that may be available otherwise than through the applicant. *The requirements of assurance from the applicant may be waived if the applicant demonstrates to the satisfaction of the State agency, subject to subsequent approval by the Surgeon General, that to furnish such services is not feasible financially.*[10] [Emphasis added.]

The imprecision of the regulation has meant that community mental health centers can provide little or no service to the poor. How much care is "reasonable" is never spelled out; and although formal exemptions have rarely, if ever, been requested, the existence of such a loophole is enough to indicate that the regulation has no teeth. Martin Keeley put it very well: "The 'reasonable' amount of services regulation doesn't hold any water. . . . If it's going to work, let's be damn specific how much we mean. . . . Then there's got to be a funding mechanism to carry it out." What's wrong with the centers, he went on, "is that non-paying patients get thrown into the state hospital system. People get excluded on the basis of a fiscal reason which has nothing to do with treatment. As the legislation is set up, it is detrimental to the treatment of indigent patients!"[11]

It is not merely the legislation or the vacuity of the "reasonable volume of services" regulation that excludes the poor, however. In many cases, even where mental health services are desperately needed, a community mental health center may be inaccessible because of language barriers or because of the barriers imposed by racial, cultural, and class prejudices. Because the centers program as a whole embodies a fundamentally middle-class model, individual centers are often irrelevant to the poor and minority groups. Traditional programs, planned and operated by middle-class professionals, are of dubious appropriateness to poverty-area residents who may not conceive of their problems as "emotional" or "mental" as defined by professionals, and whose experience has taught them to mistrust the existing "helping" institutions of the dominant white society.

A number of studies during the past two decades have demonstrated the pervasiveness of a middle-class bias in the presumably "scientific" formulations of mental health and illness. One such study, an examination of the content of mental health educational pamphlets, found that the values of adjustment, conformity, thrift, respectability, and control of emotions were used to describe the characteristics of mental health, and concluded that the mental health movement "is unwittingly propagating a middle-class ethic under the guise of science."[12] Looking at this phenomenon from a historical perspective, the authors point out that:

> The moral, religious, and economic underpinnings of "traditional" middle-class society have altered appreciably during the past fifty years. It is of particular significance that with the decline of these old supportive institutions there has emerged a new movement giving "pseudoscientific" authoritative support to the new "middle-class" way of life. In many respects the mental health movement represents the functional equivalent of religion in the traditional middle-class structure.

> When the foregoing remarks are viewed from the standpoint of the formal goals of the mental health movement, a significant paradox is evident. If, as many sociologists and culturally oriented psychiatrists maintain, one of the primary roots of mental disorder lies in socially structured strains, then it may very well be that the mental health movement is helping to support a social system that is producing a high incidence of mental illness.[13]

Nevertheless, the whole legislated package of the centers program—from predefined "communities" to "essential services" to "comprehensive programs"—reveals its underlying middle-class nature. It is unfair to impute this problem only to individual centers for, as E. Fuller Torrey pointed out in a paper presented to the American Orthopsychiatric Association, it began at a higher level:

> It began at the very conceptualization of the Community Mental Health Centers. It began when the architects of the Act unconsciously and ethnocentrically perpetuated the dominant-class, dominant-culture, dominant-caste model of mental health services as The Model. This works as long as the Mental Health Centers are serving Wellesley or White Plains or Palo

Alto. But it is irrelevant when they are to serve Roxbury or the South Bronx or East San Jose.[14]

The extent to which the poor and ethnic minorities are excluded, and the various ways in which they are excluded, is amply illustrated by the Metropolitan Community Mental Health Center in Minneapolis. The closest this center comes to serving the community is in its name. Both a recent NIMH-funded evaluation conducted by the Health Planning Advisory Center (Health-PAC) and a June 9, 1972, NIMH regional-office site-visit report reveal that this center, built in 1968 for around $1.68 million, operates almost exclusively as an inpatient facility for the patients of private psychiatrists.[15] The great majority of inpatients come from outside the catchment area through referrals by private psychiatrists; in no year of its operation has the percentage of inpatients from the center's own catchment area ever exceeded 25 percent of the total number of inpatients.[16]

The Metropolitan Community Mental Health Center is jointly sponsored by two private voluntary hospitals, Swedish and St. Barnabas. The center (a streamlined, modern building with a glassed-in courtyard and a swimming pool*) is located on a tract of land adjacent to the two hospitals. In a telephone interview, the director of the center, Dr. Donald Daggett, stated that the two private hospitals had been seeking for some time to expand their own inpatient facilities. Because they did not comply with state guidelines requiring, among other things, more comprehensive community-based (i.e., non-hospital) services and a policy-making board of citizens, the two hospitals could not qualify for state or Hill-Burton construction funds. "The only funding mechanism for construction was the comprehensive community mental health centers program," explained Daggett.[17] Nevertheless, the two hospitals had no intention of changing their inpatient orientation and embracing a comprehensive community approach. "The model for treatment at the mental health center will be the model of the private psychiatrist in private practice,"[18] wrote the director in a planning

* The Metropolitan Center is one of two federally funded centers in the country with a swimming pool; the other is in Orlando, Florida.

proposal. Dr. Daggett further remarked: "Right from the beginning it was our clear intention to provide basically inpatient care for the patients of the two sponsoring hospitals and that we would have to treat many people from the rest of the county [outside the catchment area]."*[19]

And so it has been. With ninety-five inpatient beds, the Metropolitan Center has nearly twice as many psychiatric beds as any other single hospital in the area. (In the first six months of 1970, the Health-PAC study reports, 72.9 percent of all admissions were admitted as inpatients, 14.9 percent for partial hospitalization, and only 12.2 percent as outpatients.)[20] Because the center operates solely on federal money and patients' fees, no one who cannot pay the average inpatient cost (about ninety dollars a day according to Daggett) is admitted as an inpatient. The large majority of the inpatients—who tend to be white women between the ages of twenty-five and forty-four—are referred to the center by private psychiatrists. The most recent statistics show that in the month of May, 1972, out of a total number of 168 patients admitted to the inpatient service, 100 were referred by private psychiatrists and an additional 5 by nonpsychiatric physicians. In contrast, 8 inpatients were referred by the county welfare department, 3 by the state employment agency, and 1 by the nearby Anoka State Hospital.[21] There is no evidence that the center has established any working relationship with the state hospital, much less had an impact on the admissions to the state hospital from its catchment area. The NIMH site-visit report states that the center has "no linkage with the state hospital for people from the service area." The site-visit report further notes that many patients from the catchment area who initially contact the County General Hospital "are never offered alternative service at Metro, but are routinely transferred to Anoka." The report concludes, "This practice defeats the essential philosophic treatment concept of the Center program. Instead of changing the patient flow away from state hospitals and inpatient service, the emergency component supports the traditional status-quo of service delivery."[22]

* According to a June 9, 1972, NIMH site-visit report written by Martin Keeley, however, "the intent of the construction grant to the hospital was to provide an inpatient unit for the specific geographic area described in the grant application."

According to its director, it is the clear policy of the Metropolitan center to refuse to admit indigent patients for inpatient care. When we reminded Dr. Daggett that the federal regulations require centers to treat patients without regard to their ability to pay, Daggett replied that his center had an agreement with NIMH that it would treat only paying inpatients.[23] According to the two directors of NIMH's regional offices in Kansas City and Chicago (responsibility for the Metropolitan Center was transferred from the Kansas City regional office to the Chicago regional office in 1970), there was never such an agreement.[24] Virgil Shoup, head of the Kansas City regional office, stated that, on the contrary, the Minneapolis Center had to sign an agreement binding them to treat indigent patients. Nevertheless, Dr. Daggett insists that his center will continue to treat only paying inpatients "until the county sets up a scheme to take care of the payments for indigents."[25]

The service the Metropolitan Center most frequently provides to indigents is outpatient service. The extent of this "service" to the poor throughout most of the operation of the center is indicated by the statistic that as recently as February, 1970, the center was treating a total of five outpatients per month![26] Daggett contends, however, that the center has significantly expanded its outpatient service since then.

The Health-PAC study of the Metropolitan Center found that the aged, youth, and Indians are the three groups in the center's catchment area in greatest need of mental health services. Yet the center frowns upon accepting these kinds of patients. In 1970, only 8 percent of all center admissions were over sixty-five and only 4 percent were under eighteen.[27] This is not surprising, since the center lacks any treatment program for children. For Indians, services are even more inaccessible. With some 12,000 Indians, Minneapolis has one of the highest urban concentrations of Indians in the country; most of this population is located in the downtown area near the Metropolitan Community Mental Health Center. Yet in the eighteen-month period, from October, 1970, to May, 1972, out of a total of 3,127 patients admitted for any kind of care to the Metropolitan Center, only 25 Indians were seen. These figures indicate that the Metropolitan Center sees an average of one Indian patient every two weeks.[28] During the same eighteen-month period, the Metropolitan Center saw 47 blacks, or 1.5 percent of the total number of patients admitted; 3 Mexican-Americans; and 1 Syrian male.

The pattern of services provided to minority groups is mirrored in the makeup of the center's staff. Of 120 individuals connected with the center, 118 are white. Two—a female receptionist and a female M.A.-level sociologist—are black.[29] All the psychiatrists connected with the center are also in private practice, with most of them spending the bulk of their time outside the center treating their private patients. Five of the seven psychiatrists listed in the current NIMH staffing grant application are members of the prestigious Minneapolis Clinic of Neurology and Psychiatry. Located outside the catchment area next to a lake and golf course, this clinic for private group practice is widely known among professionals throughout the city as the "cartel." According to the Health-PAC study, "this group plays a powerful role in setting prices and standards for psychiatric services in Minneapolis and throughout the state."[30]

According to NIMH regional office official Martin Keeley, the top staff at the Metropolitan Center were never interested in treating the indigent. Keeley stated that the psychiatrists "focused all their attention on the construction grant." Now that the building is finished, Keeley believes that the regional office has little leverage over what kinds of services the center provides and to whom. "I get the impression that these guys don't even value the staffing grant. They got what they wanted—a nice building. . . . They would probably be glad if we took the staffing money away. Then they wouldn't have to worry at all about treating the indigent."[31]

Financing Community Mental Health Centers: Running out of Steam

The fact that so many centers do not open their doors very wide to the poor is based, in part, on an economic imperative: they cannot afford to do so. As Dr. H. G. Whittington candidly remarked:

> A center director who sees indigent patients is not behaving logically. I see indigent patients on the basis of idealism and

commitment, not logic. Economic incentives to see them are simply not there. If NIMH provided economic incentives to see people like this so that we at least broke even and so that virtue was rewarded, we'd have a more workable system.[32]

By the late sixties, as the oldest centers were entering their third and last year of federal staffing grant support, it had become obvious that the financial situation of the program was close to disastrous. Even centers in affluent areas tended to have increasing difficulty coming up with sufficient nonfederal funds as the NIMH grant declined to zero. State and local governments, with their own budgetary restraints and other social priorities, were simply not willing or able to carry the centers, and the limitations of most health insurance plans mean that such reimbursements make a negligible contribution—particularly to any center that tries to be innovative. This "running out of steam" syndrome has a number of implications.

For some centers, the financial squeeze alone has forced a reversion to a private-practice format; that is, in order to stay financially afloat, they must raise patient fees and make the ability to pay those fees (either directly or through insurance coverage) a major criterion for admission. Other centers, located in urban or rural poverty areas whose residents often cannot arrange third-party payments, are faced with grimmer alternatives: They must drastically cut back on services and staff, phase out operations altogether, or receive a continuing heavy federal subsidy. In any case, the inadequacy of the financing mechanisms for community mental health centers has presented one of the severest challenges to the program's viability.

An NIMH-contracted study undertaken in 1968 and 1969 by Stanford Research Institute (SRI) looked at the actual and potential sources of funds for centers. It studied sixteen centers in fourteen states serving catchment areas of varying sizes and socioeconomic characteristics; all were in or approaching their third year of staffing support. The documentation in this study suggests that the expectation that states and local communities would ultimately assume full financial responsibility for the centers was based largely on wishful thinking. All the centers in the sample, despite varying fiscal patterns, continued to rely on federal support, even in the third year of the original staffing grant (in some cases the declining federal share was buttressed with growth and other supplemental grants). Though state funds were the major source of replacement as the federal share declined, the study found that most states, under pressure to fund other social programs, are unlikely to increase substantially their support of community mental health centers. According to the SRI study:

> In some states, legislative leaders indicated that mental health programs have reached a plateau in terms of popularity and that further increases in appropriations would require clear demonstrations of effectiveness. Federal matching programs, particularly seed money programs, are being viewed with increasing suspicion by state legislators, a number of whom made it clear that the legislature was under no obligation to provide additional program funds merely because federal support was declining.[33]

It is also unlikely, even if the community mental health centers program were greatly expanded and even if it succeeded in reducing the need for state hospitals, that substantial sums of money would therefore be diverted from state hospital budgets to community programs. In almost every state a large and well-entrenched bureaucracy has grown up to administer state hospitals, and the extent of its resistance to budget cuts is not to be underestimated. It is possible, even probable, that state mental hospitals will change in character—but that they will disappear completely (thus freeing all those dollars) is another matter. As Robert Connery *et al.* remark in *The Politics of Mental Health*, "While it is all very well to argue that in the long run community mental health centers will contribute to a 'withering away' of the large state mental hospitals with a consequent freeing of funds, the immediate financial irrelevance of this position is evident."[34]

As for local support, the SRI study found that direct contributions to community mental health centers by local government units was piddling.[35] This should have been anticipated. Historically, local governments have relied on the state to provide most mental health services; and everything else considered—the needs in education, housing, transportation, physical health care—mental health (particularly as a separate system) is not among their highest priorities. Furthermore, local governments, with relatively narrow and inflexible tax bases, could not begin to meet the expense of the program even if it *were* a high priority. Indeed, the trend has been in the opposite direction—that is, for the federal government to assume an ever-larger share of the fiscal responsibility for social problems that are considered to be national in scope. In this sense, the emphasis on local fiscal responsibility in the centers program is a curious reversal. Given the already obvious inequalities in wealth among localities and the great inequities in property tax on which so much local revenue is based, it is highly questionable that community mental health should be financed through local taxes if the goal of the program is really to end the double standard of care.

Another potential source of funds for centers is health insurance. But although private, nonprofit centers have tapped it to some extent, this source has generally proven to be disappointingly dry. SRI found that private insurance reimbursements together with patient fees accounted for 20 percent or more of the total revenues in only five of the sixteen centers studied, and these five were privately operated.[36] (Not surprisingly, centers operated under public auspices were found to rely far more heavily on government funds than those operated under private auspices.) Private insurance, provided by most major employers and by unions, carries a number of crucial restrictions against mental health coverage. Typically, it covers just inpatient hospital services; outpatient and partial hospitalization coverage is very limited or nonexistent. Furthermore, private insurance normally will not cover the services of nonmedical mental health professionals—psychologists and social workers, primarily—not to mention paraprofessional therapists, all of whom can play large roles in providing comprehensive care in community mental health centers. At any rate, there is danger in too great a reliance on insurance plans that concentrate coverage on "medical" care provided by M.D.s. The kinds of financial sources a center has will inevitably define the kinds of services provided. And should the main source be existing insurance plans, that will inevitably subvert the broader community orientation of the centers.

The prospects for including outpatient mental health services in the national health insurance plans now before Congress are grim. Of all the various proposals, only one (the Kennedy bill) provides for such ambulatory care. The official position of the American Psychiatric Association (probably the most powerful mental health lobbying group) on mental health coverage under national health insurance is discouraging. The APA calls for hospitalization benefits equal to those for medical and surgical illnesses, and defines mental health services as "medical treatment" to be provided by, or under the direction of, psychiatrists or other physicians. This is clearly a regressive policy, for it will only hinder efforts to provide alternatives to hospitalization and shore up the already formidable barriers to providing a broader human services approach to mental health problems. Whether the APA plan is adopted or not, the battle for adequate coverage of mental disorders is likely to be long and arduous, and will leave millions of people uncovered.

Revenues from Medicare and Medicaid have been negligible for most centers, accounting for no more than 3 or 4 percent of total income. The most obvious reason that Medicare has not been a factor is that few centers provide services to the aged. Medicaid, like private health insurance, is limited in its coverage of mental disabilities, and its ceiling on payments varies from state to state. In a number of states, community mental health centers are not certified providers of psychiatric services under Medicaid (certification for Medicaid is left up to the states) and so cannot bill for it even where it might be appropriate. Other states will cover only those on public assistance.* Furthermore, since Medicaid has proven to be far more expensive than was anticipated, many states are limiting rather than expanding coverage.

An additional problem, particularly for those centers operated by a government agency (state, county, or local), is the lack of any incentive to collect Medicaid (or indeed, any third-

---

* In addition to those actually receiving public assistance, who are automatically eligible for Medicaid, there are those who meet all of the eligibility requirements *except* income level for one of those categories. Depending on the income ceiling set by the states, such people may also be eligible for Medicaid.

party) reimbursements. In many cases, such revenue goes into a general fund rather than to the individual center; and often the state or county will deduct whatever it has to pay on Medicaid from its share of the federal matching grant. Consequently, many centers simply don't bother to collect the fees to which they're entitled. Other centers, according to the SRI study,

> . . . because of philosophical attitudes . . . have not pursued these revenues. Staff of a number of centers expressed the opinion that an aggressive collection program was not appropriate for a center that receives significant government or philanthropic support or that serves an area of low income. This was reported also to be the reaction of the general public. . . .[37]

As for philanthropic support from private charities such as the United Fund and the Community Chest, no more than token contributions can be expected unless normal contributions soar or other worthy causes cease to exist. As the SRI study discovered, most philanthropic organizations "do not support programs that are operated by government jurisdictions or that receive substantial amounts of government funding."

The precarious financial situation of existing centers and the need for expanded and extended assistance to poverty areas were highlighted in hearings held by the House Subcommittee on Public Health and Welfare in 1969. It was recognized that both NIMH officials and their supporters in Congress had been too optimistic about the development of nonfederal funding resources and somewhat blind to the need to provide higher percentages of federal matching funds to poverty area centers. Accordingly, Congress amended the Community Mental Health Centers Act in 1970, extending the period of federal staffing-grant support and increasing the level of that support in poverty areas. The 1970 amendments also authorized construction grants for another three years, allowing the federal government to bear up to 90 percent of the cost in poverty areas. Staffing-grant support to all centers was extended for eight years, and broadened to include part of the operating and maintenance cost as well. For poverty areas, support was authorized for up to 90 percent of the costs for the first two years; 80 percent of the costs during the third year; 75 percent for the fourth and fifth years; and 70 percent for each of the remaining three years. In addition, Congress authorized one-year initiation and development grants of up to fifty thousand dollars to urban and rural poverty areas for assessing local needs, designing a program, and obtaining local financial and professional assistance.

Although these amendments took the immediate financial pressure off existing centers and bought time for the program, as a whole, the seed-money concept was staunchly adhered to. It was evidently presumed that a few more years would be enough time to generate full nonfederal support. As Creed C. Black, HEW Assistant Secretary for Legislation, told the subcommittee, "The program was started as a seed money concept, and we want it to continue that way."[38]

Overall, federal funds for community mental health centers have flowed less freely during the Nixon Administration. In fiscal 1971 no money was spent on new construction, and the $90 million appropriated for staffing grants went to centers previously funded. For fiscal 1972, Congress appropriated $15 million for construction over two years and $135 million for staffing. Few new poverty areas were funded in fiscal 1972, however, since $92 million of the staffing money went to 283 centers already receiving staffing money, $24 million to 65 previously approved but unfunded centers (some of which have been waiting for two years), leaving only $19 million for new centers. Of this remaining money, $13,637,000 went to 12 poverty-catchment areas.

Poverty Redefined

After the 1970 amendments were passed, "poverty" was redefined, and the designation of poverty areas left up to NIMH. According to Saul Feldman, "Assessing need is in the eye of the beholder. It depends on your definition of poverty."[39] The new definition, spelled out in revised regulations issued in February, 1972, is based strictly on family income. Each state ranks its catchment areas in terms of average family income. The 25 percent with the lowest average income are automatically designated poverty areas by the Secretary of Health, Education, and

Welfare. Catchment areas which do not qualify under the new guidelines can apply directly to HEW for a poverty designation under additional criteria. They must demonstrate that:

(i) At least one-half of the population of such area lives in one or more impoverished subareas;

(ii) The percentage of families with incomes below the poverty level . . . who live in such impoverished subareas is at least 1½ times greater than the percentage of families with incomes below the poverty level living in the least poor of the areas of that State initially designated as poverty areas. . . .

(iii) The project, facility, or program of services for which the applicant seeks support does or will focus on the needs of such impoverished subareas.[40]

Armed with these broad definitions of poverty, NIMH now claims that more than 50 percent of its funded centers are in poverty areas. It is perhaps not mere coincidence that shortly after the GAO report was released charging that not enough centers had been funded in high-need areas, NIMH changed its definition of need. Saul Feldman brushed aside the GAO report as being based on the old definition of need embodied in the state plans. "State plans are falling into disrepute, and rightly so, I think," said Feldman. "I'm not sure they're relevant to the real world."[41]

Several states, however, have claimed that the new regulations are not relevant to the real world, since they are based on 1960 census data which, in many cases, do not accurately reflect present income levels. Other states have complained that certain areas known to be poor do not appear to qualify. This criticism has been dismissed by NIMH as being due "in most instances to the fact that the state had either failed to apply the additional poverty area designation method . . . or had applied it incorrectly."[42]

In addition to the new poverty definition, the revised regulations also enlarged upon the "reasonable volume of services" requirement. But a careful reading reveals that this regulation has simply been painstakingly rewritten; the verbal elaboration makes it, if anything, more incomprehensible than it was. According to the new regulations, "a reasonable volume of services to persons unable to pay therefor" means a volume which, together with services otherwise available to residents of the catchment area, is sufficient to meet the total need for such services in the catchment area except that the Secretary may in particular cases determine that a volume of services to persons unable to pay therefor which meets less than the total need for such services in the catchment area is "a reasonable volume of services for persons unable to pay therefor" where he finds, on the basis of information supplied by the applicant, that such lesser volume of services is the maximum volume which the center can provide, for such period as the Secretary may determine, without placing such a severe financial hardship on the center as to jeopardize its continued operation.

And, the regulations continue, this requirement may be waived altogether, if

the Secretary finds, on the basis of information set forth in the application, that the furnishing of any such services by the center would place such a severe financial hardship on the center as to jeopardize its continued operation.[43]

The 1970 amendments, along with the revised regulations, in no way altered the basic problems of the community mental health centers program. Beyond the increasing numbers and the inflated rhetoric, the same structural problems have remained. And it is precisely these problems that should be corrected if the program is to receive additional federal money beyond 1974.

7

Evaluation
and Accountability

In recent years, one of the most popular recommendations of observers both inside and outside the federal bureaucracy has been to call for increased evaluation of programs. Its hypothetical appeal is irresistible. How else can citizens hold their public institutions accountable? How else can policy-makers make rational decisions? Without evaluation, decisions are made on the basis of guesswork and in some instances on far worse criteria—personal prejudice, cronyism, political deals, and the like.

From the sole perspective of the desirability of evaluation, it would be simple to assess NIMH's deficiencies. But this would *not* be a realistic appraisal, for the subject of evaluation raises complex issues that cannot be adequately understood from any single perspective. A clearer understanding of both NIMH's deficiencies in evalution and what the Institute should be doing is gained when the logical necessity for evaluation is weighed against both its political and its scientific feasibility.

Only in late 1969 did NIMH start any evaluation of the community mental health centers program. The impetus for this effort came not from within NIMH but from Congress, which earmarked up to 1 percent of the appropriations for a number of HEW programs, among them the centers program, for evaluation. Forced to evaluate, NIMH contracted with various consulting firms and individuals for twenty-six studies during fiscal years 1969 and 1970. Without these funds, it is highly unlikely that the Institute would have initiated evaluation efforts on its own. As Dr. William Tash, chief of NIMH's newly created Program Evaluation Branch, explained to us, "I and my staff wouldn't be here if it weren't for the one percent money [from Congress]."[1]

Why did it take congressional action to budge the Institute from its inertia? Certainly, the Institute was fully aware that evaluation of all its programs was sorely needed. In 1955, the National Advisory Mental Health Council recommended that "a high priority should be placed on evaluative research and [that] a much larger part of total funds should be used for this purpose."[2] Making specific reference to the centers program, the Joint Information Service noted in 1964 that "the one area in which there seems to be substantial deficiency across the board is perhaps the most consequential of all, namely, a means of determining the effectiveness of their services."[3] And when Bertram Brown was deputy director of NIMH, he quoted in 1965 before a conference on community mental health centers the conclusion of a then-recent study that "not a single facility exemplifying the community mental health center has been subjected to rigorously controlled experimentation."[4]

Perhaps the fundamental reason that NIMH did not begin evaluation efforts on its own initiative is that evaluation does not serve the Institute's bureaucratic self-interests. Like any government agency, NIMH is primarily concerned with the maintenance and expansion of its programs. Because the Institute has from the start claimed great success for the centers program, evaluation is a great liability, since any negative findings can be used by opponents of the program as evidence of ineffectiveness and failure. Moreover, as Bertram Brown has confessed, there is an inherent embarrassment in asking Congress for more money to evaluate a program whose success was all but guaranteed in order to obtain congressional approval in the first place.[5] Since historically Congress has never made increased NIMH appropriations contingent on evidence of effectiveness, why risk embarrassment? Evaluation might even antagonize staunch supporters of the Institute, as one NIMH administrator, who asked not to be identified, explained to us: "The lack of evaluation results in part from the fact that you're looking at the whole psychiatric field and you're starting to ask hard questions and you're treading on holy ground."

NIMH's reluctance to study the effectiveness of the centers is understandable in the context of a Congress that generally does not base its mental health appropriation decisions on hard information, opponents who would comb any evaluation studies for compromising information, and staunch supporters who might feel antagonized by questioning. Nevertheless, such reluctance is in no way to be condoned, especially for an agency that publicly prides itself on its scientific integrity.

There is an additional reason for the lack of scientifically valid evaluation of the effectiveness of community mental health centers that is both understandable and pardonable: the inherent difficulty of evaluating broad social programs. In a letter to a member of this Task Force, Dr. Ernest Gruenberg of Columbia University outlined the preconditions for a scientifically valid and meaningful evaluation of a social program.[6] First, says Gruenberg, the goals of the program "must be stated in such a way that objective data can indicate whether or not the desired state of affairs is present." For the centers program, in other words, specific aims must be stated which lend themselves to scientific measurement. Second, there must be "a way of judging what would have happened with respect to the objective if the program had not been instituted and executed." In addition, any study must be replicated many times to produce a meaningful overall picture of the program. Gruenberg writes:

> In general, scientists do not arrive at a definitive conclusion regarding the nature of the real world from a single investigation, no matter how "crucial" the experiment or reputable the

investigator. Scientists want to see repetitions of experiments by other investigators to reduce the probability of an undetected fluke in the experimental situation. The single, isolated evaluation research has the same weaknesses as the single laboratory experiment; it may not mean what it appears to mean. Evaluation studies tend to build an accumulated new picture of the effect of an activity on a defined objective; individual studies only add to the building process.[7]

And finally, Gruenberg observes that present evaluation methodologies are in a "primitive state of development."

Gruenberg clearly feels that a scientifically valid evaluation of the community mental health centers program is unfeasible at the present time, and if one accepts his conditions for the successful conduct of a scientifically valid evaluation of a social program, one is forced to come to the same conclusion. NIMH has prescribed only the vaguest of goals for community mental health centers. Moreover, there are no widely accepted and dependable methodologies for measuring the effectiveness of either mental health treatment or service delivery. According to Robert A. Walker, associate director of the Minneapolis Rehabilitation Center, "When you measure program performance you are putting your value judgments on the line for all to see."[8] Thus, it would make little sense to berate NIMH for its lack of scientifically valid evaluations of its entire centers program.

In addition, there are certain built-in administrative obstacles to NIMH's evaluation efforts. For one thing, it should be noted that after Congress earmarked the special 1 percent funds, a departmental decision was made by the comptroller of HEW that these funds would be used entirely for outside grants and contracts, not for in-house staff. No procedures were established whereby NIMH staff would systematically plan and monitor this evaluation activity; as a result, careful monitoring (evaluation of the evaluation) has received very little attention. The legal requirements for competitive bidding on government grants and contracts dictate that when an area has been designated for evaluation, NIMH must publish a Request for Proposals (RFP) soliciting qualified researchers. RFPs are either advertised in *Commerce Business Daily*, a publication of the Department of Commerce, or sent to a preselected group of bidders.* The danger is that competitive bidding can often lead to the hiring of researchers who are adept at competitive proposal writing, but not necessarily adept at (or interested in) studying the particular area NIMH wants evaluted. Many researchers prefer to follow their own interests, and are thus inclined to relate current research to their own past work rather than to a context specified by NIMH administrators.

Moreover, all NIMH-designated topics for research must be approved by both the Health Services and Mental Health Administration and the Department of Health, Education, and Welfare. The intervention of two higher administrative echelons means that some projects can be rejected, funds redirected, or evaluation strategies revised. While this kind of supervision can be valuable, it also carries the liability of having no central, ongoing responsibility for coherent evaluation efforts. Within the federal bureaucracy, evaluators and mental health administrators are, as psychologist Thomas J. Kiresuk, director of program evaluation at the Hennepin County Community Mental Health Center in Minneapolis, points out,

> involved in a dismal, annual festival of numbers presentation and budget reclassification and realignment. There are no folk heroes in this celebration, only anonymous workers pushing an ever increasing mass of data and words upwards through administrative ecological levels leading to an icy, snow-capped top. There, the festival reaches its own climax when the mental health staff find themselves unbelieved, untrusted, second guessed, unrewarded, and facing a demand for more and different data; their recommendations go ignored or are replaced by decisions of other individuals ("who know best"). On their way back down the administrative mountain, they can hear that year's juggernaut rumbling behind them, while all about them lie the dust and debris of memos, worksheets, and revised or adandoned reports.[9]

On the other hand, there are certain aspects of NIMH's present evaluation program, as defined by the Institute itself,

* In some cases it is determined that there is only one qualified source for a particular area to be studied; in such cases NIMH awards a "sole source" contract, which must be justified according to standards established by the Federal Procurement Regulations.

that are clearly deficient and whose reform is just as clearly within the realm of political and scientific feasibility. First, a distinction should be made between *scientifically valid* evaluation as narrowly defined by Gruenberg and the gathering of hard information which can help policy-makers to make more rational decisions, enable citizens to gain a better knowledge of what the community mental health centers are doing, and aid future researchers in their assessment of the long-term impact of the program. In other words, a principal criterion of the success or failure of NIMH's evaluation program is whether it collects the kind of information useful to policy-makers, local citizens, and researchers. A second criterion is the availability and accessibility of this information to the public. And a final criterion concerns the utilization of this information—namely, whether it is used to make specific changes and to hold individual centers accountable, or merely "buried" in the bureaucracy. We shall judge NIMH's evaluation program on these three criteria.

According to Harry Cain, director of NIMH's Office of Program Planning and Evaluation, eight contracted evaluation studies have been completed, another twenty are in the process of being completed, and at least a score of additional studies are being either contemplated or contracted out on problems dealing with community mental health centers. Censored copies of most of the completed studies—in nearly all cases center names and individual identities were deleted—were made available to this Task Force by NIMH. As far as they go, these studies provide useful information to the general public; we have used parts of several NIMH studies as substantiating documentation. In general, they indicate that a number of centers are experiencing serious problems. One study showed that state and local funding sources will not be adequate to guarantee the future operation of many centers.[10] Another study observed that citizen involvement in many centers is nonexistent or minimal and further that the centers' "middle-class" model of citizen participation is inappropriate in poverty areas.[11] The same study and another one concluded that indigent patients are not receiving adequate services in many areas.[12] A further study found that centers are not readily accessible to people,[13] and another identified the lack of continuity of care as a major shortcoming.[14] Still another study found that the great majority of centers do not offer comprehensive services for children.[15]

These conclusions should hardly be surprising to NIMH officials and others who are intimately acquainted with the program. NIMH official Harry Cain expressed to us his disappointment in the quality of many of the completed studies; he felt that although parts of some studies were helpful to him, the studies should have been more analytical and better designed.[16] Cain is correct. Though these studies offer much useful information to the uninitiated, they provide little of the hard data which both the public and federal officials should have at their disposal. This is a failing that also seems to apply to the NIMH studies in progress, those currently contemplated by the Institute, and the Institute's biometry inventory (statistical information compiled from questionnaires filled out by the centers). The NIMH project descriptions of their studies in progress or currently contemplated, the published results of their biometry inventory, and the nature of the biometry questionnaire all indicate that they will *not* provide the Institute in the foreseeable future with the following kinds of basic information:

1. Admission, readmission, and discharge rates to and from state hospitals of the residents of every community mental health catchment area in the country.
2. The percentage of catchment-area residents admitted to state hospitals who are first screened by a center; the percentage of catchment-area residents discharged by state hospitals who are immediately seen in the rehabilitative programs or other services of a center.
3. The kinds of social and economic problems faced by individuals admitted to any given center.
4. Where patients released from state hospitals go (whether they are sent to nursing homes, foster care homes, community mental health centers, families, etc., or merely left to fend for themselves).
5. What happens to individuals when they cease being clients

of a community mental health center. (Do they find a job? A place to live? Do they go back to their families, or are they merely left to fend for themselves?)

6. Utilization rates of community mental health centers compared to other facilities in the community.

7. Comparative costs per length of stay or unit of service for persons with similar problems in centers, state hospitals, general hospitals, and any other facilities by catchment area, county, and state.

8. Evidence or the lack of evidence that the five essential services are the most needed services for every community in the country.

9. The appropriateness of the 75,000-to-200,000 population limits defining catchment area. The impact of these limits on coordination with other agencies and on the delivery and accessibility of services.

10. The extent to which current catchment-area boundaries correspond or conflict with existing governmental boundaries; the neighborhood lines of ethnic, cultural or racial groups; and the target areas of other federal programs like Model Cities and OEO neighborhood health centers.

11. The accessibility of centers compared to general hospitals, clinics, state hospitals, and other facilities.

12. The travel time necessary to get to centers by public transportation from the furthest point in the catchment area.

13. The kinds of information and training citizens need in order to manage effectively their own community mental health center.

14. Information on the quality of care provided by community mental health centers compared to the care provided by general hospitals, private psychiatric hospitals, state hospitals, clinics, and private practitioners.

15. The effectiveness of present NIMH mechanisms of supervision and accountability.

16. Information on the long-term impact of community mental health centers on the delivery of services. (All current studies are limited to one or two years.)

17. What indispensable training, skills, treatment techniques, or other expertise privy only to the psychiatric profession

are utilized in the solution of the kinds of problems that are most generally encountered in community mental health centers.

This is only a partial list suggesting the kind of basic information that NIMH's evaluation program should be, but is not, providing.* Moreover, the Institute appears unwilling to share with the general public and researchers the limited information it *does* have. The contract evaluation studies become public information only after every reference to a specific center, individual, place, or organization is deleted. This policy of complete anonymity was made, according to Harry Cain, because these studies are part of "the national program evaluation; the issue is not an individual center."[17]

But the individual center is exactly the issue. Virtually all of the studies in NIMH's evaluation program look at only a handful of centers; some look at two or four, though eight or nine are the most popular numbers. According to the public statements of many top NIMH officials, centers vary a great deal; no two are alike. Thus, studies of a handful of centers may tell one a lot about individual centers, but they probably do not offer a statistically significant basis for the agency's evaluation of its entire national program. Yet this is what Cain insists they do.

NIMH's policy of complete anonymity subverts any real understanding of the complexities of local centers. Through various sources and our own investigation, we were able to uncover all the identities of all the centers and nearly all the individuals and other organizations referred to in the censored copies as "Dr. A," the "Valley View Center," or the like. Had we not been able to do this, it would have been impossible for us to understand the centers' operation. For example, one NIMH-contracted study on citizen participation looked at the Area B Community Mental Health Center in Washington, D.C.

---

* An important qualification is needed here. We do not suggest that the Institute embark on a massive and indiscriminate data-gathering program. We propose that the Institute collect data for which NIMH officials, consumer representatives, or outside researchers can affirmatively answer the following questions: Should this data be collected? Will it help us to answer important questions? Will this data be used?

It seems absurd, at the very least, to expect anyone to understand the lack of citizen involvement at this center out of context—that is, without knowing that District residents do not elect their city officials, have no voting representative in Congress, and live in a city whose activities are closely controlled by a few powerful federal officials and members of certain committees in Congress. (See Chapter 8 for our own investigation of this center.)

A last criterion of NIMH's contract evaluation studies is whether the information is used to make substantive changes and to hold individual centers accountable. There have been some minor changes in federal regulations as a result of evaluation studies: the regulations now contain vague mentions of citizen participation and require centers to publicly announce to communities that they are open for business. Beyond this, there have been no substantive changes. Furthermore, the Institute has yet to act to correct the deficiencies of individual centers that were detailed in the evaluation studies. When we asked William Tash, chief of the Program Evaluation Branch, what disciplinary steps the Institute was going to take, he replied that such decisions take time and were in the process of being determined.[18] Three months later, NIMH official Saul Feldman wrote this Task Force that "the monitoring of community mental health centers for compliance with the law, regulations, and the specific terms of the grants is a Regional Office responsibility." Feldman further noted, "Monitoring is accomplished in several ways, including site visits, ninety-day follow-up visits, the review of continuing applications, and the Biometry Inventory."[19]

Following receipt of Feldman's letter, we conducted long telephone interviews with officials in nine of the ten NIMH regional offices. These interviews revealed that regional-office officials feel that they have neither adequate staff and money nor the legal sanctions to monitor individual centers effectively. "We're so short-staffed, we're not able to do the things we're supposed to do," stated Ann Toomey, director of the Boston regional office.[20] "The first thing that [goes] is site-visiting, if we are faced with a deadline for getting in an application," observed Doreen Loso, deputy to the director of the San Francisco regional office.[21] According to Loso, her office visits about half the centers in its region each year. "Our monitoring is more theoretical than actual," stated one official in the Philadelphia regional office, who asked not to be identified. This official explained, "Monitoring in this region for the last three or four years has just been overwhelmed by our struggle for mere survival."

Furthermore, while most of the regional office officials interviewed agreed that monitoring was their responsibility, they were quick to point out that monitoring was not their *prime* responsibility. "We have never seen our prominent role as an enforcement agency," asserted Dr. Howard Siple, director of the Chicago regional office. "We have always seen it as program development."[22] The primary emphasis placed on "program development" was echoed by nearly every regional-office official interviewed. All this is not to say that regional offices should not emphasize program development; it is merely to recognize the fact that accountability seems to be no one's primary responsibility at NIMH.

Even in those cases where regional-office staff vigorously strive to enforce compliance, they are frequently hamstrung by the lack of sanctions and mechanisms of accountability. For example, Katharyn Fritz, director of the Dallas regional office, observed that a major problem of the centers in her region was the lack of citizen involvement. "Some places are just dragging their feet," she said. But she added that her office could do very little to promote citizen involvement because of the lack of sanctions in the regulations. "We really don't have much of anything [in the way of sanctions]."[23] Her comments were echoed by Martin Keeley of the Chicago regional office, who told us that "the community involvement regulation means practically nothing. . . . There are no teeth in it. . . . I tried to do that [community involvement] in some areas a couple of years ago," he went on, "and I got shot down by both the center people and NIMH central headquarters."[24] Besides informal cajoling and persuasion, the only sanction regional offices have to enforce compliance is the withdrawal of funds from a community mental health center. And this has happened very rarely. We are aware of only three instances in which a

center's funds have been temporarily suspended for any reason.*
(A larger number of centers have been *threatened* with suspension of funds.)

With limited resources and with so few supervisory mechanisms, it is not surprising to find an emerging body of evidence
documenting misuse and mismanagement of grant funds and
lack of center program responsiveness to consumers. For example, in its 1971 report the General Accounting Office found
that two centers—the community mental health center of
Temple University in Philadelphia and the West Philadelphia
Community Mental Health Consortium—built as part of general hospitals spent an unwarranted $168,000 to construct
hospital facilities that center patients rarely, if ever, used.
According to the GAO study, the Temple University center
improperly allocated about $90,000 to defraying the cost of its
hospital's business office, automatic data processing room, and
recreational facilities. The GAO also found that the West
Philadelphia Community Mental Health Consortium charged
the federal government $79,000 for the construction of its
hospital's operating room, an inhalation therapy room, and
other services that mental patients almost never used. Since it
was found that center patients accounted for less than 1 percent
of the use of these areas, the GAO determined that less than
$1,000 of their construction cost could have been legally charged
to federal tax dollars.[25]

Beyond legal and fiscal accountability to the public, the
mechanisms for which should be strengthened and stringently
enforced, is accountability for the quality of care provided by
community mental health centers. It should be recalled that
the community mental health centers program marked the
advent of the National Institute of Mental Health into the
delivery of direct services to the public. Until then, it had
concerned itself with the funding of research and professional training. It was assumed, of course, that the public
would be the ultimate beneficiary of the research; but the Institute's "consumers" were a relatively small professional group.

* The NIMH central office could not (or would not) supply us with this
information, so we have had to rely on an informal canvass of the regional offices.

The concept of a more direct and immediate "accountability" to the general public is therefore a new one at NIMH. Unfortunately, historical precedent is strong: NIMH tends to award community mental health center grants primarily to the professional community it has always dealt with; they, in turn, rarely consider that they are accountable to anyone. Beneath the recent rhetoric of citizen involvement there presently exist, as this report documents, no mechanisms ensuring citizens a legitimate voice in mental health programs at any level.

As mental health care grows more expensive to taxpayers and individual consumers, and as the tools and techniques (chemical, electrical, and surgical as well as psychological) available to the practitioner grow more varied and sophisticated, the need for some sort of quality control becomes crucial. At the very least there should be greater responsibility on the part of ethics committees and the development of adequate internal peer review. Sociologist Eliot Freidson has aptly pointed out that only the requirement of formal, periodic, internal review of the quality of their work is likely to stimulate practitioners to look closely at what each is doing and to evaluate it according to some systematic, self-conscious standard. In addition, formal, periodic review should be undertaken by *outsiders* who represent the highest possible standards of the profession as a whole. In Freidson's view, outside professional monitoring should concern itself not only with such mechanical matters as completeness of records and referral and consultation patterns but also with "the propriety, skill, and decency of the practitioner's manner of dealing with patients."[26]

As a result of the stepped-up demand for mental health services, the rise of consumer movements, and, perhaps most of all, the demands of major insurance carriers, the ethics committees of local medical and psychiatric societies are in fact increasingly active, and peer review—monitoring of professionals by their colleagues—is being discussed more and more. But peer review by itself is not enough. Precisely because it is administratively initiated and professionally implemented, it reflects what insurance carriers, administrators, and professionals see as the best interests of the patient, and may too easily overlook what patients themselves feel to be their interests. We can no longer rely solely on the professions and their own systems of self-regulation to provide a responsible system of care, or to provide sufficient protection against unscrupulous or incompetent practitioners. If we are to have built-in accountability and effective quality control in the value-laden area of mental health care, citizens must be responsibly involved in promulgating explicit standards of quality and in overseeing professional performance.

It should be pointed out that while "quality control" is often presented as though it rested on sound scientific or objective criteria, it is better described as an abstraction that covers what is at heart a political phenomenon. As psychiatrist Jack Zusman pointed out in a paper presented to the American Orthopsychiatric Association,

> The definition of quality or the choice of one definition from a group of possible ones determines in whose interest quality control will operate. The individual or group which defines quality is placed in an extremely powerful position and this position is one worth fighting for. In our society, the fighting goes on through the political process. The medical profession has recognized this very well and is already working as hard as it can to influence the process.[27]

So long as we rely exclusively on peer review, we perpetuate the system in which all the defining and all the reviewing are on one side. Moreover, peer review as generally practiced refers to a mechanism of checking in specific cases that are being questioned for one reason or another; in this rather narrow function, peer review is of limited usefulness. However, it has not as yet led to the development of explicit, agreed-upon standards which are routinely applied in order to modify or upgrade the quality of care.

In order to protect the interests of consumers and to preserve the integrity of professionals, the defining of quality and the setting down of standards by which to measure performance should be openly and explicitly negotiated among the various interest groups concerned. Once such standards (which are not immutable, but subject to change as the nature of the standard-setting body changes and as the state of the mental health care art advances) have been established, the process of evaluation must be ongoing; quality ratings for any program, facility, or practitioner should be public information. The role to be played by consumer representatives in this process and on peer review committees is not merely a token bowing to a current fad; it is essential.

A few promising models in this direction have recently been put into practice. One, developed by Dr. Thomas J. Kiresuk, director of program evaluation at the NIMH-funded Hennepin County Community Mental Health Center in Minneapolis, is a disarmingly simple system for establishing concrete goals and measuring performance. "Goal Attainment Scaling," as it is called, has implications for individual treatment, for broader program evaluation, and for administration.[28] Briefly, Goal Attainment Scaling is based on the careful and explicit formulation of problems specific to an individual and a range of possible goals to be achieved through treatment. For each defined problem to be solved, there is a brief, behavioral description of possible treatment outcomes ranging from the least favorable to the most favorable on a five-point scale. At the heart of this system is an acceptance of the individual as the standard for his own measure; that is, Goal Attainment Scaling is primarily a method for setting standards based on reasonable expectations for a specific person—not arbitrary standards based on an absolute or predefined notion of "health" that may or may not be relevant or attainable for that individual.

As originally conceived, Goal Attainment Scaling involved only the clinician in the goal-setting process. The basic structure, however, is malleable, and an adaptation of it—called "Contract Fulfillment Analysis"—has already been developed by Dr. Jose R. Lombillo, director of the Collier County Mental Health Clinic, Inc., of Naples, Florida.* Here, the achievement of individual goals is defined and measured by a "contract" negotiated between client and therapist.[29] This has the advantage of involving the client more directly at the outset, necessitates thorough discussion of the expectations of both

* The Collier County Mental Health Clinic receives no grant funds from the National Institute of Mental Health.

parties, and facilitates a collaborative relationship in an atmosphere of mutual trust. Both systems also have explicit mechanisms for follow-up. Moreover, the potential applications of systems like these are far wider than individual one-to-one therapy. Through the use of such "contracts," tangible program goals can be negotiated among center staff and administration, between the center and community representatives, between the center and related care-giving agencies, etc.

There is clearly much to recommend in this idea, aside from its compelling simplicity. In a field where highly personalized services are offered, providers have a major responsibility to overcome mistrust on the part of their clients—this means, in part, setting realistic and agreed-upon goals, and demands an uncommon degree of openness and honesty on the part of the provider in place of the mystification that too often shrouds mental health services. Perhaps the most important thing about a contract mechanism is that it makes explicit a joint commitment to the accomplishment of specific goals, and serves to diminish the vagueness that has historically helped to insulate mental health services in general and psychotherapy in particular from any realistic appraisal of effectiveness.

Part Two
CASE STUDIES

8

Washington, D.C.[1]

The city of Washington, D.C., is a prime testing ground of NIMH's commitment to assure, through its community mental health centers program, adequate and accessible mental health services for the poor. For it is here in the Institute's home town that NIMH has had the best opportunity to participate in the planning and implementation of such services. Long before the Institute came on the scene, the inadequacies and inequities of the District's mental health programs and their administration had been obvious. These are precisely the problems that the community mental health centers program was largely designed to alleviate; their resolution, or nonresolution, will reveal whether the Institute's propensity for rhetoric exceeds its concern for human beings.

Washington has, since World War II, experienced rapid growth and a marked change in the racial composition of the

123

population. As the city has become more urbanized, the privileged classes have moved to the suburbs, so that the District's total population is now 71 percent black—and, although it is the nation's capital, increasingly poor. It is also increasingly needful of human services, mental health services among them.

Ironically, Washington has the highest per capita concentration of psychiatrists of any city in the United States, boasts a number of federal and private medical training and psychiatric residency programs, and is the home of the National Association for Mental Health, the American Psychiatric Association, the American Psychological Association, and, of course, the National Institute of Mental Health. In metropolitan Washington there are ten hospitals and fifteen separate agencies and clinics (exclusive of community mental health centers) to provide various mental health services. Psychiatry is big business in Washington, where approximately three million federal employees have access to one of the nation's most comprehensive insurance plans for outpatient psychiatric care, which pays up to 80 percent of the cost of psychotherapy or psychoanalysis. It is widely acknowledged that many people come to the District of Columbia to take federal jobs so that they can afford the high cost of psychotherapy. For the same reason, the city attracts psychiatrists, who find no dearth of patients and the assurance that their services will be properly paid for. Yet with all of these rich resources, mental health care for the District's poor is close to nonexistent.

A major reason for this has to do with the political setting of the nation's capital. Washington is unique in that there are no elected city officials: the mayor and a nine-member city council are appointed directly by the President, while the directors of city departments are appointed by the mayor.* Thus, the citizens of the District of Columbia have no procedural means by which to influence governmental response to local problems, though the city depends on the federal government for approval of every detail of its annual budget. Congress, through

* Aside from elected officials on the Board of Education, there is one elected delegate to Congress, but he may vote only in committee, not on the floor of the House of Representatives.

its appropriations process, controls all of the District's funds, not merely those guaranteed by specific federal grants—which means that both the total revenue and the setting of priorities for its expenditure are in congressional hands. In addition, a number of federal agencies are directly involved in the city's affairs—the courts, the Parks Service, the Department of Health, Education, and Welfare, and a number of special-purpose federal agencies that perform local functions, such as the National Capital Housing Authority. Federal involvement in local affairs without explicit accountability to the local public has encouraged, by and large, pervasive indifference to the needs of the city's residents.

This indifference is shared by nonfederal institutions, and is particularly glaring in the areas of health and mental health care. For example, neither the psychiatry departments of the three local medical schools (George Washington, Georgetown, and Howard* universities), nor the many psychiatrists in private practice, nor NIMH has ever shown any but the most superficial concern for the predominantly poor and black population of Washington. Though part of the city's budget goes to support the medical schools, they, along with the privately practicing physicians, have tended to serve the white suburbs.

For its part, NIMH has traditionally been interested in solving the nation's mental health problems at a safe distance. Saul Feldman, associate director of NIMH's Division of Mental Health Service Programs, was hard pressed to tell this Task Force anything about the so-called national model in the District. "I know less about the centers in D.C. than in other parts of the country," he explained. "Your best bet is to contact the regional office in Philadelphia for information."[2]

Thus, by default as it were, mental health care for the poor and black has been left entirely to the D.C. Mental Health Administration, which is part of the Health Services Administration, which in turn is part of the D.C. Department of Human Resources (DHR). Buried inside this mammoth bureaucracy, mental health services have never been given much priority—to

---

* Howard, a private black university, was established by an act of Congress, and continues to receive approximately 60 percent of its annual operating budget from the federal government.

put it mildly. According to the 1970 *Mayor's Task Force on Public Health Goals,*

> Mental health services in a comprehensive way go beyond the Health Department into the Welfare Department, the schools, the prisons, the juvenile justice system. They have to be brought out into the community, and even more than physical health care, they have to involve the community. Something radical has to be done in the District to make mental health services visible, effective, and relevant, and soon.[3]

This, it should be noted, was in 1970, several years *after* "something radical" had been done—that being the establishment of the community mental health centers program. Washington was one of the first cities in the country to be funded, receiving in 1964 a federal demonstration grant of more than two million dollars for the development of comprehensive community-based mental health services.

Such services were and are desperately needed. Until the 1960s, the only public psychiatric services available were at the city-run D.C. General Hospital, whose psychiatric unit, overcrowded and understaffed, functioned primarily as the diagnostic arm of the courts and as a traditional 240-bed receiving hospital. Treatment at D.C. General was minimal. Because of an increasingly large indigent population, it was imperative that patients be released quickly to make room for the next group of admissions; most patients who needed further care were sent to the federally run St. Elizabeths Hospital, a long-term custodial institution with a 7,500-bed capacity.

With the passage of the Community Mental Health Centers Act in 1963, the D.C. Department of Public Health* set out to develop a master plan for community mental health services in the District. It began with an administrative reorganization designed to integrate the few fragmented public services that

---

* The Department of Public Health as such no longer exists. In 1970, the Department of Human Resources was formed by combining Public Health, Welfare, Vocational Rehabilitation, Veterans Affairs, and the Narcotics Treatment Administration into one superdepartment. The Department of Public Health became the Health Services Administration, which was then divided into the Hospital and Medical Care Administration and the Mental Health Administration.

existed in the city under various health department bureaus. The Bureau for Mental Health was renamed the Directorate for Mental Health (and would later become the Mental Health Administration); its planning staff, following federal guidelines, divided the city along basically geographic lines into four catchment areas and called them Areas A, B, C, and D. All four centers are now operating, with the last one, Area A, having just begun operating fully in January, 1972.*

Significantly, the private universities and hospitals, unlike their counterparts in many other cities, did not see the Community Mental Health Centers Act as an opportunity for aggrandizement, and offered the Department of Public Health no competition for the control of federal funds. The result is an almost citywide service monopoly, rather than the more typical monopoly within a single catchment area. The center's program for nearly all of Washington is centrally administered by one city agency and has inspired little or no competition with the private sector.

Area C

The health department applied for its first federal grant early in 1964, before Congress had actually appropriated funds for the centers program. It was encouraged to act quickly by President Kennedy's message of 1963, which promised special funds to the District of Columbia. A comprehensive plan, ranking the four catchment areas according to need, was drawn and speedily approved. Top priority was designated to Area C, comprising that part of the city which included D.C. General Hospital and those services under its auspices that had traditionally administered short-term psychiatric care to the District's poor. This catchment area, predominantly poor and black, contains some 250,000 people (a special compensation to go over the population limit was given to the District of

---

* The Area A center is the only one in the city with a predominantly white catchment area. Located in Washington's fashionable Georgetown section, this fledgling center is likely to have access to richer resources than the others. To date it has received no federal funds. For that reason, and because it is so new, it is not discussed in this book.

Columbia); it also contains three large urban redevelopment areas, which have caused considerable dislocation of neighborhoods and loss of housing to those people.[4]

A proposal was submitted to NIMH requesting funds, not for construction, but to augment the staff and services at D.C. General. The new community mental health center was to be housed in the acute psychiatry unit of the hospital, a wing that had been constructed in 1958. Prodded by the White House, NIMH announced in the spring of 1965 that it would approve a five-year demonstration grant for Area C, funding the center to the tune of $2,679,686[5] and proclaiming that this community mental health center would be a model for the entire nation.

With more than $2.5 million and the reputation of the Institute at stake, NIMH attached a few strings to the demonstration grant. The major stipulation was that the director of the new center had to be approved by NIMH before grant funds would be released. There ensued a period of considerable uncertainty, during which health department officials and NIMH officials regarded one another with suspicion while both ignored the "community." No public hearings were held, and only health department officials and the scientists and professionals at NIMH were involved in the planning that was to answer the needs of the public.[6] NIMH sent top officials from its central office and prominent outside consultants to advise the Directorate for Mental Health and to make recommendations for the development of mental health services for this model center. Most of these visits took place prior to the appointment of a director and dropped off soon thereafter.[7]

A director was finally approved in October of 1965. While a traditionally oriented and predominantly white staff made faltering attempts to develop a "community orientation," the new director, caught between the demands of NIMH and the health department bureaucracy, could exercise little leadership of his own. Lacking direction and without clear and agreed-upon goals, the staff quickly became fragmented, competitive, and demoralized. The formal dedication of the Area C Community Mental Health Center took place in May of 1966, and was followed almost immediately by an official site visit from

NIMH. According to former health department official John Schultz, "NIMH took one look at the psychiatric services at D.C. General and screamed—this was not community mental health, and this was not the model it had in mind."[8] Shortly thereafter, the director resigned.

Area C has never managed to overcome its bad beginnings. It has had a succession of directors, all of whom have been undercut and overruled by the authorities "downtown" at the Department of Human Resources. It has faced large and continual staff resignations and mammoth confusion over its goals. An article in the *Washington Post* in December, 1967, reported that the center had in no way reduced referrals to St. Elizabeths; rather, admissions to that institution had doubled between 1966 and 1967, and many more patients were going directly to St. Elizabeths because they could not get treatment at District facilities.[9]

A 1968 study of the Area C Community Mental Health Center, prepared jointly by the Catholic University School of Social Services, the program evaluation unit of Area C, and the D.C. Department of Human Resources, illuminates other problems of the center. One part of the study, for example, asked staff members and a sampling of adult outpatients to suggest ways of improving Area C. Their responses, highlighting the most basic deficiencies, were strikingly similar, and included such comments as (from a patient): "There are not enough people working at Area C. They didn't have time to really listen to me," and (from a staff member): "Organize more psychiatric treatment time for individual psychotherapy." Another recommendation had to do with simple housekeeping. A patient said, "They should keep the place up better. The bathrooms were filthy"; a staff member stated, "Improve the physical facilities. . . ." The problems created by a predominantly white staff's working in a black ghetto community were also identified by both. Said a staff member, "Hire more black staff . . . who are sure of their racial identity, who can instill a sense of black identity among patients. More staff familiar with white racism, poverty, and the culture of patients." A patient put it more poignantly: "There is no place in the city of Washington where a poor black person can go and feel like

a person. Educate secretaries and nurses in human behavior."[10]
Summing up, one of the authors of the study commented:

> The work of Area C is a band-aid upon a mighty social
> sore. . . . The quality of life in the catchment area of the Center
> is a sad reflection of American impotence in dealing with the
> basic needs of all its citizens. For the objectives of Area
> C are intimately connected with and frustrated by the inade-
> quate income levels of individuals coming to the Center,
> the lack of decent housing where families can feel secure, the
> discrimination against individuals who are black and poor,
> the paucity of educational opportunities in the ghetto area, and
> the absence of meaningful vocational opportunities, especially
> for men.[11]

In the spring of 1969, another NIMH-funded study of Area
C was released by the D.C. Judicial Conference Committee on
Laws Pertaining to Mental Disorders. A major problem, the
committee found, was the center's selective admissions policy.
Since there was no overall policy offering guidelines for admission, each program or unit (alcoholism and drug addiction,
geriatric, adult, adolescent, and children) had set up its own
requirements regarding the suitability of an individual for
treatment. Generally they were willing to admit only "good"
patients. Alcoholics with delirium tremens, for example, or
geriatric patients who required intensive nursing care, or those
who posed a "management problem" were unacceptable to the
center. Similarly, anyone who didn't fit readily into a particular
program was likely to be refused admission. The committee
questioned "whether the Center is acting in a truly representative capacity in serving all those with mental health problems in
the catchment area, and whether indeed the 'walking wounded'
or those most desperately in need of help are not being deprived
of their 'entitlement to services' by such a selective admissions
policy."[12]

The study also critized the location of the center in an
isolated quadrant on the grounds of D.C. General Hospital,
separated from the community it was supposed to serve, making
it virtually inaccessible to many people. Moreover, the study
noted, there were few if any night or weekend programs or
emergency facilities, so that the center was unavailable to anyone who had a daytime job.

But the strongest criticism took up the environmental generalizations made by the Catholic University–Area C-DHR study and pointed to the gross irresponsibility of the center itself. According to the Judicial Conference Committee, there had been no effort on the part of the Area C staff to identify, let alone make use of, existing community resources that might help to meet a patient's needs, including his social and economic needs—such as inadequate housing and legal aid:

> Clearly it is important that a unit of the Center, or a special consultant on the staff of the Center, be assigned the task of promoting a coordinated and systematic program of identifying the social and economic needs of the patients and developing a complete awareness of the public and private community supportive resources existing in the District so that they may be utilized on behalf of the Center patients.[13]

In May, 1970, Area C came under attack once again—this time by citizens, the press, members of Congress, and its own staff. The uproar was over an apparently arbitrary decision by DHR officials to move patients of the Narcotics Treatment Administration (NTA)—an agency administratively separate from the Directorate for Mental Health—onto the fifth floor of Area C, without consulting the staff and without considering the effects on center patients or programs. According to WTOP–TV news reporter Jim Michie, the takeover by NTA caused serious cutbacks in programs, staff resignations, and other problems such as "male and female alcoholics having to use the same bathroom, patients being turned away because of the loss of space and disgusted staff, and the demoralization of remaining staff and patients."[14] Michie quoted a spokesman of the Senate Committee on the District of Columbia, who called the situation "a clear example of abysmal administration."[15]

By then the National Institute of Mental Health had long since stopped talking about a "model effort in mental health care for the nation" and had begun instead to threaten to cut staffing-grant funds if the most serious deficiencies were not corrected. Following a site visit in July, 1970, by NIMH's regional office in Charlottesville, Virginia, NIMH official A. Naomi Kennedy wrote to then-Director of Public Health Raymond Standard that the site-visit team was "seriously disturbed by some of the administrative and programmatic shortcomings of the Center."[16] The site-visit report enumerated the "major concerns" of the Institute and demanded that a new plan for the center's operation be submitted within two months. Among these concerns were the lack of a qualified full-time director with sufficient authority, ambiguity of the role of a citizens' "policy-making" board, too many referrals being made to St. Elizabeths, poor relations with D.C. General for medical coverage of center patients, and the fact that continuity of care was "entirely lacking" in some parts of the center's program.[17]

Although many of the same problems remain unresolved today, NIMH has evidently been content with plans and promises, for its "demands" have not been enforced and funds have flowed uninterrupted into Area C. As part of the city bureaucracy, the center has indeed survived the reorganizations, the critical attacks by NIMH and others, even serious staff rebellions. Under the circumstances, however, survival is an accomplishment of questionable worth. Area C has never been able to turn its conflicts into creative resolution, and as a result the same conflicts reappear under different guises. The community expects little from the center. An "advisory board" which has fluctuated in popularity, and whose representativeness is doubtful, has no say in policy. No by-laws outline the extent of its responsibility or authority; consequently, the board tends to function apathetically and at the whim of the center administration. When questioned about the involvement of the current board, the center director told us, "They're about as involved as I want them to be."[18] At a public hearing held in May, 1972, to review the District's latest "Comprehensive Mental Health Plan," Veronica Brown, speaking on behalf of the Area C community board, complained that the board had been repeatedly ignored by center directors and by the city Mental Health Administration and charged that the mental health plan was no more than a piece of paper. (Indeed, the 1971 plan reads very much like the 1965 plan. The same problems not only remain but have gotten worse, and there are the same obstacles to their resolution.) Among the Area C staff, there is pervasive uncertainty, rigid hierarchy, secrecy, and competition.

In 1973, the squat brick building that was new in 1958 shows definite signs of age. In physical appearance, moreover, the Area C Community Mental Health Center looks precisely like what it was originally constructed to be: an acute psychiatric service, a locked-ward facility by design and a place one would not be inclined to go to by choice. Set off on the far side of the grounds of D.C. General Hospital, it is a structure that intimidates. There is a tight circular driveway in front and a sea of concrete parking lots all around, unrelieved by grass or trees or any sign of growth. Inside are straight, silent, gray-green corridors, dimly lit, lined with offices. Nothing about the center is bright or warm or welcoming. Instead, both inside and out there is an atmosphere of gloom and a haunting sense of the "total institution" whose era was to have been banished by the community mental health center.

There are, of course, some differences. And at Area C a few hopeful changes have, with difficulty, been made. The most significant of these has been the establishment of three outreach teams. While one of these teams was assigned a target area and works under the close supervision of the center director and DHR officials, the other two, composed of small groups of primarily black workers, have quietly disengaged themselves from the center and set up storefront operations in neighborhood health centers. Their job, as they see it, is prevention—which means being visible, accessible, and involved. They have trained a number of indigenous paraprofessional workers and are attempting collectively to confront some of the environmental problems of the catchment area. These teams have not had the blessings of the center staff. On the contrary, they have been regarded with considerable hostility as irresponsible upstarts, threatening traditional professional wisdom. Indeed, in the spring of 1971 communication and cooperation between the center staff and the satellite teams had broken down to the point where, allegedly, desks were rifled, bomb threats were made, and mutual suspicion marked every encounter. The teams have been protected, however, by the tacit approval of NIMH (they are virtually the only innovative aspect of Area C's program) and by the qualified support of the center director.

But the strong, often arbitrary controls exercised by the D.C. Mental Health Administration and Department of Human Resources have meant that serious morale problems infect the outreach teams and the rest of the staff as well. Such centralized authority has also been responsible for serious discontinuities in patient care. In November, 1971, for example, an alcoholic detoxification unit for females—to serve the entire city—was moved into Area C, again without consulting the director, the staff, or the community board. On a day's notice, patients were moved and staff reassigned, including seven staff members from the outreach teams. According to then-director Dr. Jefferson McAlpine, the change affected approximately four hundred patients who were in therapy with the reassigned outpatient and day-care staff. McAlpine and the staff protested by way of an angry but futile memo to Dr. Essex Noel, director of the Mental Health Administration:

> Since we have understood for years, from NIMH and others, that the utmost priority for the Center was the outreach teams, the transfer of these persons severely depletes staff. . . . We feel that the transfer which has been ordered reflects the prejudice with which psychiatric patients are treated, especially when they are poor and black.[20]

Problems in continuity of care are also created by Area C's continued reliance upon St. Elizabeths Hospital. To the Richardson Division, Area C's 615-bed "backup service" at St. Elizabeths, are referred those patients who are extremely disturbed and agitated, as well as chronic, often geriatric patients—in other words, the undesirables. Although nobody seems to know exactly how many Area C patients are currently in residence at St. Elizabeths, estimates are in the neighborhood of three hundred. Because relationships between the two hospitals leave much to be desired, records may or may not follow patients, and the question of who has responsibility for continuity of care remains a question.

Responsibility for keeping tabs on formerly hospitalized Area C patients is shared by the St. Elizabeths' foster-care unit (an administrative entity distinct from staff on the wards), the Mental Health Administration Outplacement Unit, and Area C.

In spite of—or because of—the shared responsibility, follow-up services for most patients remain mostly an abstraction.

Moreover, there is no consensus about the proper relationship between the two hospitals. The staff at St. Elizabeths claims that the hospital is used primarily as a "dumping ground" for undesirable or "hopeless" patients. Ethel Beaman, the admissions unit nurse at St. Elizabeths, remarked to this Task Force, "Of course Area C is quiet. Anyone who speaks above a whisper they send to St. E's."[21] At an Area C staff meeting attended by this Task Force in the summer of 1970, Dr. Arthur Kiracofe, then acting director of Area C, stated:

> Whether they [NIMH] like it or not, it [St. Elizabeths Hospital] is a state hospital for the District. The administrative policy must be changed and it must be made easier to get patients in. Short-term crisis intervention is our mission and we can't do it if we have to deal with chronic schizophrenics.[22]

Area B

The Area B Community Mental Health Center, assigned second priority in the District, is located in the far northwest section of the city. The building is glum and dilapidated. There are few signs to indicate what it is, and little to suggest that anything therapeutic goes on within its walls. It is mostly a collection of grim offices, open from 8:30 A.M. to 4:30 P.M., Monday through Friday.

Like Area C, the catchment area contains over a quarter of a million people, most of them poor and black, though the largest part of the District's growing Spanish-speaking population is located here, too. Unlike Area C, Area B has within its boundaries a number of major general medical and psychiatric facilities, both public and private. These include the Howard University College of Medicine and Freedman's Hospital, Children's Hospital, Walter Reed Army Medical Center, Providence Hospital, the Washington Hospital Center, Children's Convalescent Hospital, and the new Veterans Administration Hospital. For reasons that are primarily political and financial, however, Area B has no firm or ongoing relationship with any of these institutions. Instead, it relies on D.C. General

Hospital and on St. Elizabeths, both of which are miles away, and outside its catchment area.

A plan to develop mental health services in Area B was initiated in 1967. Originally, the D.C. Department of Public Health and Howard University jointly proposed a comprehensive mental health plan to NIMH. The proposal, which was to have made extensive use of Howard's psychiatry department as well as its medical and laboratory staffs and emergency room, was approved by NIMH, and funds were made available to provide a staffing grant for the new Area B Community Mental Health Center. Shortly after the grant application was approved, however, Howard University and the health department became embroiled in unresolvable struggles over control of the center. Howard pulled out, and since then has had little to do with the Community Mental Health Center.

Once again, things were left solely up to the D.C. Department of Public Health, and once again the community was not part of the planning. Original health department plans called for the construction of a new building of eighty thousand square feet to house the center. An application to NIMH for construction funds was provisionally approved. These plans also never materialized, due to conflict within the health department over a suitable site and, according to health department officials, failure to get the necessary budget support for the D.C. share. Meanwhile, an inpatient unit for Area B residents was established at D.C. General, while a small administrative staff occupied rented space in the catchment area.

The health department's next move was to purchase, for approximately $1,300,000, the former Hebrew Home for the Aged, a decrepit, abandoned nursing home. The building was bought without consulting either the community, NIMH, or even the staff of Area B, and the transaction created an understandable furor on the part of all three groups. According to the 1970 *Mayor's Task Force Report on Public Health Goals*, "The condition of the structure upon actual takeover by the Department of Public Health was, to put it mildly, deplorable."[23]

It was clear that extensive renovation would be necessary, and the health department approached NIMH for funds. NIMH refused, calling the structure "generally inadequate for use as a Community Mental Health Center" and complaining that there had not been "an adequate plan for the coordinated utilization of the funds granted in 1967 for new construction . . . and the funds applied for this application."[24] The Institute, however, reserved $100,000 for renovation and gave the District until the end of fiscal year 1970 to submit another plan and to have matching funds available.*

Because of the rejection, the funds that had been reserved to support the D.C. contribution to the renovation (about $217,-000) were redirected "by Departmental decision" (since, it was claimed, matching money must remain unspent until an application is approved). Part of the money was used for a neighborhood health center in Anacostia, and what remained went toward renovation of the Hebrew Home.[25] With minimal renovation accomplished, the staff was directed to move in and begin operating in August, 1969—a directive that was greeted with dismay by the staff and angry picketing by community people. The anger was not sustained, however; instead, it has been added to a widespread, simmering resentment at what community residents see as a general pattern of second-rate facilities and inadequate funds for services in the District's poor black areas. Compounding the resentment, the Department of Human Resources took it upon itself to transfer $100,000 in federal funds which had been earmarked for Area B to wealthy Montgomery County (the Maryland suburb where NIMH's offices are located) to help pay for a mental health facility under construction there. According to the *Washington Post*, the transfer was initiated by Philip J. Rutledge, then DHR director, who told the *Post* that "We just did not have the money in our budget to make the grant. Rather than lose it completely, we let it go to a nearby Maryland county that services a lot of District residents."[26] Federal regulations do permit transfers of allotments from one state to another. They read as follows:

A state [or a jurisdiction like the District of Columbia] may submit a request in writing to the Surgeon General that its al-

---

* $100,000 is annually made available to states from NIMH for the construction or renovation of community mental health centers, subject to an approved application.

lotment or a specified portion thereof be added to the allotment of another State for the purpose of meeting a portion of
the Federal share of the cost of a project for the construction
of a community mental health facility in such other State. In
determining whether the facility with respect to which the
request is made will meet the needs of the State making the
request, and that use of the specified portion of such State's
allotment, as requested by it, will assist in carrying out the
purposes . . . of the Act, *the Surgeon General shall consider
the accessibility of the facility and the extent to which services
will be made available to the residents of the State making the
request.*[27] [Emphasis added.]

Under the circumstances, the legality (not to mention the
ethics) of this particular transaction seems dubious at best—
but, according to a former health department official who asked
not to be named, "It happens all the time—the point is to get
the money, then you can 'redirect' it as you see fit." Neither the
Surgeon General nor NIMH evidently raised any strenuous
objections to this transfer, although one might wonder about
the likelihood of a welfare recipient in Area B traveling some
twenty miles to a wealthy white suburb for mental health
services. It is perhaps merely coincidence that Mr. Rutledge,
along with a number of NIMH officials, lives in Montgomery
County.

The precipitous transfer of federal funds led to further investigation by the Washington press. Tallying up the losses to
Area B, WTOP–News reported in 1970 that the center had
missed out on more than half a million dollars since its inception due to mismanagement and lack of planning within the
DHR bureaucracy, if nothing else. According to reporter Jim
Michie, "An official involved in the renovation planning [said]
he is completely frustrated because of the bickering and confusion among Health Department officials over the project."[28]

The staff at Area B continues to try to implement what
programs it can in a still-unfinished and grossly inadequate
building. Because of poor and fluctuating leadership (the center
has had, like Area C, a succession of directors; after nearly a
year without a full-time director, one was finally appointed in
June, 1972) and the grim physical conditions, staff turnover

and absenteeism have been high, morale low. Services provided by Area B are limited at best and extremely fragmented. Aside from a therapeutic nursery for preschool children, there are no day-care or inpatient facilities for children or adolescents (although older teenagers are occasionally placed in the adult inpatient unit at D.C. General). An adult day-care program has recently been moved to the center,* and alcoholics are routinely referred to an affiliated treatment center in the catchment area or to one of several alcoholism services run by the city.

Area B's consultation and education programs have been skeletal. A few services (largely administrative) are provided by an official staff of one. And although staff in other units engage in some consultative efforts aimed at the schools and the juvenile courts, there is no unified, planned program.

There is no twenty-four-hour emergency service available in the catchment area. For night or weekend emergencies, one must go across town to D.C. General, where the central admissions unit at Area C does emergency screening for the city as a whole. Because emergency services and facilities are limited, this usually involves an unfortunate game of pass-the-patient. According to Murray Levine, a psychologist at Area B, 60 to 80 percent of the people who go to D.C. General for psychiatric emergency admission are referred elsewhere (sometimes with a tranquilizer to tide them over).[29] Usually the referral is to the outpatient unit of the center in their catchment area, where there may or may not be a waiting list. But in any case, there is no follow-up to see that help is actually provided. Consequently, most people just give up. What happens too often is that one must be disturbed enough to require hospitalization before adequate help, or any help at all, is available.

For those who do make it to Area B, frustration is likely to supersede treatment, or at least accompany it. Programs are organized along categorical lines (adult, children, inpatient,

---

* An adult outpatient and day-care program was provided to a subsection (80,000) of the catchment area under contract to an OEO-funded community action agency called Change, Inc. People living outside the boundaries of Change, Inc., could partake of a limited day-care program at D. C. General. Day-care programs, however, were and are geared to patients just released from the hospital, with little effort to use it as a means to prevent hospitalization.

outpatient, alcoholic, etc.) with little communication among staff assigned to different programs. (When this Task Force went to interview a psychologist at the center and had trouble finding him, three employees we asked didn't even know who he was, reinforcing the impression of isolated people in offices.) Not surprisingly, the kinds of problems presented by the community are largely multiple "life problems"—housing, nutrition, drugs, family disorganization, and usually several ongoing crises at once—which do not lend themselves to simple categorization. According to one staff member, "most people in the center really feel afraid—the problems presented are too many and too large, their inability to come up with solutions makes them feel helpless. . . . There is a prevailing attitude that the patient is the enemy. He always makes demands that usually can't be met—so people tend to hide in their offices, behind their titles."

For paraprofessionals on the staff, discouragement has followed close on the heels of optimism about the center's "new careers" program. Despite an inservice training program, with its (perhaps unfairly inflated or misunderstood) promises of upward mobility, salary and recognition have not been commensurate with increased responsibility or accomplishment.*

Understandably, the community has remained, for the most part, skeptical. There is a token community advisory board with a small core of actively concerned members. The board, however, has no policy-making powers and is not adequately representative of the Spanish-speaking population within the catchment area. It meets sporadically and tends to have a rapid turnover of membership. Indeed, because the center has done so little outreach work, it is doubtful that more than a handful of the 250,000 community residents are even aware of its existence, much less that of an advisory board to represent their interests.

Recently there has been an effort on the part of some staff

* This is complicated by the fact that city employees (and all community mental health personnel are employed by the city), like federal employees, are civil servants with G.S. (Government Service) numbers. Getting one's number—and thus one's salary—raised is, particularly at the low end of the scale, an endless bureaucratic process.

members to confront some of these obstacles. Community out-reach teams have been organized (though due to budget cuts the teams are neither as large nor as well equipped as had been hoped). These teams, which are to be highly mobile, will be concerned primarily with crisis intervention, early detection and prevention, and coordination with other city agencies. The goals are admirable. The problems are immense, however, and the resources exceedingly slim. As one team member said, "Sure, we can go out into the community and locate problems, but there is little support from Area B—that is, no facility where those problems can be effectively dealt with."

A large number of the problems in the catchment area turn out to be chronic medical ones, or to have medical components. Due to the lack of easy access to any medical facility (despite the abundance of such facilities in the catchment area), two part-time internists joined the staff in August of 1971 to provide medical backup for center patients. Since then, they have been waiting for basic equipment. According to one of the internists, Dr. Timothy Tomasi, the list of deficiencies is long. "We're at about the level of an emergency unit at an army field camp," he said.[30] Area B is the only community mental health center in the District to have its own medical unit (such as it is), and this is evidently causing some frowns on the faces of city officials, since it is considered beyond the sphere of a mental health center.

Medical problems of a more serious nature extend to Area B's inpatient unit, an acute psychiatric ward located on the grounds of D.C. General Hospital. The ward itself is over-crowded, foul-smelling, badly in need of paint and plaster. The unit has a thirty-eight-bed capacity which can be (and often is) stretched to forty-one, with three or four beds to a room. There are inadequate bathroom facilities, a constant shortage of supplies (including linens and pajamas), and what furniture there is is dilapidated.

According to Olivette Gill, the newly hired and dynamic administrative head of the unit, most of the patients are in-digent (often without even a pair of shoes or a change of clothes) and a large majority are black. Most have chronic medical afflictions, and many have never in their lives been to a doctor. Malnutrition, cardiovascular diseases, diabetes, arthritis, and hypertension are common.[31] Until quite recently there was no one on the staff to provide medical consultation (a curious problem, given the medical training required of psychiatrists), and backup services from D.C. General have been abysmal whether the need was routine or an emergency. In the past couple of years, five patients have died on the ward and although, as Gill was quick to point out, autopsy reports indicated that "they would have died anyway—no matter what," the fact is that medical coverage was simply not available. "Whether they might have died more humanely," Gill added, "is another question."[32]

None of the deaths was sudden, repeated pleas from the nursing staff for medical examinations went unheeded, and psychiatrists assigned to the unit were frequently not there. The deaths, though not publicized, caused enough of a stir among the staff to merit some investigation (i.e., autopsies were done). In one case, according to Dr. Tomasi, the patient kept having high fever and low blood pressure. After several days, he was sent to the D.C. General emergency room for tests. There, among other tests, a spinal tap was done—after which he should have been admitted to the hospital and watched closely. The spinal fluid looked normal to the resident who extracted it, however, so the patient was promptly sent back to the Area B ward, where he died a day or two later. Dr. Tomasi said further that the resident later acknowledged that he was reluctant to admit the patient because he feared the anger of his colleagues on an already overcrowded medical ward.[33]

This is perhaps a not uncommon attitude in a medical system in which the patient—particularly if he happens to be poor and black—too often comes last on the list of priorities. It is also a system which would seem to be open to abuse. For example, Dr. Ramasamy Nateson, one of the psychiatrists assigned part-time to the Area B inpatient unit, was recently investigated by the D.C. Medical Society. The reason? The forty-one-year-old Dr. Nateson collected over $100,000 in 1971 in federal Medicaid payments alone. At the same time, Dr. Nateson, as a G.S. 15, was on the city payroll at $15,000 a year for working twenty hours a week at Area B. According to several staff members at Area B, all of whom asked not to be identified, Dr. Nateson spent "precious little time" at Area B. "There is an implicit understanding on the part of a lot of psychiatrists," said one staff member, "that they don't have to work as much as they're paid."

Federal regulations stipulate that a psychiatrist can collect a maximum of $23.04 per psychiatric hour for treating a Medicaid patient ($7.20 for each patient in group therapy). This means that either Nateson ran exceedingly large groups, or that he would have to have worked a minimum of eighteen hours a day, 365 days a year to fill all his obligations. Nateson told *Washington Post* reporter Bob Woodward, however, that he works between twelve and fourteen hours a day, six days a week. Asked to explain the apparent contradiction, Nateson replied, "If I had made $1 million in business, would you ask that lousy question?"[34]

It has long been acknowledged that the D.C. Medicaid program, which has no review system despite a federal law requiring it, is open to flagrant abuse. Some critics, druggists and physicians among them, have said that "the failure to establish a review system is no less than a license to steal."[35] Although the medical society has not yet released its findings to the public, Nateson's case is dubious at best. Even if the investigation should find no proof of deliberate fraud, one can question the effectiveness of any form of psychotherapy for patients like those in Area B—particularly since Dr. Nateson, who is from India, speaks English that is barely comprehensible to native Americans.

This particular sort of abuse may be somewhat curtailed at Area B due to Olivette Gill's efficiency and determination. Everyone, she says, must now check in and out with a time-keeper. "Everyone has a designated time to work and if they're not there when they're supposed to be, I know about it."[36] Furthermore, referral decisions are now made jointly by "therapeutic teams" of staff and patients, and very few are made to private physicians.

But this, after all, is only a small unit and even with a devoted staff is a pathetic answer to the human problems that repose there. Though theoretically a short-term treatment ward, many patients have no money, no families, no place to go. Some simply stay. Others are referred to the Nichols Division, Area B's backup service at St. Elizabeths for patients needing long-term hospitalization. But because the inpatient unit is usually filled to capacity, a number of acutely ill patients are also referred to Nichols, and its 325 beds are frequently full, too.

Again, the responsibility for continuity of care tends to fall between the cracks in this unwieldy tripartite system in which the three major facilities are widely separated by distance, and in which the staffs are both too limited and too fraught with internal problems to have time left over for communication or systematic follow-up.

Compounding these problems is the fact that Area B contains 60 to 80 percent of the city's foster homes. When, under pressure from NIMH in the late sixties, St. Elizabeths began to develop the idea of foster homes as an alternative to long-term hospitalization, people from all over the city were placed in homes in Area B—an environment unprepared to accommodate them. One block in the catchment area contains so many foster homes that neighborhood wits refer to it as "St. Elizabeths Row." Ex-patients, once in foster homes, are theoretically the responsibility of the community mental health center. According to Gill, the catchment area has far more than its share of chronic schizophrenic and geriatric patients, and the most inadequate facilities in the District. Consequently, those who most need it receive, at best, only the most minimal after-care.

The tragedy is that with the overwhelming need for services in Area B, it has suffered most at the hands of the city bureaucracy—and with little or no support from NIMH—from gross mismanagement of funds, to appallingly bad and often inaccessible physical facilities, and uncoordinated services. When reminded of the fact that in the more hopeful days of the early sixties the District of Columbia was to have been made a national model in mental health care, Olivette Gill smiled a small, wry smile. "What we need," she said, "is a miracle."

Area D

Area D, the third community mental health center to extend services to residents of the District of Columbia, is unique.

Located on the grounds of St. Elizabeths Hospital, it is operated by St. Elizabeths and is thus the direct responsibility of NIMH rather than the D.C. Department of Human Resources. (NIMH took over the administrative control of St. Elizabeths in 1967, with the expressed goal of transforming that hospital into a "model mental institution.") Designed to serve the predominantly low-income black residents of the far southeast and far southwest sections of Washington, the center opened its doors to the community of some 170,000 in April, 1969. In the words of one of its staff members, Area D "grew right out of the hospital" without having to worry about grant applications. It occupies most of the Dorothea Dix Pavilion—a building it shares with the central admissions unit of the hospital.

Many of the staff members, including Dr. Roger Peele, the psychiatrist director of Area D, were hospital employees before the community mental health center was established. That, and the fact that it is impossible to escape the pervasive atmosphere of the "total institution"* no matter how many times it is pointed out that "this is not St. Elizabeths Hospital, this is the Area D Community Mental Health Center," account for the traditional leanings of the center, its strong ties to the medical profession, and its "hospital" identity.

If Area D is better organized, more fully equipped, and its staff more unified than its counterparts in the rest of Washington, it probably has more to do with its insulation from the D.C. Department of Human Resources (and its more secure financial situation) that with its ties to NIMH or St. Elizabeths. Contrary to what one might expect, NIMH has not seen Area D as the most logical setting in which to test the goals and explore the guidelines it has set for the nation. The Institute has not taken advantage of either its administrative control or of the proximity which could provide policy-makers with first-hand knowledge of the impact (the potentials as well as the built-in limitations) of a community mental health center in a poverty-area setting. Nor has it looked upon this as an opportunity to implement badly needed evaluation studies—not

---

* The term "total institution" was in fact coined at St. Elizabeths Hospital in the well-known study of that institution, *Asylums*, by Erving Goffman.

simply of organization, patient movement, and information flow, but of the quality of care.

In short, the Institute has not been interested. When this Task Force questioned several high-ranking Area D staff members about the role of NIMH in Area D's development, they shook their heads. "I cannot cite you one instance in my experience that NIMH has come in to help," said one. The sense that NIMH has chosen to interpret its responsibility to the center in the narrowest possible way was corroborated by Saul Feldman, the NIMH official with general responsibility for the centers program. "I know the director and some of the people," said Feldman, "but you see, it does not receive a grant from us. It's under the St. Elizabeths Hospital Administration, it's a division of St. Elizabeths, so I don't know much about it."[37]

While Area D, judged against the goals of accessibility, availability, and comprehensiveness proclaimed by NIMH, provides well-integrated but fairly conventional clinical services, it is a triumphant success compared to other local centers. For one thing, all of its services are located within the catchment area (though the services themselves tend to be organizationally decentralized). And although the stigma of being on the grounds of the local "insane asylum" has presented a large obstacle to community acceptance, hospital facilities, including medical facilities, are readily available to center patients.

Area D patients are clearly segregated from other patients at St. Elizabeths. Those who live within the catchment area are the responsibility of the center; if they are admitted as inpatients, they are admitted to Area D—which has 110 inpatient beds—regardless of age or diagnostic label ("chronic, acute, we take 'em all," said one jovial staff member). There is perhaps just a touch of irony in the fact that Area D is the only community mental health center in the District that does not have a "back ward" (or backup service as it is usually called) at St. Elizabeths—something the staff is very proud of and quick to point out—since it is also the only community mental health center in the District that is part of St. Elizabeths. It also shows the highest readmission rate of all the centers in the District, according to a recent study.[38]

The most innovative aspect of the Area D Community Mental Health Center is its successful translation of the "team" concept into a workable reality. The bulk of the staff is sub-divided into four treatment teams, each of which has an in-patient component (consisting of a psychiatrist, mental health counselors, nurses, and aides) and an outpatient component (a psychiatrist, psychologist, social worker, and mental health counselor) which is also responsible for consultation and educa-tion. Each of these teams serves a geographically determined subsection of the catchment area. In addition to these teams, there are specialized programs for children and adolescents, alcoholics, and drug addicts.

Although geographically determined, the amount of time the teams spend providing direct services outside of the Dix Pavilion tends to be limited, and there are no satellite clinics. Similarly, the specialized programs have not begun to be more than a Band-Aid on the needs of the community—in terms of the numbers of disturbed children, the increasingly high in-cidence of addiction, and so forth. The basic structure, how-ever, which is aimed at keeping administrative red tape at a minimum and continuity of care at a maximum, tries to com-bine comprehensive and categorical services without necessarily sacrificing one to the other.

Whether the programs and services offered are effective, however, is an important but unanswered question. A program evaluation director was optimistically hired, but lack of sup-portive staff and lack of a workable system has precluded the development of any ongoing program evaluation. Dr. Peele termed evaluation "pathetic," and indicated that, insofar as Area D is concerned, NIMH has been indifferent to the issue. When asked if he got any support or advice from NIMH, Peele said, "They just tell me to keep my big mouth shut."[39]

NIMH seems also to have remained indifferent to the issue of citizen participation in the center's programs—both in terms of a policy-making board and in terms of paraprofessional training. Although nearly two-thirds of the staff is black, pro-fessional control is clearly white, and in this respect Area D stands out from the other two poverty-area centers in the Dis-trict. The center recruits much of its professional staff from the training division of St. Elizabeths—which is almost entirely white and which is run directly by NIMH. Area D is "working on" establishing career ladders and inservice training programs for paraprofessionals, but none have been widely or effectively implemented to date.

The more formal mechanism of citizen participation through a board of community representatives presents a somewhat more complex situation. Although the community did not share in the initial planning of the center, the Area D staff very early sought to involve community residents in the establishment of priorities. Beginning with an open and well-attended but heated meeting shortly after Area D opened its doors, an active board of elected representatives has evolved. According to Vivian Smith, community liaison and public education officer, "At first, it was a matter of who could scream the loudest— there had to be more structured input." For the next year or so, the staff and community worked to build a structure. "Now," says Vivian Smith, "well, it's a good board."[40] Indeed, the Area D Citizens' Board, after nearly three years, has developed a reasonably stable, collaborative relationship with the Area D center staff, its major priorities being increased drug treatment programs and expanded services for children. The board is even beginning to test the limits of its policy-making power. It has developed its own by-laws and is seeking to become legally incorporated.

To requests by the staff for NIMH guidelines on citizen participation relating specifically to Area D, the Institute has responded by sending a copy of its general policy statement on consumer participation, extolling its own "long-term commitment . . . to consumer participation in NIMH programs,"[41] but declining to comment on the concrete issues at stake. Requests by the Citizens' Board for legal advice from the St. Elizabeths lawyers meet with stalling and silence, according to one board member. It seems that NIMH, for all its professed dedication to the community mental health centers program, both nationally and locally, has given every indication that it is in fact more interested in community mental health centers as an Institute *program* than with the real mental health needs of real communities.

Unfortunately, the institutionalized insensitivity of NIMH is matched by that of the service delivery system in the District.

In addition to the community mental health centers, Washington has a number of centralized programs which serve the entire District—including alcoholism, narcotics treatment, and suicide prevention—none of which has ever been effectively integrated with the mental health centers, and most of which tend to be hopelessly inadequate. Indeed, one of the major problems is that the community mental health centers program demands a decentralization of authority and responsibility that is totally at odds with both the city structure and with the point of view of city officials. Dr. Essex Noel, the first black to head the city's Mental Health Administration, has inherited massive problems, among them a faltering community mental health program to whose structure he is reluctantly bound and by which he feels frustrated. According to Noel, NIMH has been thoroughly disappointed by the District's failure to develop a model program. "I find myself the victim of their biases," he told this Task Force.[42] Noel tends to be rigidly professional. In June, 1972, a professional advisory council to the Mental Health Administration was organized. The suggestion of psychiatrist Robert Butler that this council might properly include nonpsychiatric professionals, such as social workers, psychologists, and nurses, met with a decision to change the name to the Psychiatric Advisory Council, just so there would be no mistake about who would be included among its members. In a letter dated June 28, 1972, to Dr. Robert G. Kvarnes, director of the Washington School of Psychiatry, Noel states:

> Please be assured that I was most delighted when the Council decided to become a *Psychiatric* Advisory Council. We must be aware that we have permitted many groups to impinge upon our profession, many of whom are anti-psychiatrists and anti-physician. My analysis of this trend indicates that it is counter-productive and will only lead to diminishing respect for the profession, with consequent dilution of our solidarity and ability to apply our hard-earned skills where it is [sic] most needed. While I recognize and deeply value the worthwhile contributions of those who should assist us in our professional endeavors, I think we should be cognizant that ours is the ultimate responsibility, and with that responsibility should be vested commensurate authority.[43] [Emphasis in original.]

Noel's heavy-handed wielding of authority and his instinct to guard jealously what little actual power he has are inappropriate to say the least. To illustrate: alcoholism is a major health and mental health problem, Washington ranking number one in alcoholism among the nation's ten largest cities.[44] Yet services, which are not community-based, have been minimally effective, as evidenced by the extremely high readmission rate to both the Detoxification Center and the Rehabilitation Center for Alcoholics (RCA). The latter, a residential treatment center for chronic alcoholics in Occoquan, Virginia, is a 715-bed institution that was created in 1966 as a national model. According to the *Washington Post*, the RCA "has deteriorated to the point where it will soon be able to offer alcoholics little more than a place to eat and sleep."[45] The deterioration has been attributed to inadequate funds as well as to lack of autonomy in the development of programs.

According to Dr. Robert Butler, the District's drug program has usurped both space and money from the alcoholism programs and the community mental health centers. What all of this points up is that in Washington, mental health and other service programs are neither strictly autonomous *nor* coordinated with each other in any meaningful way. And the problem is by no means primarily financial. Not counting the $5.5 million spent on the drug program, the District of Columbia has a per capita mental health expenditure higher than that of any state, its total mental health funding being comparable to, if not greater than, that of most urban areas.[46] The four community mental health centers alone are currently funded at a level of around $8 million per year in a total District mental health budget of approximately $40 million. But in Washington, the community mental health centers program has proven to be largely a simple renaming of traditional and, at that, inadequate psychiatric services. It is very hard to see where all the millions of dollars allocated to community mental health centers have gone—since in no catchment area of the city (with the exception of Area D) are comprehensive services available.

It is a byzantine (and often ruthless) system, full of bureaucratic redundancies and devoid of any real accountability to the public. Decisions are made unilaterally, and primarily on the basis of political expediency. Indeed, Washington, D.C., provides a superb example of mental health as pure politics. And it is a political arena in which NIMH is unlikely to wage battle for the poor and disadvantaged. Although the District has no voting representative in Congress, it is not without its supporters on Capitol Hill and in the White House. If NIMH were to break the precedent of federal indifference to the poor and radically challenge the running of District programs, the local politicos might well try to influence their friends in Congress and the White House to withdraw their support for the Institute. Why should the Institute take this chance of eroding its own political support simply for the sake of one city? As one NIMH official said frankly to this Task Force, "You pick your battles."

Moreover, in addition to the politicking that goes on in and among NIMH, the D.C. Department of Human Resources, and congressional committees, there operate subtle (and not-so-subtle) race and class distinctions. Historically, public health officials in the District have not been graduates of the prestigious medical schools that have spawned NIMH officials and the researchers that make up the most influential community of mental health professionals. Instead, they have in general been trained at the less elite institutions, and remained in public service (which is in itself considered rather low-brow) in a city structure that is more fragmented and bureaucratized than most. Even when the D.C. health department was all white (which until quite recently was the case), its officials were never on intimate terms with NIMH. As one former health department official put it, "We were never part of the national scene, with meetings in San Francisco and New Orleans. . . . We did not belong to the club."[47]

As the black population in Washington has increased, a large black middle class, with its share of professionals and professional bureaucrats, has grown up. Blacks now dominate the Department of Human Resources, but there is little evidence that they are any less directed than their white predecessors to bureaucratic empire-building or any more committed to the provision of human services. And with the increased demand for psychiatrists on the part of the black middle class, there is always the retreat into private practice when the system becomes too much for the few who do care. The poor, meanwhile, without a voice, are hidden in the back wards of St. Elizabeths Hospital and in the "back wards" of the ghettos in the nation's capital.

Although the District of Columbia has been proclaimed a "national model" of just about every federal program that has addressed itself to a social challenge—a model in crime prevention, drug abuse treatment, alcoholic rehabilitation, mental health care—the harsh conditions under which the poor continue to exist point to a reality that is, if anything, a model of racism, exploitation, and the arrogance of power.

9

Kern View Community Mental Health Center and Hospital, Bakersfield, California[1]

The San Joaquin Valley is the heartland of what has come to be called "agri-business," California's richest industry. From this valley come cotton, potatoes, grapes, and other crops. Although oil production and processing contribute to the region's economy, agriculture sets the tone and style of life. For most people, everything depends on a good season, a good crop, a good harvest. There are basically two kinds of people in the Valley: the growers and their families, and the farm workers,

153

most of whom are migrants. While the growers dominate the economic life of the Valley, their sons and grandsons, cousins and nephews dominate the professional and political life, which tends to be fervently conservative. The Valley is a heartland of fundamentalist religion and the John Birch Society. The prevailing ethic is that of the frontier; any challenge to that ethic, which extols the virtues of the rugged individual, tends to be viewed as a Communist conspiracy. One native daughter, author Joan Didion, described the Valley as "the California where it is possible to live and die without ever eating an artichoke, without ever meeting a Catholic or Jew. This is the California where it is easy to Dial-a-Devotion, but hard to buy a book."[2] For the farm workers, who are predominantly Mexican-American, Filipino, and black, the Valley way of life means powerlessness and poverty, chronic ill health, and flagrant discrimination.

The first beginnings of change for both growers and workers were ushered into the Valley in the mid-sixties by Cesar Chavez and the grape pickers' strike, which originated in the little town of Delano and grew to national proportions. The strike was resisted violently, brutally, and for as long as possible by the growers. And in the wake of Cesar Chavez, it was unlikely that a community mental health movement giving priority to the poor would be welcomed much more graciously.

The Kern View Community Mental Health Center, one of the first poverty-area centers in the country to be funded by NIMH, is now in its eighth year. The state community mental health plan divides Kern County—one of the largest counties in California—into two catchment areas, with the boundary line running through the city of Bakersfield. The Kern View Center is responsible for the western half of Kern County, an area of some 4,000 square miles with a population of approximately 170,000, including roughly half of Bakersfield plus several outlying rural communities, among them Delano, which is about thirty miles away. There are a number of other serious pockets of rural poverty like Delano in West Kern, as the area is officially called, characterized by low income, low educational achievement, and substandard and overcrowded housing. There are many chicanos in the area, and sprinklings of blacks and Filipinos.[3] Some minorities live in Bakersfield, but most are farm laborers concentrated in small agricultural settlements. Public transportation is abysmal; to get anywhere, one must have a car or access to one.

Located in downtown Bakersfield, the Kern View Community Mental Health Center is the only mental health facility in the catchment area. Kern View is responsible for serving all the residents of its catchment area, and it has been given a total of $752,000 in NIMH money to do that.[4] But the center has been hopelessly inadequate in meeting the needs of chicanos and other minority groups, according to a recent NIMH-funded evaluation contracted to the Tufts University School of Medicine. Since it began operation in 1966, the Kern View Center has been beset with organizational, operational, and ideological conflicts that have made its services inaccessible, both geographically and psychologically, to a large majority of the residents of the catchment area. In fact, for the first three years of its existence, Kern View was run strictly as a private psychiatric inpatient hospital; not until June, 1969, was its official name changed from Kern View Hospital to Kern View Community Mental Health Center and Hospital. The local psychiatric community looked upon the center as a private inpatient facility, and has continued to resist any change. Conflict with the private sector has had wide ramifications and is at the heart of the center's past and ongoing problems.[5]

The seeds of this conflict were planted in the early sixties, when the Mennonite Mental Health Services began to initiate plans for a psychiatric hospital in Bakersfield. The Mennonites had sponsored mental health programs in various parts of the country, including a psychiatric hospital called Kings View Homes in Reedley, California, about a hundred miles north of Bakersfield. Because a number of the Kings View Homes' patients were from the Bakersfield area, the Mennonite Mental Health Services decided to open a similar facility there. Negotiations were begun with the Greater Bakersfield Memorial Hospital Association to establish a separate unit affiliated with that hospital. The Mennonites also contacted several psychiatrists in private practice in Bakersfield. They enthusiastically approved the idea of an inpatient psychiatric hospital. Accordingly, a new building (including a twenty-five-bed inpatient unit) was constructed adjacent to Bakersfield Memorial Hospital, financed through federal hospital construction funds matched by the state. All the interested parties agreed that the new facility would provide no outpatient services (since that was the preserve of private psychiatrists and county facilities), but would be operated as a private inpatient hospital for the patients of local psychiatrists and would be governed by the Kings View Homes Board of Directors.[6]

Shortly before the center officially opened in 1966, financial pressure led the Mennonites to apply to NIMH for a community mental health center staffing grant, which was subsequently approved; the funds were made available a few months after operations began. The conditions of the NIMH staffing grant, requiring four additional essential services, imposed a new mandate upon the center and set forth goals that were diametrically opposed to the original conception of a private facility devoted strictly to inpatient care.

It is not altogether clear what the Mennonite Mental Health Services—the legal grantee—understood by community mental health or comprehensive services. In any case, the Mennonite board of directors remained outside the catchment area, nearly a hundred miles away, and focused its attention on broad financial matters, leaving the development of services and programs entirely to the discretion of three full-time psychiatrists who had been hired to run the facility.[7] Adhering closely to the original plans, they used the center for private practice and limited its services to inpatient care. According to Lawrence Yoder, the present administrator:

> After the psychiatrists started here, this place slowly evolved into a private inpatient hospital. It was really difficult to say what part of their practice was community mental health center work and what part was private practice. . . . The three psychiatrists were each making about $60,000 per year. They were being paid for services to patients who could not pay, but they took the amount from the Mental Health Center grant. Also for each medical round they made, they were paying themselves $6 each time. There were all sorts of tricks they were doing.[8]

This situation continued until 1969, when an NIMH site-visit team discovered to what extent the Institute's goals had been perverted by the staff at Kern View. NIMH sharply attacked the center for the most obvious indiscretions: it was not offering the five essential services, was not providing comprehensive care, and was catering only to the rich while sending indigent patients to the county hospital located outside the catchment area. NIMH was also critical of the board of directors, which, composed entirely of Mennonite members, was hardly representative of the local community.[9] A number of changes were made. A local board of directors was appointed and later expanded to include some community leaders who were not members of the Mennonite Church; a new administrator, with several years of experience as assistant administrator of a Mennonite clinic in Indiana, was brought in. The new board decided not to renew contracts for the three psychiatrists.

At this point, local psychiatrists would have nothing to do with the center; a medical director was with some difficulty recruited from Fairview State Hospital outside Los Angeles. The three psychiatrists left with a great deal of bitterness. The ousted director of the center expressed outrage at the turn of events. He stated:

> I would like to see a good private psychiatric hospital here. . . . I think doctors should be in charge of the program, they could then make the decisions about electroshock therapies. . . . I really wish the federal support would stop funding Kern View. We need a good private psychiatric hospital. Kern View is not in a ghetto. They were brought in to take care of the same kind of patients that Memorial takes care of. But they never realized this.[10]

According to another local psychiatrist:

> Kern View keeps moving in the direction of going into the outpatient business and this may or may not be a real threat to those of us who are in the outpatient business. At any rate, I think this is the main thing that's at the core of the problems that the private psychiatric community has had with Kern View. The fear is that it will become a service, with a lot of ancillary people who will hurt us. This is the major issue and it has caused the most conflict. It is an extremely emotionally charged area.[11]

Hostility toward the center has continued on the part of the psychiatric community, which fervently endorses private practice and feels threatened by the idea of "a social work type of thing."[12] Because local psychiatrists have considerable political clout, the center is vulnerable to threats of sabotage and "revenge" by the professional community—in the form of a boycott of the center or by influencing the county to withhold funds from Kern View. Indeed, Yoder indicated that a number of local psychiatrists have recently formed a corporation and are in the process of building their own psychiatric hospital across the street.[13]

In terms of county funds, the threat is not an idle one. Due to financing mechanisms peculiar to California and the close ties between the various county mental health agencies and local private psychiatrists, the role of the county in the affairs of the community mental health center is crucial. The County Mental Health Advisory Board, though it theoretically functions in an advisory capacity to the County Board of Supervisors and the County Mental Health Services Department, in fact is the major policy-making body.[14] The board includes several powerful private psychiatrists, who are thus in a position to influence how county funds are spent.

Kern View has become increasingly dependent upon financial support from the county, given the federal staffing-grant formula for declining funds. Support from the county, however, is derived not through direct financial commitment but through individual contracts for specific services. Moreover, the only state funds available to the center are through these same contracts, under the Short-Doyle Act.* Although at the height of the conflict at Kern View, there was some pressure from the County

* The California Short-Doyle Act of 1957 created the original financing mechanism by which responsibility for mental health services would be placed at the local (county) level, with reimbursement from the state, initially on a 50/50 basis. The act was modified in 1969, to increase the financial participation of the state to 90 percent, in an attempt to further promote the establishment of mental health programs on the local level. However, private facilities can participate in the Short-Doyle program only to the extent that their services are contracted for by the county. Because Kern View is licensed as a private psychiatric hospital, it falls into this category.

Mental Health Advisory Board to "punish" the center by deny-ing county contracts,[15] the center now has several fairly sub-stantial contracts with Kern County to provide, among other things, a methadone program, a partial hospitalization program, and inpatient services to county residents.

Significantly, the County Mental Health Advisory Board, by a policy that probably stems from a deep-rooted suspicion of federal intervention in regional affairs,* does not recognize catchment-area boundaries in providing services to county residents.[16] Thus, under contract, Kern View takes a consider-able number of the county's partial hospitalization patients and some of its inpatient load. This contractual arrangement, coupled with the fact that the center is located in Bakersfield only a mile west of the catchment-area boundary, means that its patient load is divided between the two catchment areas, with the heaviest concentration of patients coming from the immediate vicinity of Bakersfield. A 1970 site-visit report from the NIMH regional office in San Francisco indicated that only 40 percent of the people treated at the center were from the catchment area. By 1971 the figure had risen to 47 percent, according to Kern View's 1971 staffing-grant application.[17]

State legislation requires all counties with populations of 100,000 or more to develop countywide community mental health services, and requires that "county Short-Doyle plans shall provide for the most appropriate and economical use of all existing public and private agencies and personnel."[18] Pre-sumably the state would encourage the integration of private facilities such as Kern View into the county's overall program. But state legislation does not mention catchment areas, and

---

* Distaste for federal intervention, it should be noted, is often aroused by social programs. When it is a matter of financial aggrandizement in the form of crop subsidies, no one seems to mind. Some of the state's largest landowners have concentrated their holdings in Kern County (the Kern County Land Co.), which is one of the top eleven subsidy receivers in the nation. In 1970 the Kern County Land Co. received sev-eral hundred thousand dollars from the federal government in crop sub-sidies, in addition to reaping beneficial and disproportionate subsidies in the form of property tax breaks, etc. See Robert C. Fellmeth, *Politics of Land: Ralph Nader's Study Group Report on Land Use in California* (New York: Grossman Publishers, 1973), for full documentation.

what is meant by "the most appropriate and economical use" is left to the county to interpret. Kern County currently utilizes the Kern View Community Mental Health Center, but strictly on its own terms. In a telephone interview, Dr. David A. Grabski, director of the Kern County Department of Mental Health Services, stated that while he was glad to see NIMH money coming into the community, he was not enthusiastic about the federal program and expressed a hope that nobody would try to set up another community mental health center in the eastern half of the county.[19]

The county's strong desire to keep federal influence at a minimum is revealed by the "Five Year Plan" drafted by the County Mental Health Advisory Board in 1970. The plan strongly advocates building up a "county-centered" program that would rely less and less on other sources and outside contracts:

> Involvement in Federal Programs, except perhaps research grants, should be avoided. . . . The County Mental Health Program should be essentially a County centered program as contrasted with a program of contracting with outside vendors. The reasons for favoring a County centered program include lowered costs, greater visibility and control, overall higher quality of care. . . . Non-county agencies should be utilized to provide back up or overflow services where the county centered program is unable to meet a need.[20]

If this policy is followed, it will force the Kern View Center to revert completely to a private, profit-making facility in order to survive at all.

Lawrence Yoder, administrator of Kern View, and the center's medical director, Dr. Sigmund Kosewick, together have attempted to resolve some of the more egregious problems that were originally built into the center. There are, according to Yoder, an expanded day-treatment program, increased services for adolescents (though very few services for younger children), and a drug program that attempts to respond to the growing incidence of drug abuse in the community. A bilingual (English and Spanish) psychiatric social worker has recently been added to the staff, and outpatient services have been developed.* Still, virtually all services are contained within the six-year-old building. And, according to the SRI study, "the amount of effort devoted to inpatient services significantly exceeds that for all the other services combined."[21]

In the past, the center has suffered from lack of recognition in the larger community, as well as from internal conflicts. With many of the internal conflicts somewhat assuaged, the staff now asserts that its goal is to make the center known and available to everyone in the catchment area. In a telephone interview, Yoder stated that educating the community about the center and its services is a high priority. It wasn't so long ago, he indicated, that psychiatry in general and community psychiatry in particular were looked upon as a "Communist plot" by many people in Kern County. To "remedy" this situation, one staff member currently devotes about half his time providing consultation to such local agencies as the juvenile court and the public school system. In addition, a new public relations department puts out brochures and pamphlets, and educational seminars are held at the center on an average of once a month.[22]

According to Ernest Solano, the chief psychiatric social worker and head of the consultation and education program, conflict with the private sector has abated somewhat, and Kern View's alliances with the county are now more stable than they have been in the past. In a local atmosphere of lessened hostility and resentment, and with a continuation grant from NIMH approved for two more years, the center has optimistic plans to establish satellite clinics in three outlying rural areas: one in Delano, one in Taft, one in Shafter. According to Solano, these clinics will be heavily staffed with paraprofessionals, and each will have its own representative community advisory board.[23] At this stage, the center has encountered little overt resistance to its proposed outreach program. Historically, however, neither Kern View nor the county has given much priority to outreach programs, and at present virtually all mental health facilities, such as they are, remain clustered in Bakersfield. The latest

* The most recent NIMH site-visit report (February, 1971) indicated that during 1970 the outpatient load was two patients per week; this was in the *fourth* year of the center's operation.

figures (1971) regarding the center's services to minority groups reveal that in 1970 *fourteen* nonwhite patients were seen out of a total of 284 new patients.[24] Outreach clinics are evidently aimed at correcting this situation. Even with outreach plans duly made by Kern View, center staff are seriously limited as to what they can do without full-fledged support from the county. It should also be noted that these plans are already several years old; that "suitable locations" have not yet been found for the satellites-to-be; that, as Yoder put it, "you have to have enough political clout to provide services to indigents."[25] Meanwhile, the center continues to remain largely inaccessible to the indigent rural population.

Furthermore, lessened hostility does not necessarily mean strong advocacy or active support. And that is what it will take if Kern View is to live up to its stated goals. Whatever the center's potential might be, the facts point to a more sobering reality. It is not an integral part of the county mental health program, and for this reason its future is precarious at best. Because it is licensed as a private psychiatric hospital (as opposed to a general hospital), it is ineligible for Medicaid reimbursement for inpatient services; as mentioned earlier, it can participate in the Short-Doyle program with state reimbursement only through the county. Therefore, the center is dependent for the bulk of its income (60 percent) on patient fees and private insurance, inpatient revenues accounting for 80 to 85 percent of this.[26] Should financial support from the county decline, and should federal funds not be continued, it will be forced to raise those fees, further excluding the poor. In the long run, the viability of the center is dependent upon permanent financial support from both county and state, and the cooperation of the local psychiatric community. Without such support, as the SRI study points out,

> the only apparent alternative appears to be reversion to a private psychiatric hospital; and without the benefit of federal support under this alternative, it seems questionable that Kern View could remain financially viable even operating in that mode.[27]

Despite two evaluation studies and a number of site-visit reports criticizing the center and pointing out many of the political and financial problems, NIMH continues for the most part to reassure itself that Kern View is making progress. Both contracted evaluation criticism and critical site-visit reports usually end on a note of "they-are-sincere-and-trying." The site-visit report of December, 1971, for example, ended thus:

> In summary, it should again be stressed that Kern View has made tremendous progress in the past 18 months. The Board and staff should be extremely proud of that progress and take the above suggestions as the site visitors' earnest endeavor to support their efforts and to give consultation rather than criticism of either the direction or rate of Kern View's progress.[28]

Aside from its uncertain financial future, Kern View has a rather dubious relationship with the community it professes to serve. Citizen participation in setting the center's program goals and service priorities seems to exist exclusively in future plans. There are no paraprofessionals on its staff, and no inservice training programs. There is no community advisory board. The board of directors is still far from being representative. General control is in the hands of this governing board and the top center staff; but even with the change in staff and the reversal of the center's original narrow orientation, and even though the board of directors has been enlarged, there exist no mechanisms for accountability to community residents. NIMH has gently urged the development of an advisory board, but has evidently not insisted. So this too remains an item on the agenda for the future. According to one member of the present board of directors:

> There is a lot of feeling that unless the advisory committee has some power and something to do, you'll just end up being another committee to the board. We've been thinking about how you carry this out. We really don't know. We haven't come to a conclusion as to what they should do. We have lots of Mexican-Americans and Negroes here and they all have a little "hate" with them. I guess if they don't, they're not really with it. Our board is a little scared of this. What do you do with them? I think some of the members of the advisory committee should be members of our board. But it still comes down to how they can help us.

If you have a committee like that and they just get together once a month to talk, you'd soon get bored. I think we can get help from all sorts of people. No one is so dumb that you can't learn something from him. I learn something when I talk to my truck driver or my salesman.[29]

Change, perhaps, comes more slowly to some parts of the country than to others; and attitudinal change has a way of lagging behind organizational change. The Kern View Community Mental Health Center and Hospital has, under pressure, somewhat modified its organizational structure and its stated philosophy. The extent to which it can—or will—take an aggressive role in challenging the attitudes and assumptions that perpetuate the powerlessness of the poor and minorities is highly questionable given the middle-class orientation of its governing board. Conflict and competition with the psychiatric community, compounded by a politically conservative local power structure, add further obstacles to the possibility of genuine change insofar as issues of accountability and service delivery are concerned. Kern View is still a very long way from providing services that could by any stretch of the imagination be called comprehensive, and from providing any services at all to those most in need of them.

10

South Central Community Mental Health Center, Atlanta, Georgia[1]

The South Central Community Mental Health Center is relatively new. Beginning operations in September, 1970, it was the first center established in Georgia, which was the last state in the union to be funded. The center serves a catchment area of eighty thousand—60 percent black, 40 percent white—on Atlanta's Southside, an area whose poverty belies the outward symbols of affluence and the progressive spirit of Atlanta as a whole. The genesis and early development of the center involved a number of agencies, institutions, power groups, and people, with various concerns and interpretations of community

165

mental health. Interagency planning and coordination issues were and are crucial. Powerful conflicts of interest characterized the early life of the community mental health center and are likely to remain key factors in its precarious future.

The South Central Center was born out of an Office of Economic Opportunity neighborhood health center funded through Economic Opportunity Atlanta (EOA), a Community Action Agency. The Atlanta Southside Comprehensive Health Center was developed in 1966 and directed by Emory University in conjunction with the Fulton County Medical Society (since renamed the Medical Association of Atlanta). The mission of the center was to provide comprehensive medical and dental care, and very limited mental health care, to the black poverty area of some 22,000 that makes up the core of the present mental health catchment area. The small mental health unit had just begun to function under the directorship of psychiatrist Peter Bourne, associate professor of psychiatry and assistant professor of preventive medicine at Emory, when it was learned that an NIMH staffing grant might be available for an expanded mental health center to serve a much larger area.

From the outset, a number of interest groups and agencies clashed over the very prospect of the community mental health center. Officials at Model Cities,* a program of the Department of Housing and Urban Development, who since the late sixties had been actively concerned with the development and coordination of new services and the involvement of Atlanta community residents in them, were initially dubious about a mental health center funded by NIMH. According to Peter Bourne, "they saw this as another evidence of strengthening the hands of the colonial empire—Emory's medical school."[2] They were appeased in the early stages of planning, however, by Bourne's commitment to the idea of a consortium of community residents, including professionals, agency representatives, and consumers to organize and control the community mental health center. Bourne was determined that neither

---

* Atlanta was among the first cities in the nation to be designated a "Model City," and the first target area in Atlanta fell within the Southside mental health catchment area and overlaps with the area designated by the OEO Community Action Agency to be served by the comprehensive neighborhood health center.

Model Cities nor the medical school would control the proposed center. But there was the critical problem of who *could* be the legal applicant for the staffing grant.

At this point, with an NIMH deadline fast approaching, there also entered on the scene the Fulton County Health Department and Board of Health, Grady Hospital (the county-run inner-city hospital that is also Emory's chief teaching institution), the State Health Department, the Atlanta University School of Social Work (primarily black), and the Metropolitan Atlanta Mental Health Association. All these groups are in one way or another directly related to the community mental health center and all were involved in the initial planning. Although there was no formal community input, a number of community residents did participate in the early confusion.

Both the county and the state (whose approval and long-term financial support were essential) quickly scuttled the idea of a consortium.[3] They wanted one existing agency to have control. While it would have been possible for the county to assume responsibility and become the applicant, the county declined to do so because of the implied possibility of a long-term financial commitment. It was also clearly impolitic for Emory to become the direct applicant or delegate, in part because of a past history of failure to relate to the black community (and the community's manifest suspicion that its residents would be used as "guinea pigs" by Emory) and in part because of strong opposition on the part of Atlanta University's School of Social Work—which saw itself as potentially having a substantial role in the center and which feared domination by the medical school.*

Eventually the only plan that was politically acceptable (though it was of questionable legality) was for the OEO comprehensive health center to become the applicant, with the money going directly to the mental health center. Although the Fulton County Health Department, and particularly its County Board of Health, resisted, being generally uninterested in a poor,

* According to Mary King, Program Analyst for OEO, Emory by this time had no more desire than the county to get involved with the community mental health center. Having had both financial and public-relations problems with the OEO health center, the University was ready to wash its hands of the "whole community bit" and had to be persuaded to lend its support.

mostly black catchment area at a time when none of the other
(white) catchment areas in the county had centers, it was
finally persuaded, along with the county hospital that would
provide the necessary inpatient beds, to sign a formal contract
guaranteeing future funding.[4] It was determined from the start
that Model Cities (which has a loophole allowing HUD supplemental funds to be counted as local funds) would provide the
matching money, and that the OEO health center would continue to contribute its mental health budget (twenty-five personnel slots) to the new mental health center.

The role of Model Cities is important: it had done general
planning for social projects in the area, was philosophically
committed to some form of community control, and had previously contracted with the Atlanta University School of Social
Work to do specialized mental health planning for its area in
the hope that it would counter the influence of the medical school
and be more sensitive to local needs.[5]

The Emory medical school played a crucial if obsecure role.
Since it already administered the OEO health center which
parented the community mental health center, it became, in
effect, the controlling institution of the community mental health
center, although without strict legal responsibility. For example,
top center staff were recruited with the promise of professional faculty appointments to Emory's department of preventive medicine and the combined staffs of both the health
center and the mental health center were on Emory's payroll.
Derril Gay, a sociologist and coordinator of community mental
health programs for the Georgia Department of Public Health,
commented on the arrangement:

> The ultimate governing board is the Emory University board
> of trustees, and that presents very hairy problems. I don't
> know what the final authority is because the organizational
> concept is so complex. . . . When I look over the proposal and
> think about it I really shudder, because there's no commitment
> anywhere from the medical school or its board of directors.[6]

The county health department, for its part, was no less
worried about the role of Emory. According to Dr. Mildred
Keene, Fulton County mental health commissioner:

The medical school has had *inordinate* control for its size over the health affairs in the county. But I suppose that is the kind of situation that arises whenever you have one medical school in a city. There is a lot of jealousy and hard feelings about it. Some groups will fight occasionally, but they have always lost and it has always seemed to come out on top.[7] [Emphasis in original.]

According to Peter Bourne, the potential for conflict between the medical school and the school of social work was and is considerable, the major issue being one of white versus black control. Dr. Bernard Holland, chairman of the department of psychiatry at Emory, though he became involved reluctantly, has some stake in the community mental health center. He oversees the professional staff of the center and depends upon part of its staffing grant as a resource for the training of psychiatry residents. Dr. Holland is somewhat wary of the problems that will inevitably accompany the involvement of the county and state health department bureaucracies and is inclined to proceed cautiously where the black community is concerned.[8]

As if this were not already sufficiently complicated, the neighborhood health center, as originator of the mental health center and applicant for the NIMH staffing grant, has seen the developing mental health center as being clearly within its province and has assumed a sort of parent-child relationship between the two. According to Mary King, a close observer of the developments, the OEO center has attempted to control the mental health center in a manner repetitive of EOA's attempts to control the OEO center, and suggestive of long-standing patterns of control over minority interests in Atlanta.[9]

A determining factor in the ultimate organizational structure of the South Central Center was the way in which decisions were arrived at in the early planning stages. Because of the time pressure, political considerations and personal prejudices necessarily played a more prominent role than they otherwise might have. Most of the important decisions were made not by attempting to resolve differences or to find a common ground, but by politically expedient (and insincere) compromises and financial trade-offs. For example, Grady Hospital's psychiatric unit provides and controls inpatient services for the community mental health center on a contractual basis (six beds are reserved for the center), although it is located outside the catchment area. The hospital is administered by the county, which contracts with Emory to provide all professional services. Dr. Doug Skelton, director of the psychiatric unit, is not on the staff of the community mental health center, but is on the faculty of Emory's department of psychiatry. Dr. Skelton has little to do with the community mental health center, feels that its impact on his unit will be minimal, and tends to view the whole thing as a strictly business arrangement:

> The arrangements that were made for the NIMH grant were satisfactory. For some time we have had need of a 24-hour observation unit where patients could be kept for an intensive kind of observation and intake proceedings. What will happen is that we will use the money coming from the National Institute of Mental Health grant to build our 24-hour observation unit. In return for that we will care for Dr. Bourne's patients.[10]

This contractual agreement has provoked strong criticism (though not for the dubious ethics of using NIMH staffing money to build an observation unit), since the county hospital was already obliged to accept and treat all county residents. The fact that there is no organic relationship—but only a paper contract—between the inpatient unit and other center programs means that there are formidable problems in providing continuity of care.

Similarly, a twenty-four-hour-a-day telephone emergency service is provided by the Fulton County Emergency Mental Health Services. According to Peter Bourne, referrals to the community mental health center are erratic, with the county usually referring people automatically to the Grady Psychiatric Service even when they live within the community mental health center catchment area. As for the acute emergency room, the staff has little communication with the mental health center staff, which means that follow-up is entirely a matter of chance.[11]

Although the South Central Community Mental Health Center is by nature dependent upon four major agencies and several related ones, none of these identifies itself as being part of a community mental health "system." Grady Hospital sees it as a matter of "them" and "us"; Emory has a more paternalistic attitude, as does the OEO health center; and the county is reluctantly responsible for supporting a program over which it does not have unilateral control. Moreover, the concept of community mental health is interpreted differently by nearly everyone. There is totally lacking the kind of cohesiveness among agencies and the individuals on their staffs that is essential if such an organizational structure is to work for the benefit of the community. According to Peter Bourne, a large part of the reason for this in Atlanta is that there is a basic lack of understanding of what community mental health is all about.[12] The South Central Center was the first venture of its type in Georgia, and there remains a strong tendency to see the county charity hospital as the only legitimate health care provider for those who cannot afford to pay for a private physician. Any public program outside of Grady is therefore seen as being fundamentally illegitimate, so that by and large the South Central Community Mental Health Center is treated as though it does not exist. Ironically, this attitude appears to coexist easily with the competing interest-group struggles for control.

Despite the inherent difficulties of planning and coordination within the context of fragmented authority, conceptually the South Central Center is one of the very best in the country. Its staff very early took an aggressive role in finding out what the mental health needs of the community were and in attempting to meet them. The original idea of a consortium was implemented to act as an advisory board, and satellite clinics (there are now six), were spread through the catchment area. Designed to respond to the localized needs of their subcommunities, these were staffed heavily by trained paraprofessionals along with the part-time services of a psychiatrist, a psychologist, and mental retardation workers. A halfway house for alcoholics was set up and is run totally by paraprofessionals, most of whom are ex-alcoholics.

These programs have continued, and are successful as far as they go, though the use of paraprofessional workers has declined since the directorship of the center has been turned over by Dr. Bourne (who is white) to Barbara King, a black social worker. Although King herself declined to speak with this Task Force, she is, according to one staff member who asked not to be identified, more concerned about educational levels and credentials, and stresses the importance of black professionals over paraprofessionals. Accordingly, the alcoholism program is now supervised by a social worker, and new paraprofessionals are encouraged to go to Atlanta University for training rather than being trained on the job. Along with the change in directorship, a larger organizational change has occurred. Under pressure from NIMH, Emory, and the Fulton County Health Department, the grant has been transferred from the OEO health center to the Fulton County Health Department, which has subcontracted the center program and administration to Emory University.

Although this is a more straightforward and sounder legal arrangement, it raises certain fundamental issues. For purposes of administrative simplicity, the mental health center is now run by Emory through its department of preventive medicine as part and parcel of the comprehensive health center. This is likely to limit the possibility of mental health needs being given much priority at a time when the developing mental health center has begun to seek its own identity and, more important, its own control. Since the mental health catchment area extends well beyond the OEO target area, and since the community mental health center is at this point more stably funded, there is, as Peter Bourne suggests, "a situation where the tail is wagging the dog." The OEO health center has not expanded its medical and dental services to cover the entire catchment area; and although it will treat acute medical problems from outside its area when they present themselves, there is virtually no medical backup for most residents of the catchment area. Instead, they must rely on the inadequate facilities and reluctant staff of Grady Hosiptal. As Bourne commented laconically, "If someone comes in from outside the OEO area, we have to tell him, 'well, we can give you some Thorazine for your schizophrenia, but we can't fix your teeth or give you glasses,' even though these services are available in this building to others from a different part of the community."[13]

Moreover, the original consortium that Dr. Bourne envisioned as the body that would eventually control the mental health center has been absorbed by the "policy board" of the neighborhood health center, although it represents only one-third of the catchment area. This may in the long run prove fortuitous, since OEO seems to have a far stronger commitment to citizen participation than does NIMH, and the policy board, which is in the process of becoming incorporated, is likely to be effective in wielding responsible power. There is, however, a danger that without citizen representation the mental health needs of a large part of the catchment area will be neglected, and a further danger that the community mental health center, lacking a strong board of its own, will fail to be clearly accountable to consumers.

On Atlanta's Southside, the biggest irony is that three federal agencies—NIMH, OEO, and HUD—all dedicated to comprehensive programs and coordinated planning on the local level, have not only not done much to further broad local cooperation, but have provided a wonderful example of fragmentation at the federal level. Without a central focus of authority, accountability of any kind is extremely difficult; without a strong representative citizens' policy-making board, conflict over control is inevitable, and the battles over power for its own sake are likely to usurp considerations of human service to the community. When we queried Dr. Bernard Holland about the fragmented health and mental health care despite all the federal help, he stammered, "Are you kidding? It's those three agencies that are *creating* the fragmentation. They all have different catchment areas, different funding mechanisms, and they all want visibility for their own programs. It's a mishmash, it's just awful."[14]

11

The Lincoln Hospital Revolt, New York City

Early in March of 1969, a determined band of more than 150 mental health workers, led by black and Puerto Rican nonprofessionals and supported by a handful of professionals, seized control of the Lincoln Hospital Mental Health Services (LHMHS) in New York City. The occupation of the mental health center signaled the eruption of a long-seething situation fueled by a welter of problems, including inefficient management of funds, a rigid internal hierarchy, racial tensions, job insecurity and lack of career advancement, and university and city bureaucracies traditionally unresponsive to the needs of disadvantaged communities.[1]

Though not a complete surprise to those most immediately involved, the takeover by mental health workers in the name of community-worker control came as a rude awakening to many others. For the Lincoln Hospital Mental Health Services, affiliated with Albert Einstein College of Medicine of Yeshiva University, was widely hailed as an innovative, community-oriented program. In 1968 the American Psychiatric Association awarded LHMHS a silver achievement medal for "its innovative efforts in making mental health services available when and where they are needed . . . demonstrating how to reach the unreachables."[2] NIMH designated the community mental health center at Lincoln Hospital one of eight national model centers, giving special tribute to its program to hire and train community people for "new careers" in mental health.

Lincoln Hospital is situated in a rapidly decaying ghetto in the South Bronx, an area that since the turn of the century has been a way station on the road to upward mobility. In one five-year period from 1960 to 1965 more than 50 percent of the people of the South Bronx moved from the area; as soon as resources became available, residents simply packed up and left.[3] Little wonder—for every statistic about the area testifies to the daily misery of its inhabitants. The median income is a third less than that of the rest of the city, unemployment is two-thirds higher, twice the number of people are on welfare, infant mortality is a fifth higher than in the rest of the city, venereal disease nearly twice as common, and admissions to mental hospitals are 50 percent higher.[4] Today the population of the South Bronx is about 70 percent Puerto Rican and 20 percent black, with various other ethnic groups making up the remaining 10 percent. Many of the Puerto Ricans speak little or no English.[5]

Lincoln Hospital, whose squalid physical plant mirrors its surroundings, is the only general hospital available to the 350,000 people in the South Bronx. It is among the most physically deteriorated, ill-equipped, and understaffed of all New York City hospitals. And its frightfully inadequate emergency room—the second busiest in the nation, with about 300,000 patients' visits each year—is one of the reasons local citizens call Lincoln the "butcher shop."[6]

Mental health services for Lincoln Hospital were begun in

1963 as an outpatient clinic housed in the hospital complex, funded by the New York City Department of Hospitals through an affiliation contract with the Albert Einstein College of Medicine of Yeshiva University. Thus, from the beginning the Lincoln Hospital Mental Health Services functioned under the mandates of a number of supraordinate bodies. On the one hand, it was funded by a city bureaucracy connected with and partially responsible to a variety of state and federal agencies. On the other hand, responsibility for service delivery was borne by the Department of Psychiatry of Albert Einstein, which is ultimately responsible to the Board of Trustees of Yeshiva University. But early on, the questions of who the administration was and who had authority to do what were submerged in the rush to get the services going.

On paper, LHMHS, whose budget grew fourfold from $830,000 in 1964 to $3.4 million in 1968, looked impressive and combined traditional and innovative approaches to mental health services.[7] The traditional approach consisted primarily of an outpatient psychiatric clinic located in the renovated second floor of an abandoned nurses' residence at Lincoln Hospital. The innovative program was begun in 1965, when the Office of Economic Opportunity funded three storefront centers in what had formerly been a linoleum store, a post office, and a dance hall. These "neighborhood service centers," designed to attract people whom the clinic had been unable to reach, were centrally located, easily accessible, informal, and lacked any of the usual appurtenances of a hospital or psychiatric service.[8]

The mental health services recruited and trained 140 indigenous nonprofessionals, mostly black and Puerto Rican, under the "new careers" program. Supervised by professionals, they were to staff the centers. Initially, the new careerists were enthusiastic about the promise of further education that would push them up the career ladder, possibly even to the ranks of professionals. But as the program developed, a number of conflicts arose between professionals and nonprofessionals. According to two former associate directors of LHMHS, the underlying problem was a "clash of cultures," which made communication and mutual respect difficult for the two groups.[9]

More important, the administrators of the program failed to keep their promises of job advancement and further education. This effectively quashed the expectations of the nonprofessionals, and instead fostered frustration and mistrust.[10]

In this early phase of their work in the neighborhood service centers, however, the workers were proud of their work—helping people find jobs or apartments, talking with them about family problems or tracking down a missing welfare check, organizing tenants and voters—despite the broken promises about career opportunities. In an evaluation of the program Stanley Lehmann, then associate director of research at LHMHS, found that the centers were indeed oriented to the problems of community people. "A community service that attracts three times the expected number of clients with previous psychiatric histories is doing something right insofar as psychiatric interests are concerned," he observed. And he concluded:

> The centers were eminently successful in attracting large numbers of people with problems typical of a disadvantaged community. They were especially successful in attracting those who had prior psychiatric problems. In this way, they accomplished their primary aim and managed to serve a segment of the population that is not reached by other means. They did this by being accessible and informal, by establishing an open-door policy in respect to problems and people, and by using people from the same community to perform most of the services.[11]

Early in 1967 it became apparent that the three-year OEO demonstration grant that supported the neighborhood service centers would not be renewed at the end of the year. Top administrators of LHMHS began making plans to turn their program into a community mental health center based on the federal model, and they applied for an NIMH staffing grant. This grant was formally awarded in July, 1968, six months after the termination of the OEO grant, and provided for the continued employment of the nonprofessional staff who otherwise would have been dismissed for lack of funds. The storefront centers, however, were phased out.

According to Drs. Robert Shaw and Carol Eagle, former director and assistant director, respectively, of the Children's

Mental Health Services at Lincoln Hospital, the development of the community mental health center staffing grant forced a change in the conceptualization of the program.[12] The federal guidelines were interpreted in such a way, they maintain, that the innovative emphasis on social action shifted to a more conventional medical approach, differing very little from a traditional psychiatric hospital. They observe that this change to "a much more traditional model defeated the very purpose of the nonprofessional training program, of the social action modality, and of the attempts to raise self-esteem within the ghetto."[13] These concerns were also expressed by a number of nonprofessionals who began to question what was being done with the grant money. Said one of the frustrated workers:

> When I first came here we dealt with people's needs. If a man was depressed and he lived in a rat hole, we went out and we helped move him. We carried his bed on our backs. In other cases, we started putting pressure on landlords. And then the word came down. . . . we don't move patients anymore— Einstein says we're not covered by insurance. Pressure on the landlords? We've been ordered to cool it. In the case of one of the landlords, word came from high up. We found out later that the landlord was a big contributor to Yeshiva.[14]

In a book published in August, 1973, Drs. Seymour Kaplan and Melvin Roman, two former associate directors of LHMHS, deny that with the NIMH staffing grant the program retreated back to hospital-based care. They argue that their plan called for an extension of community services, with a greater proportion of staff moving out of the hospital-based clinic into neighborhood satellite clinics.[15] But whatever the intentions of the LHMHS administration at this time, a number of problems reached a climax during 1968–1969 that wreaked havoc with the implementation of community mental health services, innovative or otherwise.

To begin with, only one of the three neighborhood satellite clinics provided for by the federal grant had actually been established by 1969. According to Dr. Roman, this was largely due to the delays and inefficiencies of the city administration.[16] But since the inception of mental health services at Lincoln Hospital the inefficiencies of Yeshiva University and LHMHS had caused serious problems and eroded staff morale. Vendors and consultants were not paid for months. The staff at one storefront center were nearly evicted for nonpayment of rent. Most frustrating of all were the frequent delays and errors in paychecks. The feelings of the staff were expressed in a memo by one mental health worker:

> I have been in the Lincoln Hospital Mental Health Program for two and a half years and each day the business and personnel aspect of the program becomes worse and worse and has prompted me to Phase One of my campaign, which is to demand that on pay day I receive my check on time, no later than 12 noon so that I won't have to hang around the payroll office like a beggar begging for crumbs from the rich man's table. I work hard for my money . . . and when I receive the check, many times I do not have time to get to my bank before it closes.[17]

In May, 1938, the nonprofessional workers staged a sit-in at the business office of Lincoln Hospital demanding that new payroll procedures be developed and educational release time and free tuition be established. The professional staff supported the nonprofessionals through a work stoppage, and the demands were met by Yeshiva University. A short time later, in what was known as the "palace revolt," the senior professional staff demanded greater authority and more participation in policy-making. In addition, the nonprofessional staff called for specific plans for community participation and staff elections for members of a "policy planning and review board," which would have final control over all major program policies, including hiring, firing, and fiscal arrangements for the staff.[18]

Throughout the summer of 1968 intense discussions were held to establish procedures and the composition of the board. The final plan was accepted by the entire staff, including the director of LHMHS, Dr. Harris Peck. But on October 4, just one day before the balloting, the general counsel of Yeshiva University sent a letter declaring that the establishment of a staff policy-planning and review board involved a proposed delegation of powers of the university and the college of medicine without authority of either the university's Board of Trustees or the College Board of Overseers, that this authority could not be delegated beyond present limits without their consent, and that the consent had not been given.[19]

This experience, which embittered the entire staff, was followed by five months of escalating conflicts and grievances, including charges of racial discrimination against nonwhite workers. Finally, in early March of 1969, after the LHMHS administration dismissed four black, nonprofessional workers in unrelated disciplinary actions, the situation exploded. Nonprofessional workers occupied LHMHS and replaced professionals in administrative capacities and as heads of services. In addition, three psychiatrists who were chiefs of services continued to work as technical consultants to the dissident nonprofessionals for the two weeks of the occupation.

During the occupation, the hospital administration's unresponsiveness to staff workers and to the community became the leading issues. The workers also complained of inefficient coordination of existing programs and failure to develop many of the programs that had been described on paper. Their central demands, however, called for removal of the director, Dr. Harris Peck, and his two associate directors; the establishment of a policy-planning and review board; and a "meaningful community board with significant decision-making power and responsibilities over the administration and policies of Lincoln Hospital and LHMHS."[20] The demand regarding community control was particularly wrought with political implications. A citywide teachers' strike in September, 1968, had pitted the right of local communities to control their schools versus the teachers' demands for job security, and in the following months the South Bronx continued to be torn by strife over this issue. The issue was further complicated by an inherent ambiguity about who truly represented the community and competition between blacks and Puerto Ricans for political control of the area.

The response of NIMH to the crisis that gripped one of its model centers sheds light on the Institute's regard for public accountability and its own priorities. To begin with, it was not until July 9, 1968, after more than four months of total disruption of services, that NIMH formally entered the scene. In a site-visit report released to the media, NIMH blasted the LHMHS administration for eight "major deficiencies" in meeting federal standards which were described as being "of such a magnitude as to ordinarily warrant suspension of the grant." In one instance, $136,000 had been provided for establishing a psychiatric emergency-room service. The site-visit team reported that "a visit to the emergency room did not reveal any of the federal staffing grant personnel as physically present, accessible, and available. . . ."[21]

In another instance, $137,000 had been earmarked for a "liaison staff" for the center's adult inpatient service located at Bronx State Hospital. The site-visit report stated that, "Not only was there no liaison staff, but the inpatient service was apparently completely separate and not coordinated with the rest of the Community Mental Health Center Services."[22] NIMH also criticized LHMHS for deterioration of relations between center administrators and the community, and lack of adequate services provided to the community.

NIMH officials made no distinction in their site-visit report between the disruption of planned services caused by the strike and those deficiencies that had always characterized LHMHS. They did not explain why they had waited so long after the occupation even to visit the center, nor did they delve into the conflicts and issues that caused it. Furthermore, NIMH made no attempt to resolve the fundamental problems besetting LHMHS and made no substantive recommendations for change. Instead, NIMH officials focused their attention on the lack of "an identifiable community mental health center separate from the rest of the mental health services of Lincoln Hospital" and demanded that "the Lincoln Hospital Community Mental Health Center . . . be clearly differentiated from other Lincoln Hospital mental health programs immediately."[23] Instead of insisting that fundamental changes in the administrative structure be made, NIMH simply recommended that funds for the mental health center be separated from those for the rest of the hospital program. To NIMH, the visibility of its own program took precedence over how the community could determine its needs and how these needs could best be met.

12

North Oakland Community Mental Health Center, Pontiac, Michigan[1]

Oakland County, Michigan, encloses some of the wealthiest suburbs in the United States, an abundance of middle-income housing developments, and a few pockets of poverty in a sprawling territory just north of Detroit. Mostly rural before World War II, it has become a bedroom community for many of its inhabitants who each morning commute to the auto plants in neighboring Detroit and Flint. The rapid growth of the county over the last several decades is inextricably linked to the transformation of Detroit from a small city with a fairly diversified economy to a large metropolis dependent upon automobile manufacturing as its single most important industry. During the economic prosperity of the 1950s, which made it possible for many middle- and working-class people to move to the suburbs, the population of Oakland County increased by 74 percent. Most of these new suburbanites came from Slavic and southern European stock; others were from the southern United States; all were fleeing as much from the migration of blacks to Detroit as they were from the decay of the inner city.

An NIMH evaluation study contracted to the Health Policy Advisory Center (Health-PAC) of New York describes the bleakness and the urban blight that has accompanied this un-planned-for growth. Oakland County's air and waters are dangerously polluted; rows of quickly and poorly built tract housing are spread across the area, particularly its southern end; commuter traffic clogs its highways, which have become lined with endless processions of hamburger havens, bars, and discount shoe stores. Without a car there is little mobility in or out of Oakland County, for there is very limited public trans-portation to link its thirty-some townships or to provide access to Detroit. In addition to the rapid growth of the population and the spread of urban development, there has been a marked shift in the age composition of the population, with the greatest increase among those under fifteen years of age.

The population of Oakland County is basically a white, middle-class one whose economic life is relatively secure, al-though both the long General Motors strike in 1970 and cur-rent inflation have been deeply felt. While most working-class families have tended to settle in the southern part of the county, in recent years there has been a discernible movement north-ward, again, ahead of the movement of blacks. The bulk of the county's black and poverty-level population is concentrated in the county seat of Pontiac. Directly south of Pontiac is the township of Bloomfield Hills, one of the wealthiest in the nation, rivaling Grosse Pointe as the favorite residence of top auto executives. North Oakland County, somewhat more sparsely populated, contains a number of small rural and semi-rural townships. It remains virtually all white.

The economy of Oakland County is dominated by the automobile industry; in addition to serving as a bedroom community
for Detroit and Flint, Oakland County has three major factories
of its own: the Pontiac Motor Division of General Motors, a
Fisher Body plant, and a GM truck and coach plant. There are
also a number of smaller auto plants across the region. More
than 40 percent of the working population is employed in
manufacturing, and most of the work force, directly or indirectly,
is dependent on the auto industry. Industry domination is not
solely economic, but extends into local politics and social
services as well through the exercise of more informal but
quite effective power. Social service agencies tend to remain in
the private sector and are maintained by local philanthropy,
most notably the United Fund. General Motors supplies about
70 percent of the Pontiac Area United Fund gifts, and is the
mainstay of non-United Fund agencies as well.[2] According to
Ken Morris, regional director of the United Auto Workers
(UAW), "We are owned by GM in this area. Not only does GM
control the politicians, but they control doctors and professionals
of all kinds. . . . It's a subtle operation."[3]

Whether or not they are "controlled," Oakland County has
an abundance of doctors, including psychiatrists. Although
county health officials were unable to provide us with precise
figures, there was general consensus among a number of informants that the county has in recent years become one of
the most richly endowed in the state in terms of medical and
psychiatric manpower. Despite this richness, however, mental
health services in Oakland County are fragmented and largely
inaccessible to the poor and working-class population. Most
psychiatrists are in private practice, serving primarily the
wealthier suburbs. Until 1967 there were only two major public
facilities: Pontiac State Hospital (PSH), which provides the
bulk of inpatient mental health services, and Pontiac General
Hospital, which has a small (twenty-four bed) locked inpatient
ward and provides some outpatient services.

Into this dearth of available public services came in 1967
the county's first and only "community" mental health service—
the North Oakland Community Mental Health Center. From its
inception the North Oakland Center has been located in, and

physically indistinguishable from, Pontiac State Hospital, which looms before the eye as the archetypal state mental hospital. It is a complex of red brick Victorian buildings dating back to the 1870s and set safely back from the road on a small rise. The hospital serves ten counties, including Oakland, and is administered directly by the state; local agencies have little or no involvement with its operation. Yet it was in this state hospital—isolated physically from the community and administratively from local agencies—that community mental health services were established.

When word of the soon-to-be-launched federal community mental health centers program began to spread in the early sixties, Michigan passed Public Act 54, which authorized local governments to carry out some previously state-administered mental health functions. This 1963 Michigan act created local (that is, county-level) community mental health boards to administer public funds for mental health services. While these boards were to have primarily a coordinating and evaluation function, they were also free to provide direct services. As county boards were being established, the State Department of Mental Health was busily engaged in drawing up the first comprehensive state plan for Michigan's community mental health centers. Curiously, the state plan indicated that state hospitals would be the most appropriate existing facilities for the development of these new centers. According to Dr. Philip Smith, an official in the State Department of Mental Health, the state felt that maximum use should be made of existing resources and manpower. "If we were going to move into the centers business, we had to move quickly," said Smith. "The issue was not money. The issue was who was going to run them, and how."[4] The state plan divided Oakland County into two large north-south areas and left it to the newly created Oakland County Community Mental Health Services Board (OCCMHSB) to decide on the specific catchment boundaries.[5] This board, appointed by the county commissioners, consisted of a twelve-member lay board and a nine-member paid staff. The lay board is made up of judges, business executives, a lawyer, a newspaper publisher, a couple of civic-minded women, and a single labor representative, the regional director of the

UAW. The last, Ken Morris, described in a recent interview what the board does: "They scratch surfaces. I know because I'm a member. . . . They are a do-gooder, do-nothing board, with absolutely no concern except for doing the traditional things."[6]

When NIMH community mental health center staffing grant funds became available in 1966, both PSH and the OCCMHSB, the two major public mental health agencies in Oakland County, were likely applicants. According to Dr. Donald Martin, medical superintendent of PSH, the State Department of Mental Health "deliberately held back, hoping that the County Board would take the initiative on the application."[7] When it did not, and time was running out on the NIMH deadline, the state urged Martin to apply and he hastily submitted an application to NIMH.

Once the application had been approved, however, there ensued several months of intensive negotiations between PSH and OCCMHSB, which belatedly felt that its new powers had been usurped and wanted "a piece of the action."[8] An agreement was finally reached whereby OCCMHSB would assume responsibility for providing consultation and education services, emergency outpatient services, and a few additional services through other agencies.

Not so clear, however, was the issue of the catchment-area boundaries. No one involved seems to agree on how or why or by whom the boundaries were determined. Dr. Martin claims that OCCMHSB made the decision and made it non-negotiable; Dr. Lino Romero, psychiatric director of the OCCMHSB, says that the State Department of Mental Health drew the boundary lines; others claim that PSH, afraid of being overwhelmed with patients, had something to do with it; still others maintain that it was assumed Pontiac General Hospital would establish a second center and wanted the southern part of Oakland County for its territory.

At any rate, the catchment area excludes the bulk of the population, and particularly the low-income and black population of Oakland County; indeed, the boundary line goes carefully around the city of Pontiac (which means that the center, located in Pontiac, is outside of its own catchment area!), but dips down to include the wealthy suburb of West Bloomfield, south of Pontiac. Pontiac General Hospital has never developed a center, nor any plan for one—which means that the poorest segment of the population is left out.

When the North Oakland Center began operating in March, 1967, with an initial federal staffing grant of $259,309, administrative responsibility was divided between PSH and OCCMHSB, the directorship of the center shared by the two directors of the parent organizations. This administrative split proved unsatisfactory, however, and in 1970 a single director of the community mental health center was appointed, although, according to Dr. Martin, he and Dr. Romero continue to hold ultimate authority. Significantly, the new director, Dr. Theodore A. Satersmoen, was recruited from the staff of PSH; indeed, he has held various positions at the hospital since 1954, when he completed his psychiatric residency there. Although administration has improved since Dr. Satersmoen's appointment, it is not surprising that the community mental health center has an operating philosophy that has little to do with such concepts as outreach or programs geared to special community needs, and functions as a traditional mental hospital.

For example, by far the most visible service of the North Oakland Center is its adult inpatient service. Dr. Martin termed it "the best unit of the center . . . smoothly run, well coordinated." He further stated that this was the only short-term inpatient facility in the area for *involuntary or indigent patients.*[9] According to Dr. Romero, the NIMH staffing grant has meant that "now people can be hospitalized at any time of the day or night."[10] Dr. Satersmoen added that "the major difference between the mental health center and the hospital is that service is more available [in the center]. Beds weren't available before because there just wasn't enough money for them. The mental health center unit of Pontiac State Hospital now has one psychiatrist per twenty-eight beds. That's better than any other part of the hospital."[11] Even an NIMH site-visit report indicated approval: "Because this program is within the State hospital, patients requiring longer-term care are easily transferred to and from the State hospital."[12]

The various service components of the center are scattered

throughout the hospital and are physically indistinguishable from it; the staffs overlap, and a number of interviews indicated that employees have, on the whole, a closer identification with Pontiac State Hospital than with the North Oakland Community Mental Health Center. Adult outpatient and partial hospitalization services for PSH patients and center patients are combined, although residence records are dutifully kept separate. Outpatient services for children are provided by the Child Guidance Clinic through a contract with OCCMHSB; inpatient services for children and adolescents are offered as part of the state hospital program. The center has created no special programs for drug addicts or alcoholics, despite the fact that these represent increasingly serious problems in the community, nor has it attempted any coordinated efforts in this area with other agencies; instead, people with any kind of addiction problem are referred to the general outpatient clinic. There is a small—fifty-patient—methadone maintenance program, but Dr. Satersmoen explained that this was a "program" only in the sense that each patient is legally required to have an identification number.[13]

Consultation and education services, provided directly by the OCCMHSB, have been geographically separated from the hospital. Until recently, a full-time staff of three was providing consultation to schools, beginning to develop relationships with the police and the courts, and, it seemed, attempting to become acquainted with the problems and pressures of the residents of North Oakland County. Now, however, the consultation and education component of the community mental health center is undergoing a major change. Over the past few months, one staff member died and another resigned, leaving only one—Dr. Aubrey Crawford, a clinical psychologist—to carry on. Instead of replenishing the staff, it has been decided to move the service into the hospital under the administrative direction of Dr. Satersmoen. (Aubrey Crawford is under the impression that NIMH requires consultation and education to be under the direction of an M.D.)[14] The rationale is that it will be preferable to mix clinical and consultative functions—that is, instead of having a full-time staff devoted to consultation, everyone will do a bit of both.

Aubrey Crawford sees the move as a step in the wrong direction. "One of the problems," he explained to us, "is that consultation and education [are] concerned with prevention—we should be out in the field, getting into communities in the rural areas, finding out what we can do that will enable people to better deal with pressure without labeling them mentally ill. People tend to react negatively to suggestions of mental illness, and if the service is administered by the hospital, identified with the hospital, people are suspicious. But the hospital philosophy is totally usurping a community orientation."[15] Indeed, despite the scattered population and the lack of public transportation, the center has established no satellite clinics and has no plans to do so.

A recent NIMH-funded evaluation of the North Oakland Center by Health-PAC found that public awareness of the center and its functions is so low as to be virtually nonexistent, both on the part of the general public and of people employed by local social service agencies or other institutions. According to the Health-PAC study, "Except for the Michigan State Mental Health Association, there was no agency whose staff recognized the name 'North Oakland Community Mental Health Center' without some explanation. In most cases, it was necessary to identify the CMHC as located at PSH and mention the federal grant in order to get any sign of recognition."[16] Moreover, none of these agencies (the Oakland County Commission on Economic Opportunity, the Pontiac Area United Fund, the Urban League, the UAW, among others) felt that their constituencies were aware of the center, and no reporter at the *Pontiac Press*, the largest newspaper in Oakland County, had ever heard of it. The center's nominal Community Advisory Board, appointed by the staff in 1970 as a concession to NIMH's discovery of "citizen participation," similarly has an extremely low public profile, no power and no real function, the Health-PAC Study concluded.[17]

In short, the North Oakland Community Mental Health Center has failed to make much of an impact on mental health care in Oakland County except that it has served well in its capacity to funnel more people to the state hospital: both the admission and readmission rates to Pontiac State Hospital have increased since the center began operating.[18] The NIMH staffing grant has been used primarily to subsidize existing services rather than to implement new ones, and the center, stigmatized by its association with the local mental hospital and isolated from its far-flung "community," remains inaccessible to the bulk of the population. This is hardly what the guidelines set forth by the National Institute of Mental Health call for. But apparently the Institute doesn't take its own guidelines very seriously. In a telephone interview, Kenneth Watanabe of the NIMH regional office in Chicago explained that few state hospitals had become vehicles for community mental health centers. "This was a brand new undertaking," he said. "Hindsight is always a great teacher." Asked why NIMH had not been more insistent that its guidelines be implemented, Watanabe stated that his office hadn't site-visited that center in a couple of years because of the pressing problems at other centers. "Anyway," he said, "you can't be Big Brother all the way through."[19]

More important than the NIMH guidelines, however, is the failure of this center to be responsive to the less tangible needs of a community in crisis. For Oakland County in many ways represents a microcosm of some of the most urgent problems facing contemporary American society.

Drug abuse among white middle- and working-class teenagers, as well as among many younger workers, has reached epidemic proportions all over Oakland County. According to the Health-PAC study:

> The most immediate social consequence of the growing number of teenage addicts, as opposed to soft drug users, is an increase in crime. Interviews suggested that the community reaction is close to hysterical. A Board member emphasized that people are afraid to leave their houses unoccupied, even to go to church on Sunday. Two informants independently cited the case of upper-middle-class parents who returned from a vacation to find their home depleted of all movable items—by a gang of addicts which included their teenage son. A staff member of the United Fund, who resides in the catchment area, said that he feared the emergence of vigilante groups if the drug problem and its resulting crime were not dealt with by legal means.[20]

Racial tensions, never very far below the surface, exploded in 1972 over the busing issue, causing violence and disruption of education for many children. North Oakland County has, according to a number of informants, an active chapter of the Ku Klux Klan, which has been accused of bombing and setting fire to school buses. The issue is particularly volatile in the town of Waterford, lying inside the catchment area just west of Pontiac. Waterford, which boasts some members of the militant antibusing NAG (National Action Group) organization, has a population of about fifty thousand—double what it was a decade ago, and many of the newcomers moved from Pontiac precisely to avoid blacks. Says Aubrey Crawford, "Anywhere you go, [if] you mention busing you see a visible, almost physical reaction. Everyone is up in arms."[21]

But the major fact of life in Oakland County is the auto plants and the men who work at them. Although the plants are, like the mental health center, located outside the catchment area, it is estimated by the UAW regional director that nearly 40 percent of the catchment area's working-class population are UAW members or families of UAW members.[22] Recent newspaper reports, sociological research, and personal interviews we conducted all point with alarming unanimity to the social and psychological disaster seething at auto factories in the Detroit area and elsewhere, particularly among the workers on the highly automated assembly lines with their anonymous atmosphere, the limitations they impose on movement, and the impossibility of conversation because of heat, noise, and tension. Boredom, frustration, anger, fear, alienation, and often outright rebellion characterize the daily lives of these workers. Industry has been exceedingly slow to acknowledge that what two United States presidents have called "America's number one health problem" pertains in any way to workers in general and to blue-collar workers in particular. The determination of management to cling to the comfortable stereotype of the "happy worker" is at least partly to blame for the current crisis, whose proportions can no longer be ignored. According to Melvin Glasser, director of the Social Security Department of the UAW and one of the proud advocates of the UAW's prepaid psychiatric care program,* as late as the mid-sixties, employers preferred to keep their heads in the sand. "Our experience in dealing with employers as we attempted to develop the benefit and to secure its underwriting through collective bargaining is instructive," says Glasser. He offers the following quotations from employer representatives as evidence:

> "Your figures about the extent of mental illness in the country may well be true, but they do not apply to our workers. They don't have the problem."

> "Such services if made available will only encourage malingering."

> "This is the government's problem, not the employer's."[23]

Where mental health is concerned, the government *is* NIMH. And whether or not the problem belongs solely to government, the emerging field of "occupational" mental health is one in which NIMH has claimed to be vitally interested. Although much of this interest has manifested itself in the sponsoring of research in industrial psychology (which has tended to share the point of view of management) and, more recently, in the problem of "executive stress," NIMH has also funded several studies on the mental health of blue-collar workers.

These studies have shown an ever-greater level of mental or emotional breakdown and a lower level of recovery among blue-collar workers and their families. Indeed, an Institute-funded study conducted by psychologist Arthur Kornhauser and published in 1965 focused on the mental health of Detroit automobile workers and found that regardless of educational level or pre-job personality characteristics, factory workers on the lowest occupational rung (that is, unskilled or semiskilled assembly-line work) revealed "extensive enough feelings of inadequacy, low self-esteem, anxiety, hostility, dissatisfaction

* The UAW benefit, developed with the help of both NIMH and the American Psychiatric Association, became operative in September, 1966. It provides coverage to nearly three million UAW members and their dependents, and includes in- and out-of-hospital benefits. Forty-five days of in-hospital care "for nervous or mental conditions" is offered. A maximum benefit of four hundred dollars is available per patient per calendar year for outpatient care provided by or under the supervision of a psychiatrist.

with life, and low personal morale to raise serious questions concerning the general condition of psychological and social health of industrial workers."[24]

A more recent (1970) study of 1,533 workers and their working conditions carried out by the Survey Research Center of the University of Michigan similarly concluded that the content and quality of the work itself—the opportunity to use one's skills and to develop new ones, to function somewhat autonomously, and to be creative—were considerably more important to the psychological well-being of workers than job security or income.[25]

These findings have been amply borne out in the past year or so. Increasingly, the plants have become centers of the drug trade and of violence. Estimates of the extent of drug usage on the assembly lines given to us by labor union leaders and workers range from 15 to 65 percent of the workers. Alcohol abuse, especially among older workers, is rampant as well, as evidenced by parking lots of the plants around Pontiac, which are strewn with vodka bottles, whiskey bottles, wine bottles, and beer cans. Fighting (between races, between older and younger workers) has become commonplace and, according to a number of informants, many workers go to their jobs armed with knives, sometimes guns.

Acute dissatisfaction with the monotony, the increased pressure to produce more and more regardless of quality, the sense of being at a dead end, has begun to be translated, especially among younger workers, into alienated behavior that is sometimes full of rage, sometimes simply turned off. As one worker—a dashboard assembler—put it, "You either conform and become deader each day, or you rebel, or you quit."[26] Absenteeism has soared over the past decade and continues to be devastatingly high on Fridays and Mondays. Turnover rates have almost doubled, and acts of industrial sabotage are becoming more and more frequent. A union steward offered the following:

> I try to understand what motivates a guy to be disturbed enough to get on drugs. Let's take his job. Say that a great big machine is in front of you and b-z-z-z-t! It runs past you. Screw two bolts and let it go. You know, b-z-z-z-t! Well, how much concentrated thought does it take to do that? It makes him feel

so unwanted; it makes him feel like part of the machinery. His energies are turned inward, like, "Nobody's concerned about me, so why should I be concerned about keeping this machine right?" He's molded like a part of the machine and it creates a kind of atmosphere that makes him say, "Well, I'll just get high."[27]

This sentiment is echoed by Walter Dance, senior vice-president of General Electric: "It involves a gut feeling on their [blue-collar workers'] part that industrial society has left them with the dull, hard, dirty jobs—and then doesn't care."[28]

What is true for General Electric is true in spades for General Motors. According to Ken Morris, regional director of the UAW and a member of the OCCMHSB board, "They're not interested in mental health; they're not even interested in physical health. Their goal is to maintain a productive process. It's like a war, someone gets injured and all they do is to patch them up and shove them back on the line."[29]

According to Detroit attorney John Taylor, who specializes in labor relations, the fear and anxiety over being injured due to inadequate safety provisions contribute as much as do monotony and lack of opportunity to the psychological responses of anger and frustration. To underscore his point Taylor cited the case of James Johnson, a young black worker in a Chrysler gear and axle plant. Johnson had previously suffered an on-the-job injury which cost him part of the middle finger of his right hand; several months later he was suspended for "insubordination" when he refused, because proper gloves were not available, to obey an order to go into one of the ovens. An hour later Johnson returned to his department with an M-1 carbine and shot and killed two foremen and a job-setter.[30] The law firm of Glotta and Adelman, which employs John Taylor, was able to overturn Johnson's conviction by claiming that Chrysler Corporation had allowed such terrible working conditions as to drive Johnson mentally ill. Johnson now makes up part of the resident population of Ionia State Hospital, Michigan's state institution for the criminally insane.

Not so dramatic are incidences of workers "freaking out." These are "very, very common," said a number of informants, who told us that freaking out is sometimes the only way an assembly-line worker can assert his humanity. According to Bob White, president of UAW Local 594 of the GM coach and truck plant in Pontiac, Michigan, such incidents happen all the time. "It's mostly due to frustration," said White. "They're nailed to the line and often the working conditions are unsafe, they have a grievance in the works but the company delays on it, and three weeks later still nothing has been done and they start losing their temper. We had three instances like that in the last month—guys climbed up on the roof and poured paint all over their supervisors."[31]

Donald Johnson, president of UAW Local 596 of the Fisher Body plant in Pontiac, noted, "In the eight years I've been union president, I've had six or seven buddies who have committed suicide. These suicides are caused, they don't just happen. I'm not a doctor, but I can tell you that all the harassment and pressure that go on in the plant help people blow up."[32] Significantly, a 1969 analysis of suicide in Oakland County prepared by the consultation and education unit of the North Oakland Center reveals that in the three-year period from 1966 through 1968, males (in a younger age-specific range than the national average) who were unskilled workers accounted for the largest number of suicides in Oakland County (41 percent). Skilled workers accounted for the next largest group (27 percent). This study also found that the catchment area served by the North Oakland Center produced the second highest suicide rate in the entire county (the area in the immediate vicinity of the city of Pontiac producing a few more).[33] While figures on suicides are generally not considered to be terribly reliable, and while this study is an extremely cursory one, the data do bear out Johnson's observations and indicate, statistically, a large population at risk.

Both Johnson and White indicated that they had had no contact with the North Oakland Community Mental Health Center in Pontiac. Indeed, White said, "I wish the federal government would take a more active interest. There are an estimated eight hundred addicts in Pontiac alone, and only a few methadone programs. I know of one center where two hundred and fifty people applied and there was only room for fifty patients."[34]

The problems in the auto plants and the larger ones of which they are symptomatic have not gone unnoticed by either management or organized labor, and have even begun to attract the attention of the general public. For all practical purposes, however, the bulk of evidence and the obvious need for social services in this environment seem to have gone unnoticed or at least have not led to action by the North Oakland Center. To the extent that center staff are aware of the social and psychological stress in the community, they do not see it as within their professional province.

Having no research component, the center has, aside from the twenty-five-page suicide study mentioned above, conducted virtually no research of its own, nor made much use of the research that does exist: it has instituted no crisis-prevention program; it has offered no educational information or outreach counseling service that might at least help to ease some of the tensions before they build to the point where spirits are broken or lives lost. Instead, locked into a traditional medical orientation that dictates waiting until a "patient" appears, the center simply waits.

The passivity of the North Oakland Center, it must be said, is not necessarily any greater or more egregious than that of any of the other social service agencies or institutions in Oakland County. Despite the awareness of union representatives and their rhetorical concern, the UAW has done precious little to challenge the working conditions that take such a toll on the physical and mental health of its members. It has bargained for, and won, expanded mental health benefits,* but it has not bargained strenuously to reduce the dehumanizing effects of automation: the deafening noise, the heat, the speed and the danger of working on assembly lines—conditions that are known to produce intolerable stress. Its failure to secure worker protection from physically and mentally unhealthy conditions makes a mockery of the UAW's alleged mental health program goals of "prevention, early diagnosis and readily available 'treatment.' "[35] For it seems patently obvious that what is needed are

---

* According to Don Johnson and others, only 1 percent of the total UAW membership utilizes the mental health benefits they are entitled to, in part because there is nobody to help them get help.

basic changes, not psychotherapy after the fact. One observer commented, "It's incredible that there are any healthy people left at all."

The lack of relationship between the North Oakland Center and the auto plants is curious, inasmuch as a UAW representative sits on the OCCMHSB. That the UAW has not put pressure on the community mental health center to be more responsive to the mental health needs of workers further dilutes the credibility of its leadership in their professed concern for human individuality and human values. When queried by this Task Force about the passive role played by both the center and the UAW, one source who has had long experience with both but who asked to remain unidentified offered an explanation. "On the part of the center," he said, "it's mostly a matter of institutional indifference. On the part of the UAW it's stark fear that outreach efforts might create some grass-roots awareness of what the real problems are."

The extremity of the real problems in Oakland County—from the general quality of life to seething racial tensions to drug and alcohol abuse to the violence in the auto plants—raises some very fundamental questions about community mental health and at least one center funded by NIMH. The failure of the North Oakland Center is not that it has done nothing about the "real problems"; there is, after all, probably little that mental health professionals can do about the policies of General Motors. Its perhaps understandable failure is that it has done nothing, period—except become a better-functioning state hospital. If ever a community was in need of accessible, relevant services, it is Northern Oakland County; but by every goal that NIMH has set for its centers program, and by every guideline it has issued, this center falls short (with the exception of certain of the five essential services). Not only has it not supplanted the state hospital, but NIMH funds have actually been used to expedite the hospital's existing services. The center is inaccessible to the community, both in terms of its negative image and its location. It has made only the most perfunctory attempts to respond to the many needs of this community or to involve its members in the planning of relevant programs. Clearly a community mental health center would not usher the millennium into Oakland County. But if there is anything at all hopeful in the ideas behind community mental health, it is incumbent upon NIMH to educate center staff in this area, and to take pains to see that appropriate and adequate community services are provided by the centers it funds.

Part Three

SUMMARY AND CONCLUSIONS

13

Those centers which are doing a better job are doing so because of their leadership, not because NIMH has required them to do so. The lack of accountability of the Centers means that all Centers, no matter what they are doing, continue to receive public money from NIMH. If a Center is not doing what it said it would, NIMH is not really interested in knowing. This is the heart of the problem—the slow, sad steps which lead to a minuet of mutual deception.

—*Internal NIMH memo*

Innovation
Without Change

A decade after Congress passed the legislation that was intended to dramatically transform and humanize the care of the mentally ill in America, many of the program's stanchest supporters have come to recognize its problems, admit its limitations, regret its failures. Yet most of them urge critics to refrain from mentioning the program's deficiencies. The Nixon Administration has its knives well sharpened for the purpose of trimming the "bureaucratic fat" off a number of liberal social programs, and community mental health centers have already lost a considerable amount of muscle along with the fat. But those who would transform the community-care ideology into a workable reality would do well to start asking some hard questions about whether the budget limitations are deserved. Indiscriminate requests for more money will no longer work. Effectiveness will have to be demonstrated, which means that the coming battles over which pieces of the program are to be salvaged will have to be carefully chosen. Not only the Nixon Administration but also state and local governments, which will bear a greater financial burden for the centers, will have to be convinced of the program's worth.

As this report documents, the community mental health center model as it was conceived at the federal level is often seriously at odds with reality at the community level. In part, this failure can be attributed to the phenomenon that psychologist Anthony M. Graziano has termed "innovation without change." Although many innovative ideas have been conceived, says Graziano,

> the *conception* of innovative ideas in mental health depends upon creative humanitarian and scientific forces, while their *implementation* depends, not on science or humanitarianism, but on a broad spectrum of professional and social politics!
>
> . . . these two aspects, conceiving innovation through science and humanitarianism on the one hand, and implementing innovation through politics on the other, are directly incompatible and mutually inhibiting factors; . . . our pursuit of political power has almost totally replaced humanitarian and scientific ideals in the mental health field. Innovations, by definition, introduce change; political power structures resist change. Thus, while the cry for innovation has been heard throughout the 1960s, we must clearly recognize that it has been innovative "talking" which has been encouraged, while innovative *action* has been resisted.[1] [Emphasis in original.]

In retrospect, the community mental health centers program was vastly oversold, the original goals quickly perverted—possibly because of the contradictory assumption that revolutionary change could be successfully wrought by those professionals and politicians with a vested interest in maintaining the status quo. At any rate, NIMH feebly communicated the original intent of the program to state and local officials; failed to coordinate the location of the centers with other HEW health and social-welfare efforts; made little attempt to train (or re-train) people for community work; avoided funding centers outside the narrow interests of the medical profession; did not engage consumers in the planning or operation of centers; and made only the most perfunctory evaluation of the program's performance. As a result, community mental health centers tend to involve only a renaming of conventional psychiatry, a collection of traditional clinical services that are in most cases not responsive to the needs of large segments of the community, and which often leave community people indifferent, sometimes antagonistic.

The short life of the community mental health centers program already bears the familiar pattern of past mental health reforms that were initiated amid great moral fervor, raised false hopes of imminent solutions, and wound up only recapitulating the problems they were to solve. The development of state mental hospitals offers an apt, if ironic, comparison. Started in reaction to the practice of locking up the poor and mentally disturbed in decaying county jails, poorhouses, and block-houses, the state-hospital system was established to ensure more humane treatment for society's castoffs. These new institutions were strongly advocated from the beginning by all the "en-lightened" professionals of the day. But little thought was given to the consequences of creating ten-to-fifteen-thousand-bed cities of the "mad," and there was no flexibility for change once the hospitals were found not to provide the most ideal setting for patients. Instead of offering humane and effective treatment to the mentally ill, state hospitals became another enormous bureaucracy catering to vested interests and embodying the worst of care and societal stigma.

Community mental health centers seem to fit the same mold. Amid flowery orations intended to generate great excitement and renewed hope, they were initiated as a reaction to the scandalous degeneration of state hospitals. Had NIMH or Congress re-sponded to the underlying lessons of past failures, or even heeded the report of the Joint Commission on Mental Illness and Health, a far more sober approach might have been adopted. There are no known, foolproof answers as to how best to care for those labeled "mentally ill"—just as there are no widely accepted answers to the question of what "mental illness" *is*. Any program aimed at reducing human suffering can only be looked upon as an experiment, a tentative step in providing better services, discovering answers. More important, any program as broad in scope as the community mental health centers program must have built-in evaluation from the very start, and enough flexibility to change, to accommodate the evolution of new methods, perhaps even to disband. This was a sober and ultimately the only *honest* strategy. It was not adopted. Instead, NIMH officials falsely fired public expectations, tagging the program not only as a "bold, new approach" to the care of the mentally ill, but suggesting that community mental health centers (and, by extension, the professionals suddenly renamed "community psychiatrists") could effectively tackle the problems of poverty, racism, drug addiction, crime, and delinquency.

In reality, community mental health centers as they are currently structured will never supplant state hospitals, much less cater to the mental health needs of all citizens. Nor is there much likelihood that they will provide any significant diminution of the problems of addiction, poverty, labor unrest, or crime. The reason is, in part, lack of resources. In fiscal 1973, NIMH obligated about $125 million for the staffing of community mental health centers (in the same year states spent more than $2 billion, more than ever before, in maintaining state hospitals); and future appropriations, if approved, will be even more spartan. But the primary reasons go far beyond the simple lack of money for the centers, or for NIMH, or for the mental health professions. Putting an end to the state-hospital system requires much more than the intervention of mental health professionals in the community.

Most important, the system of patronage and corruption which helps to perpetuate state hospitals must be challenged directly. A change in our economic priorities is essential if we are to provide the jobs, housing, and social-support programs which are vitally important to any effort to rehabilitate the victims of long-term hospitalization. Mental health professions can act as important catalysts of social change—both through personal interaction and by identifying the institutional influences on psychological development. But social and economic justice are desirable because they are essential elements of a real democracy, not because they are demanded by some sort of mental health imperative. Of course, such changes will be long in coming.

In the meantime, public policy must reflect very careful determination of how best to allocate our limited resources in mental health care. And this determination must be based on a ruthlessly honest appraisal of the limits of psychiatric (as well as related professional) expertise. Reformers, with the best of intentions, have sought to place an ever-greater number of categories of "sick" people and "behavioral problems" within the province of mental health care. Although many of these problems are undeniably more social or economic than psychological or medical, and despite the lack of evidence that psychiatric intervention can do much about drug addiction, alcoholism, crime, or poverty, mental health professionals have uncritically accepted these new tasks. In doing so, they have obtained greater social prestige as well as generous federal subsidies, but at the risk of losing their credibility before the public.

All of this follows a familiar historical trend in the mental health field. Few tangible successes have glimmered in a history composed largely of failures to produce "cures" or even very precise knowledge about the origin, nature, or treatment of "mental illness." Yet this has led only to an ever-expanding realm wherein psychiatric intervention is deemed appropriate— a realm which by now may have been extended far beyond the skills and the combined knowledge of the mental health professions. David L. Bazelon, Chief Judge of the U.S. Court of Appeals for the District of Columbia Circuit, has given the matter a very concise formulation: "The question is not whether mental health professionals are any good, but what they're good *at*." Judge Bazelon's seemingly simple question is not merely academic. As one who has written a number of landmark legal opinions regarding the insanity defense and the role of "expert" psychiatric testimony, Bazelon is concerned about the encroaching power of professionals to decide a host of complex legal, moral, and ethical questions.

If the decade of the sixties has taught us nothing else, it should have taught us that difficult problems will not go away simply because they are turned over to "experts" or placed under a new label. The growing tendency to attach medical labels to (and thus presumably to seek medical solutions for) a range of social problems helps to obscure the moral and legal issues of good and bad, fails to acknowledge the validity of competing personal values and political convictions which are the life-blood of a democratic society, and enhances the possibility that mental health professionals will be used to legitimize subtle methods of control and retribution by making them appear to be instruments of treatment.

It is clear that out of the tens of millions of individuals whom NIMH officials and others estimate need psychiatric care, only a tiny minority suffer from problems that most authorities would agree constitute "mental diseases." The much larger group of individuals who constitute the bulk of "patients" in mental institutions have problems that fall outside any rigorously defined categories of "diseases." As William Ryan notes, "the logical error we made is in dealing with such *non*-diseased persons in the same setting and with the same conceptual terminology that we have constructed for the truly *diseased* person."[2] (Emphasis in original.)

It would seem that the only way to correct this logical error is to place the great majority of so-called mental health problems outside the realm of medical responsibility. Rigid professional categories should probably be phased out altogether; we need generalists and technicians who can collaborate in providing humane care to the people who most need it. More importantly, we should concern ourselves not with the training of more "mental health" professionals, but with the development of a total coherent system of care and service delivery that will answer the basic social welfare needs of people—of which health and mental health are only a part.

The small minority of people whose problems do fall within the province of legitimate mental health concerns deserve top priority in the allocation of both financial and professional resources. Such people need a whole range of mental health facilities—from easily accessible outpatient clinics to halfway houses to top quality institutional care for the seriously retarded and the chronically ill.

In terms of public policy, what is most critical is to resist another wild swing to the next institutional fad, which will come along just as surely as did state hospitals and community mental health centers. We must also recognize that humane care given by sympathetic people in a realistic ratio to those needing help is more important than the cursory "treatment" currently provided by a pool of overworked, often overcredentialed professionals, many of whom are, by temperament and training, ill-suited to meet the real needs of most "mental patients."

For although psychiatry has always been confronted with the problems of chronic illness, it (along with most of the rest of American medicine) has persisted in thinking primarily in terms of "cure." And those whom. psychiatry has been unable to cure, it has preferred to ignore. The quixotic pursuit of ever more esoteric treatments and potential cures has completely overshadowed the development of skills to aid people with chronic disorders or diseases.

Clearly, it is time for psychiatrists and other mental health professionals to rethink their roles as "healers" and to focus their efforts instead on the effective reduction of disability. Joan Doniger, the late director of Woodley House, a first-rate halfway house in the District of Columbia, put it quite simply. "Just because someone is diagnosed as schizophrenic," she said, "he should not have to eat institutional food for the rest of his life, be regimented at meals and other times, or be shut out of the kitchens and grocery stores. His enjoyment of good food and freedom may not treat or cure him—but it may make life better."[3]

Notes

Chapter 1.

1. Thomas Szasz, *The Myth of Mental Illness: Foundations of a Theory of Personal Conduct* (New York: Hoeber-Harper, 1961).
2. Jeanne Brand, "The National Mental Health Act of 1946: Retrospect," *Bulletin of the History of Science*, May–June, 1965, p. 234.
3. Jeanne Brand and Philip Sapir, eds., "An Historical View on the National Institute of Mental Health," unpublished, mimeographed (Washington, D.C.: National Institute of Mental Health, February, 1964), p. 3.
4. Ibid., p. 5.
5. National Mental Health Act of 1946.
6. Leonard J. Duhl and Robert L. Leopold, *Mental Health and Urban Social Policy* (San Francisco: Jossey-Bass, 1969), p. 9.
7. Erving Goffman, *Asylums: Essays on the Social Situation of Mental Patients and Other Inmates* (Garden City, N.Y.: Doubleday and Co., 1961).
8. Ibid., pp. 355–356.
9. Elizabeth Drew, "Reports and Comment: Washington", *The Atlantic*, January, 1973, pp. 6–16.

Chapter 2.

1. Quoted in *Action for Mental Health: Final Report of the Joint Commission on Mental Illness and Health* (New York: John Wiley & Sons, 1961).
2. "Maintenance Expenditures—State and County Mental Hospitals, 1955—1971," mimeographed sheet. Source: R. Redick, NIMH Biometry Branch, June 30, 1972.
3. Hearings before a Subcommittee of the Committee on Appropriations, House of Representatives, Departments of Labor and Health, Education, and Welfare Appropriations for 1973, 92nd Cong., 2nd Sess., March 8, 1972, p. 97.
4. John F. Kennedy, *Message from the President of the United States Relative to Mental Illness and Mental Retardation*, 88th Cong., 1st Sess., House Document No. 58 (Washington, D.C.: Government Printing Office, 1963).
5. Quoted in *Issues in Community Psychology and Preventive Mental Health*, Task Force on Community Mental Health, Division 27 of the American Psychological Association, John C. Glidewell, Chairman (New York: Behavioral Publications, 1971), pp. 1–2.
6. David Mechanic, *Mental Health and Social Policy* (Englewood Cliffs, N.J.: Prentice-Hall, 1969), p. 63.
7. Ibid., p. 96.
8. *Action for Mental Health*, p. xxi.
9. Quoted in *Washington Post*, November 22, 1970.
10. Interview with Dr. Stanley Yolles, September, 1970.
11. Interview with Mike Gorman, September, 1970.
12. Telephone interview with Harry Schnibbe, July, 1972.
13. Hearings on "A Bill to Provide for Assistance in the Construction and Initial Operation of Community Mental Health Centers," before the Subcommittee on Public Health and Welfare of the Committee on Interstate and Foreign Commerce (March 26, 27, and 28, 1963), p. 94.
14. Ibid., p. 44.
15. Robert H. Connery et al., *The Politics of Mental Health: Organizing Community Mental Health in Metropolitan Areas* (New York: Columbia University Press, 1968), p. 52.
16. Ibid., p. 56.
17. Leonard J. Duhl and Robert L. Leopold, *Mental Health and Urban Social Policy* (San Francisco: Jossey-Bass, 1969), p. 11.
18. Jon Bjornson, "Community Mental Health Center Legislation," *New Physician*, January, 1969, p. 51.
19. Ibid.
20. Interview with Dr. Saul Feldman, March, 1972.
21. Ibid.
22. Martin Gittleman, "Sectorization: The Quiet Revolution in European Mental Health Care" (Paper presented at the Forty-eighth Annual Meeting of the American Orthopsychiatric Association, Washington, D.C., March 21–24, 1971), p. 6.
23. Hearings, House Subcommittee of the Committee on Appropriations, March, 1972, p. 147.

Chapter 3.

1. Hearings on Community Mental Health Centers Act Extension before the Subcommittee on Public Health and Welfare of the Committee on Interstate and Foreign Commerce, House of Representatives (91st Cong., 1st Sess., November 18–20, 1969), p. 38.
2. Hearings before a Subcommittee of the Committee on Appropriations, House of Representatives, Departments of Labor and Health, Education, and Welfare Appropriations for 1973 (92nd Cong., 2nd Sess., March 8, 1972), Part 3, p. 97.
3. National Association of State Mental Health Program Directors, *The U.S. Congress*, Vol. 7, No. 133 (October, 1970).
4. "Trends in Resident Patients—State and County Mental Hospitals, 1950–1968," Biometry Branch, Office of Program Planning and Evaluation, National Institute of Mental Health (Rockville, Md., 1970), p. 4.
5. "Patients in State and County Mental Hospitals in 1967," Biometry Branch, Office of Program Planning and Evaluation, National Institute of Mental Health (Rockville, Md., 1969), p. 5.
6. Robert N. Butler, "A Critique of American Psychiatry and Medicine: Ideals Versus Realities" (Paper presented at the University of Delaware Health Science Symposium, April 21, 1972), p. 35.
7. Raymond M. Glasscote et al., eds., *The Community Mental Health Center: An Interim Appraisal* (Washington, D.C.: American Psychiatric Association, 1969), p. 12.
8. Ibid., p. 54.
9. Ibid., p. 61.
10. "Objectives of the NIMH Community Mental Health Center Program" (Rockville, Md.: National Institute of Mental Health, August 8, 1970).
11. February 22–23, 1968; May 29–30, 1968; August 3–4, 1970; and September 22–23, 1971.
12. Lucy P. Ozarin, Annual Site Visit Report to Amarillo Mental Health Center, Amarillo, Texas, September 22–23, 1971, pp. 1–2.
13. Telephone interview with Dr. Lucy Ozarin, July, 1972.
14. Telephone interview with Katharyn Fritz, July, 1972.
15. Harry Schnibbe to Franklin Chu, June 30, 1972.
16. "Maintenance Expenditures—State and County Mental Hospitals, 1955–1971," mimeographed sheet. Source: R. Redick, NIMH Biometry Branch, June 30, 1972.
17. Testimony before the New York State Joint Legislative Committee on Mental and Physical Disability, October 13, 1970.
18. Transcript of Conference on Community Mental Health Centers, Washington, D.C., November 19–21, 1967, in Glasscote, *The Community Mental Health Center*, p. 43.
19. Ibid, p. 41.
20. Telephone interview with Harry Schnibbe, July, 1972.
21. "Monthly Statistical Report for October, 1971," Division of Community and Clinical Services, Saint Elizabeths Hospital, National Institute of Mental Health.
22. *Washington Post*, May, 26, 1970.
23. Team 1, Area D Community Mental Health Center, through Roger Peele, Director, Area D Community Mental Health Center, to Jessica

Epstone, Chief, Foster Care Section, Social Service Branch, Saint Elizabeths Hospital, August 19, 1969.

24. Robert N. Butler to Philip Rutledge, October 13, 1970.

25. Quoted in Butler, "A Critique of American Psychiatry and Medicine," p. 32.

26. Hearings on "Trends in Long-Term Care," before the Subcommittee on Long-Term Care, Special Committee on Aging, United States Senate (Ninety-Second Congress, First Session, April 2, 1971), p. 1106.

27. "Trends in Resident Patients—State and County Mental Hospitals, 1950–1968," *op. cit.*, p. 3.

28. Butler, "A Critique of American Psychiatry and Medicine," p. 25.

29. "Mental Health Care and the Elderly: Shortcomings in Public Policy," A Report by the Special Committee on Aging, United States Senate (Ninety-Second Congress, First Session, November 8, 1971), p. 2.

30. Hearings, House Subcommittee of the Committee on Appropriations, March, 1972, p. 158.

31. Telephone interview with Harry Schnibbe, July, 1972.

32. California State Employees' Association, "Where Have All the Patients Gone?" (a CSEA report on the crisis in mental health care in California) (Sacramento: California State Employees' Association, January, 1972), p. 8.

33. Ibid., p. 9.

34. "Reference Tables on Patients in Mental Health Facilities by Age, Sex, and Diagnosis," Biometry Branch, Office of Program Planning and Evaluation, National Institute of Mental Health, 1968, Table 2, p. 58.

35. *Science*, Vol. 179, No. 4070 (Jan. 19, 1973), pp. 250–258.

36. George Albee, "Models, Myth, and Manpower," *Mental Hygiene*, Vol. 52 (April, 1968), p. 176.

37. W. Mendell and S. Rapport, "Determinants of the Decision for Psychiatric Hospitalization," *Archives of General Psychiatry*, Vol. 20 (1969), pp. 321–328.

38. "Most of St. Elizabeths Patients Called Well Enough to Leave," *Washington Post*, August 11, 1971.

39. Erving Goffman, *Asylums: Essays on the Social Situation of Mental Patients and Other Inmates* (Garden City, N.Y.: Doubleday and Co., 1961).

40. Ernest M. Gruenberg, "From Practice to Theory—Community Mental Health Services and the Nature of Psychosis," *Lancet* (April 5, 1969), p. 722.

41. David Mechanic, *Mental Health and Social Policy* (Englewood Cliffs, N.J.: Prentice-Hall, 1969), p. 54.

42. Ibid.

43. Gerald N. Grob, *The State and the Mentally Ill: A History of Worcester State Hospital in Massachusetts, 1830–1920* (Chapel Hill: University of North Carolina Press, 1966), pp. 355–363.

44. M. Harvey Brenner to Franklin Chu, January 7, 1972.

Chapter 4.

1. William Ryan, ed., *Distress in the City: Essays on the Design and Administration of Urban Mental Health Services* (Cleveland: Press of Western Reserve University, 1969), pp. 228–229.
2. Telephone interview with Dr. Abel Ossorio, July, 1972.
3. Ryan, *Distress in the City*, p. 257.
4. New York State Department of Mental Hygiene, *Guide to Communities in the Establishment and Operation of Psychiatric Clinics* (1959), p. 4.
5. B. Pasamanick, F. Scarpitti, and S. Dinitz, *Schizophrenics in the Community: An Experimental Study in the Prevention of Hospitalization* (New York: Appleton-Century-Crofts, 1967).
6. A. E. Davis, S. Dinitz, and B. Pasamanick, "The Prevention of Hospitalization in Schizophrenia: Five Years After an Experimental Program", *American Journal of Orthopsychiatry*, Vol. 42 (April, 1972), p. 386.
7. Ryan, *Distress in the City*, p. 259.
8. Eliot Freidson, *Professional Dominance* (New York: Atherton Press, 1970), pp. 182–183.
9. Karl Menninger, *The Crime of Punishment* (New York: Viking Press, 1969), p. 19.
10. National Institute of Mental Health, "Progress Report: Community Mental Health Centers" (Rockville, Md., July, 1970).
11. Telephone interview with Katharyn Fritz, July, 1972.
12. *The Community Mental Health Centers Program: Improvements Needed in Management*, A report to the Congress by the Comptroller General of the United States, July 8, 1971, p. 23.
13. Lawrence S. Kubie, "Pitfalls of Community Psychiatry," *Archives of General Psychiatry*, Vol. 18 (March, 1968), p. 260.
14. Ibid.
15. Ryan, *Distress in the City*, p. 257.
16. Robert L. Taylor to Franklin Chu, January, 1971.
17. Raymond M. Glasscote and Jon E. Gudeman, *The Staff of the Mental Health Center: A Field Study* (Washington, D.C.: American Psychiatric Association, 1969), p. 167.
18. Robert L. Taylor, Psychiatry Training Branch, to Bernard Bandler, Acting Director, Division of Manpower and Training, NIMH, May 18, 1971.
19. Ibid.
20. J. Frank Whiting, "1970–1971 Census of U.S. Psychiatric Manpower," unpublished statistics, Division of Manpower Research and Development, American Psychiatric Association, 1972.
21. David Hamburg et al., "Report of the Ad Hoc Committee on Central Fact-Gathering Data of the American Psychoanalytic Association," *Journal of the American Psychoanalytic Association*, Vol. 15 (1967), pp. 841–861.
22. Ryan, *Distress in the City*, pp. 15–16.
23. William Schofield, *Psychotherapy: The Purchase of Friendship* (Englewood Cliffs, N.J.: Prentice-Hall, 1964), p. 133.
24. Interview with Dr. E. Fuller Torrey, April, 1972.
25. George W. Albee, "The Miracle of Loaves and Fishes Updated:

Nonprofessionals for Everyone" (Paper presented at the Annual Meeting of the American Orthopsychiatric Association, New York, 1969).

26. Freidson, *Professional Dominance*, p. 151.
27. Alan Gartner and Frank Reissman, "The Performance of Paraprofessionals in the Mental Health Field" (New Careers Development Center, New York University, July, 1971). Mimeographed. (Prepared for the *American Handbook of Psychiatry*, Gerald Caplan, ed., 1971.)
28. Arthur Pearl and Frank Reissman, *New Careers for the Poor: The Nonprofessional in Human Service* (New York: Free Press, 1965).
29. Quoted in Vernon R. James, "New Careers Development Through Systematic Study" (Paper presented at the Tenth Annual Convention of the National Association of Human Service Technologies, Dallas, October 23, 1971), p. 2.
30. *Community Mental Health Center Policy and Standards Manual* (Rockville, Md.: National Institute of Mental Health, September, 1971), pp. 2–20.
31. Quoted in Glasscote and Gudeman, *Staff of the Mental Health Center*, p. 184.
32. Interview with Dr. Joseph Perpich, June, 1972.
33. Frederick C. Redlich, "Discussion of Dr. H. Jack Geiger's Paper," in *Poverty and Mental Health*, M. Greenblatt et al., Psychiatric Research Report No. 21 (Washington, D.C.: American Psychiatric Association, 1967), pp. 66–67.
34. Franklyn N. Arnhoff, "The Boston Mental Health Survey: A Context for Interpretation," in *Distress in the City*, ed. Ryan, p. 152.
35. Gerald Caplan, *Principles of Preventive Psychiatry* (New York: Basic Books, 1964), p. 56.
36. Ibid., p. 59.
37. Leonard J. Duhl, "Psychiatry and the Urban Poor," in *Distress in the City*, ed. Ryan, p. 118.
38. Howard P. Rome, "Psychiatry and Foreign Affairs: The Expanding Competence of Psychiatry," *American Journal of Psychiatry*, Vol. 125 (December, 1968), p. 729.
39. "Trouble Ahead for CMHC's? . . . HMO's Proposed as Salvation," *Psychiatric News*, September 1, 1971, p. 3.

Chapter 5.

1. Frances Fox Piven and Richard A. Cloward, *Regulating the Poor: The Functions of Public Welfare* (New York: Pantheon Books, 1971), pp. 249–282.
2. "Community Mental Health Center Policy and Standards Manual" (Rockville, Md.: National Institute of Mental Health, September, 1971), pp. 2–4.
3. Robert Connery et al., *The Politics of Mental Health: Organizing Community Mental Health Care in Metropolitan Areas* (New York: Columbia University Press, 1968), p. 500.
4. Interview with Dr. Saul Feldman, March, 1972.
5. Code of Federal Regulations, Title 42—Public Health, Part 54.201 (b) and (c), January 1, 1971, p. 107.

6. Connery, *Politics of Mental Health*, pp. 491–492.

7. Interview with Dr. Walter Barton, September, 1970.

8. "Trouble Ahead for CMHC's? . . . HMO's Proposed as Salvation," *Psychiatric News*, September 1, 1971, p. 3.

9. Ibid.

10. Jon Bjornson, "Community Mental Health Center Legislation," *New Physician*, January, 1969, p. 53.

11. Harry R. Brickman to Richard A. Sheldon, September 11, 1970 (Appendix V of *The Community Mental Health Centers Program—Improvements Needed in Management*, A Report to the Congress by the Comptroller General of the United States, July 8, 1971, p. 64).

12. This story was told to us by Dr. Robert N. Butler, Washington psychiatrist and consultant to St. Elizabeths Hospital.

13. NIMH Regional Office (Region VII) Site Visit Report to the Mid-Missouri Mental Health Center, August 14, 1972, p. 3.

14. Transcript of Conference on Community Mental Health Centers, Washington, D.C., November 19–21, 1967, in Raymond M. Glasscote et al., eds., *The Community Mental Health Center: An Interim Appraisal* (Washington, D.C.: American Psychiatric Association, 1969), p. 44.

15. Transcript of Conference on Community Mental Health Centers, p. 63.

16. Piven and Cloward, *Regulating the Poor*, p. 278.

17. Quoted in Harvey A. Martens et al., "The Multi-Agency Community Mental Health Center: Administrative and Organizational Relationships" (NIMH Contract No. HSM–42–70–55 to the National Academy of Public Administration, Washington, D.C., August, 1971), p. 8.

18. Anthony M. Graziano, "Clinical Innovation and the Mental Health Community: A Social Case History" (Paper presented at the Meeting of the Eastern Psychological Association, Washington, D.C., April, 1968), p. 2.

19. Glasscote, *The Community Mental Health Center*, p. 19.

20. Revised Regulations, Title 42—Public Health, *Federal Register*, Vol. 37, No. 28 (February 10, 1972).

21. William Ryan, ed., *Distress in the City: Essays on the Design and Administration of Urban Mental Health Services* (Cleveland: Press of Case Western Reserve University, 1969), p. 49.

22. Ibid.

23. E. Fuller Torrey and Robert L. Taylor, "A Minuet of Mutual Deception: NIMH and the Community Mental Health Centers" (NIMH internal document, May 8, 1972), p. 14.

24. Ibid.

25. Peter Kong-ming New, Wilfred E. Holton, and Richard M. Hessler, "Citizen Participation and Interagency Relations: Issues and Program Implications for Community Mental Health Centers" (NIMH Contract No. HSM–42–70–99 to the Tufts University School of Medicine, Boston, Massachusetts, January, 1972).

Chapter 6.

1. Transcript of Conference of Community Mental Health Centers in Raymond M. Glasscote et al., eds., *The Community Mental Health Center: An Interim Appraisal* (Washington, D.C.: American Psychiatric Association, 1969), p. 91.
2. Code of Federal Regulations, Title 42—Public Health, Part 54.204 (c), (1) and (2), January 1, 1971, p. 110.
3. Testimony of Irving Chase during Hearings on the Community Mental Health Centers Act Extension, before the Subcommittee on Public Health and Welfare of the Committee on Interstate and Foreign Commerce, House of Representatives (91st Cong., 1st Sess., Nov. 18–20, 1969), p. 93.
4. Transcript of Conference on Community Mental Health Centers, p. 44.
5. Ralph Kennedy to Sharland Trotter, June 13, 1972.
6. Telephone interview with Martin Keeley, June, 1972.
7. Telephone interview with Joseph E. Coon, June, 1972.
8. Telephone interview with Katharyn Fritz, June, 1972.
9. Telephone interview with Glen Rollins, July, 1972.
10. Code of Federal Regulations, Title 42—Public Health, Part 54.210 (2), January 1, 1971, p. 114.
11. Telephone interview with Martin Keeley, June, 1972.
12. Orville R. Gursslin, Raymond G. Hunt, and Jack L. Reach, "Social Class and the Mental Health Movement," in *Mental Health of the Poor*, ed. Frank Reissman, Jerome Cohen, and Arthur Pearl (New York: Free Press, 1964), p. 63.
13. Ibid., p. 64.
14. E. Fuller Torrey, "The Irrelevancy of Traditional Mental Health Services for Urban Mexican Americans" (Paper presented at the Forty-seventh Annual Meeting of the American Orthopsychiatric Association, San Francisco, March 23–26, 1970), p. 15.
15. Health-PAC, "Evaluation of Community Involvement in Community Mental Health Centers" (NIMH Contract No. HSM–H2–70–106 to the Health Policy Advisory Center, New York, 1972).
16. Ibid.
17. Telephone interview with Dr. Donald Daggett, June, 1972.
18. Mental Health Plan for Hennepin County, Appendix 3, 1970.
19. Telephone interview with Dr. Donald Daggett, June, 1972.
20. Health-PAC, "Evaluation of Community Involvement," p. 13.
21. Telephone interview with Dr. Donald Daggett, June, 1972.
22. NIMH Regional Office (Region III) Site Visit Report to the Metropolitan Community Mental Health Center, June 9, 1972.
23. Telephone interview with Dr. Donald Daggett, June, 1972.
24. Telephone interview with Virgil Shoup, June, 1972.
25. Telephone interview with Dr. Donald Daggett, June, 1972.
26. Health-PAC, "Evaluation of Community Involvement," p. 14.
27. Ibid., p. 24.
28. Ibid., p. 7.
29. Telephone interview with Mary Jones, assistant clinical director, Metropolitan Community Mental Health Center, June, 1972.
30. Health-PAC, "Evaluation of Community Involvement," p. 28.
31. Telephone interview with Martin Keeley, June, 1972.

32. Transcript of Conference on Community Mental Health Centers, p. 92.
33. Ernest C. Harvey, ed., "Sources of Funds of Community Mental Health Centers" (NIMH Contract No. HSM–42–69–101 to Stanford Research Institute, Menlo Park, California, October, 1970), p. 24.
34. Robert Connery et al., *The Politics of Mental Health: Organizing Community Mental Health in Metropolitan Areas* (New York: Columbia University Press, 1968), p. 523.
35. Harvey, "Sources of Funds," p. 25.
36. Ibid., p. 19.
37. Ibid., p. 28.
38. Hearings on the Community Mental Health Centers Act Extension before the Subcommittee on Public Health and Welfare of the Committee on Interstate and Foreign Commerce, House of Representatives (91st Cong., 1st Sess., Nov. 18–20, 1969), p. 37.
39. Interview with Dr. Saul Feldman, March, 1972.
40. Revised Regulations, *Federal Register*, Vol. 37, No. 28 (February, 1972).
41. *Mental Health Scope*, Vol. V., No. 11 (mid-June, 1971), p. 3.
42. Interview with Dr. Saul Feldman, March, 1972.
43. Revised Regulations, *Federal Register*, Vol. 37, No. 28 (February, 1972).

Chapter 7.

1. Interview with Dr. William Tash, March, 1972.
2. *Evaluation in Mental Health*, Report of the Subcommittee on Evaluation of Mental Health Activities, Community Services Committee, National Advisory Mental Health Council (Washington, D.C., U.S. DHEW, PSH, NIH, NIMH, 1955).
3. Raymond M. Glasscote et al., eds., *The Community Mental Health Center: An Analysis of Existing Models* (Washington, D.C.: American Psychiatric Association, 1964), p. 28.
4. Ernest M. Gruenberg, ed., *Proceedings of a Round Table at the Sixtieth Anniversary Conference of the Milbank Memorial Fund, April 5–7, 1965* (New York: Milbank Memorial Fund, 1966), p. 91.
5. Ibid., p. 114.
6. Ernest M. Gruenberg to Gottlieb C. Simon, July 8, 1971.
7. Ibid.
8. Robert A. Walker, "What is Accountability and Why Are They Saying Those Terrible Things About It?" (Position Paper, Program Evaluation Forum, Minneapolis, October 5–7, 1971), p. 2.
9. Thomas J. Kiresuk, "Sisyphus Revisited" (Position Paper, Program Evaluation Forum, Minneapolis, October 5–7, 1971), p. 2.
10. Ernest C. Harvey, ed., "Source of Funds of Community Mental Health Centers" (NIMH Contract No. HSM–42–69–101 to Stanford Research Institute, Menlo Park, California, October, 1970).
11. Peter Kong-ming New, Wilfred E. Holton, and Richard M. Hessler, "Citizen Participation and Interagency Relations: Issues and Program Implications for Community Mental Health Centers" (NIMH Con-

tract No. HSM–42–70–99 to the Tufts University School of Medicine, Boston, Massachusetts, January, 1972).

12. Health-PAC, "Evaluation of Community Involvement in Community Health Centers" (NIMH Contract No. HSM–42–70–106 to the Health Policy Advisory Center, New York, New York, 1972).

13. ABT Associates, "A Study on the Accessibility of Community Mental Health Centers" (NIMH Contract No. HSM–42–70–92 to ABT Associates, Cambridge, Massachusetts, 1972).

14. Rosalyn Bass, "A Method for Measuring Continuity of Care" (NIMH Contract No. NIH–71–3–24, Rockville, Md., 1972).

15. American Psychiatric Association Joint Information Service, "A Study of Mental Health Services for Children" (NIMH Contract No. HSM–42–70–93 to the American Psychiatric Association, Washington, D.C., November, 1971).

16. Interview with Dr. Harry Cain, June, 1972.

17. Ibid.

18. Interview with Dr. William Tash, March, 1972.

19. Interview with Dr. Saul Feldman, March, 1972.

20. Telephone interview with Ann Toomey, June, 1972.

21. Telephone interview with Doreen Loso, June, 1972.

22. Telephone interview with Dr. Howard Siple, June, 1972.

23. Telephone interview with Katharyn Fritz, June, 1972.

24. Telephone interview with Martin Keeley, June, 1972.

25. *The Community Mental Health Centers Program: Improvements Needed in Management*, Report to Congress by the Comptroller General of the United States, July 8, 1971, pp. 19–20.

26. Eliot Freidson, *Professional Dominance* (New York: Atherton Press, 1970), p. 224.

27. Jack Zusman, "Mental Health Service Quality Control—By Whom, For Whom, And How" (Paper presented at the Forty-eighth Annual Meeting of the Orthopsychiatric Association, Washington, D.C., March 21–24, 1971), p. 6.

28. Thomas J. Kiresuk and Robert E. Sherman, "Good Attainment Scaling: A General Method for Evaluating Comprehensive Community Mental Health Programs," *Community Mental Health Journal*, Vol. 4 (1968).

29. Jose R. Lombillo, Thomas J. Kiresuk, and Robert E. Sherman, "Evaluation of the Effectiveness of a Community Mental Health Program" (Paper presented at the Fifth World Congress of Psychiatry, Mexico City, December 1, 1971).

Chapter 8.

1. This analysis of Washington, D.C., centers is based on a variety of materials and sources: scores of interviews with people on center staffs, past and present officials in the D.C. Department of Human Resources, private practitioners, NIMH officials, and patients, former patients, and their families.

2. Interview with Dr. Saul Feldman, March, 1972.

3. *Mayor's Task Force on Public Health Goals* (Washington, D.C., January, 1970), p. 288.

4. Lucy M. Cohen, et al., eds., *Patients in Programs at Area C Community Mental Health Center* (Washington, D.C.: Department of Human Resources, 1971), p. 30.
5. Dr. Essex Noel to Sharland Trotter, March 20, 1972.
6. Cohen, *Patients in Programs at Area C*, p. 26.
7. Ibid.
8. Interview with Dr. John Schultz, January, 1972.
9. *Washington Post*, December 4, 1967.
10. Cohen, *Patients in Programs at Area C*, pp. 78–79.
11. Ibid., p. 87.
12. "Study of Area C Community Mental Health Center, Summary and Recommendations," Committee on Laws Pertaining to Mental Disorders, Judicial Conference of the District of Columbia Circuit, Project on Community Mental Health Services and the Law, mimeographed (Washington, D.C., April, 1969), p. 3.
13. Ibid., p. 9.
14. Jim Michie, WTOP–TV News, May 30, 1970.
15. Ibid.
16. A. Naomi Kennedy, Acting Associate Regional Health Director for Mental Health, to Dr. Raymond L. Standard, August 6, 1970.
17. Ibid.
18. Interview with Dr. Jefferson McAlpine, February, 1972.
20. Concerned Staff and Patients of Area C Community Mental Health Center through Dr. Jefferson McAlpine to Dr. Essex Noel, November 29, 1971.
21. Interview with Ethel Beaman, January, 1972.
22. Area C staff meeting, August, 1970.
23. Quoted in the Area B Community Mental Health Center Orientation Manual (Washington, D.C., December, 1970), p. 8.
24. Ibid., p. 9.
25. John D. Schultz, Associate Director for Mental Health and Mental Retardation, to Mrs. Lloyd Symington, Chairman, Mental Health Technical Subcommittee, August 13, 1970.
26. *Washington Post*, August 17, 1970.
27. Code of Federal Regulations, Title 42—Public Health, Part 54.202 (b), January 1, 1971, p. 108.
28. Jim Michie, WTOP–TV News, August 7, 1970.
29. Interview with Dr. Murray Levine, January, 1972.
30. Interview with Dr. Timothy Tomasi, January, 1972.
31. Interview with Olivette Gill, February, 1972.
32. Ibid.
33. Interview with Dr. Timothy Tomasi, January, 1972.
34. *Washington Post*, April 8, 1972.
35. *Washington Post*, April 22, 1972.
36. Telephone interview with Olivette Gill, April, 1972.
37. Interview with Dr. Saul Feldman, March, 1972.
38. Andrea Gay, "Deficiencies of Community Based Facilities in Relation to St. Elizabeths Patients" (Washington, D.C.: Institute for the Study of Health and Society, April, 1972), p. 8.
39. Interview with Dr. Roger Peele, March, 1972.
40. Interview with Vivian Smith, March, 1972.
41. "Policy Statement Regarding Consumer Participation in NIMH Programs," Director, NIMH, to NIMH Staff, January 7, 1969.

42. Interview with Dr. Essex Noel, March, 1972.
43. Dr. Essex Noel to Dr. Robert G. Kvarnes, June 28, 1972.
44. *Washington Post*, April 16, 1972.
45. Ibid.
46. John D. Schultz, "The Community Mental Health Center: Future Directors in D.C.," mimeographed (Washington, D.C., April 24, 1970), p. 28.
47. Interview with Dr. John Schultz, January, 1972.

Chapter 9.

1. The background information on which this case study is based was taken from the following two NIMH-funded evaluations: "Citizen Participation and Interagency Relations: Issues and Program Implications for Community Mental Health Centers," by Peter Kong-ming New, Wilfred E. Holton, and Richard M. Hessler (NIMH contract number HSM–42–70–99 to the Department of Community Health and Social Medicine, Tufts University School of Medicine, Boston, Massachusetts, January, 1972); and "Sources of Funds of Community Mental Health Centers," by Leland H. Towle, Ernest C. Harvey, ed. (NIMH contract number HSM 42–69–101 to Stanford Research Institute, Menlo Park, California, October, 1970).
2. Joan Didion, *Slouching Towards Bethlehem* (New York: Dell Publishing Co., Delta Books, 1968), p. 4.
3. Leland H. Towle, "Kern View Community Mental Health Center," in "Sources of Funds of Community Mental Health Centers," ed. Ernest C. Harvey (NIMH Contract No. HSM–42–69–101, to Stanford Research Institute, Menlo Park, California, October, 1970), p. 104.
4. E. Fuller Torrey and Robert L. Taylor, "A Minuet of Mutual Deception: NIMH and the Community Mental Health Centers" (NIMH internal document, May 8, 1972), p. 5.
5. Peter Kong-ming New, Wilfred E. Holton, and Richard M. Hessler, "Citizen Participation and Interagency Relations: Issues and Program Implications for Community Mental Health Centers" (NIMH Contract No. HSM–42–70–99 to the Tufts University School of Medicine, Boston, Massachusetts, January, 1972), p. 64.
6. Ibid., p. 66.
7. Towle, "Kern View," p. 100.
8. New, Holton, and Hessler, "Citizen Participation," pp. 67–68.
9. Ibid., p. 68.
10. Ibid., p. 72.
11. Ibid., p. 74.
12. Ibid., p. 73.
13. Telephone interview with Lawrence Yoder, April, 1972.
14. Towle, "Kern View," p. 108.
15. New, Holton, and Hessler, "Citizen Participation," p. 74.
16. Towle, "Kern View," p. 102.
17. Torrey and Taylor, "A Minuet of Mutual Deception," p. 6.
18. Quoted in Towle, "Kern View," p. 133.
19. Telephone interview with Dr. David A. Grabski, April, 1972.
20. Quoted in Towle, "Kern View," p. 139.

21. Ibid., p. 115.
22. Telephone interview with Lawrence Yoder, April, 1972.
23. Telephone interview with Ernest Solano, April, 1972.
24. Torrey and Taylor, "A Minuet of Mutual Deception," p. 6.
25. Telephone interview with Lawrence Yoder, April, 1972.
26. Towle, "Kern View," p. 127.
27. Ibid., p. 131.
28. Quoted in Torrey and Taylor, "A Minuet of Mutual Deception," p. 10.
29. Quoted in New, Holton, and Hessler, "Citizen Participation," p. 70.

Chapter 10.

1. Parts of this case study have been taken from the Tufts University study funded by NIMH: Peter Kong-ming New, Wilfred E. Holton, and Richard M. Hessler, "Citizen Participation and Interagency Relations: Issues and Program Implications for Community Mental Health Centers" (NIMH Contract No. HSM–42–70–99 to the Tufts University School of Medicine, Boston, Massachusetts, January, 1972).
2. Ibid., p. 47.
3. Ibid., p. 51.
4. Interview with Mary King, April, 1972.
5. New, Holton, and Hessler, "Citizen Participation," p. 53.
6. Quoted in ibid., p. 56.
7. Quoted in ibid., p. 57.
8. Interview with Dr. Peter Bourne, April, 1972.
9. Interview with Mary King, April, 1972.
10. Quoted in New, Holton, and Hessler, "Citizen Participation," p. 58.
11. Interview with Dr. Peter Bourne, June, 1972.
12. Ibid.
13. Ibid.
14. Telephone interview with Dr. Bernard Holland, May, 1972.

Chapter 11.

1. See "The Health Workers Revolt: Lincoln Brigade II," in *The American Health Empire: Power, Profits and Politics,* A Report from the Health Policy Advisory Center (Health-PAC), prepared by Barbara and John Ehrenreich (New York: Random House, Vintage Books, 1970). See also Seymour R. Kaplan and Melvin Roman, *The Organization and Delivery of Mental Health Services in the Ghetto: The Lincoln Experience* (New York: Praeger, 1973).
2. Quoted in Kaplan and Roman, *Organization and Delivery of Mental Health Services,* preface.
3. Ibid., chapter 1.
4. Stanley Lehmann, "Selected Self-Help: A Study of Clients of a Community Social Psychiatry Service," *American Journal of Psychiatry,* Vol. 126 (April, 1970), p. 88.
5. Kaplan and Roman, *Organization and Delivery of Mental Health Services.*

6. Health-PAC, "Health Workers Revolt," p. 255.
7. Kaplan and Roman, *Organization and Delivery of Mental Health Services*, chapter 1.
8. Lehmann, "Selected Self-Help," p. 89.
9. Kaplan and Roman, *Organization and Delivery of Mental Health Services*.
10. Ibid., chapter 6.
11. Lehmann, "Selected Self-Help," p. 97.
12. Robert Shaw and Carol J. Eagle, "Programmed Failure: The Lincoln Hospital Story," *Community Mental Health Journal*, Vol. 7 (1971), p. 259.
13. Ibid.
14. Quoted in Health-PAC, "Health Workers Revolt," p. 257.
15. Kaplan and Roman, *Organization and Delivery of Mental Health Services*.
16. Telephone interview with Melvin Roman, March, 1973.
17. Quoted in Kaplan and Roman, *Organization and Delivery of Mental Health Services*.
18. Ibid., chapter 2.
19. Health-PAC, "Health Workers Revolt," p. 258.
20. Ibid., pp. 257–258.
21. NIMH Site Visit Report on Lincoln Hospital Mental Health Services, Jesse P. Dowling, HEW Associate Regional Health Director for Mental Health Programs, to J. Herbert Fill, Commissioner, New York City Community Mental Health Board, July 9, 1969.
22. Ibid.
23. Ibid.

Chapter 12.

1. Background information for parts of this case study has been provided by the Health Policy Advisory Council (Health-PAC), "Community Involvement in the North Oakland County Community Mental Health Center," Evaluation Report to NIMH (Contract Number HSM–42–70–106, Summer, 1972).
2. Ibid., pp. 2–3.
3. Interview with Ken Morris, April, 1972.
4. Telephone interview with Dr. Philip Smith, April, 1972.
5. Ibid.
6. Interview with Ken Morris, April, 1972.
7. Telephone interview with Dr. Donald Martin, April 1972.
8. Health-PAC, "Community Involvement," pp. 12–13.
9. Telephone interview with Dr. Donald Martin, April, 1972.
10. Telephone interview with Dr. Lino Romero, April, 1972.
11. Quoted in Health-PAC, "Community Involvement," p. 17.
12. Kenneth S. Watanabe, Mental Health Program Consultant, Annual Site Visit Report, Pontiac State Hospital Community Mental Health Center (May 28–29, 1969), p. 2.
13. Telephone interview with Dr. Theodore Satersmoen, April, 1972.
14. Telephone interview with Dr. Aubrey Crawford, April, 1972.
15. Ibid.

16. Health-PAC, "Community Involvement," pp. 24–25.
17. Ibid., pp. 19–20.
18. Admissions and readmissions figures supplied by W. L. Du Bose, Director of Patient Affairs, Pontiac State Hospital, April, 1972.
19. Telephone interview with Kenneth S. Watanabe, April, 1972.
20. Health-PAC, "Community Involvement," p. 6.
21. Telephone interview with Dr. Aubrey Crawford, April, 1972.
22. Interview with Ken Morris, April, 1972.
23. Melvin A. Glasser, "Psychiatric Disability: The UAW Response," in *To Work Is Human: Mental Health and the Business Community*, ed. Alan A. McLean (New York: Macmillan Company, 1967), p. 207.
24. Arthur Kornhauser, *Mental Health of the Industrial Worker: A Detroit Study* (New York: John Wiley & Sons, 1965), p. 261.
25. Robert P. Quinn, et al., *Survey of Working Conditions*, Report published by the U.S. Department of Labor, Employment Standards Administration (Washington, D.C.: Government Printing Office, 1971).
26. Quoted in *The New York Times*, April 2, 1972, p. 40.
27. Quoted in *Washington Post*, April 10, 1972, p. A 9.
28. Quoted in *Washington Post*, April 18, 1972, p. A 12.
29. Interview with Ken Morris, April, 1972.
30. Interview with John Taylor, April, 1972.
31. Interview with Bob White, April, 1972.
32. Interview with Donald Johnson, April, 1972.
33. "An Analysis of Suicide in Oakland County, Michigan 1966–1968," prepared by the Consultation and Education Service, Oakland County Community Mental Health Services Board, mimeographed (Pontiac, Michigan, 1969).
34. Interview with Bob White, April, 1972.
35. Glasser, "Psychiatric Disability," p. 206.

Chapter 13.

1. Anthony M. Graziano, "Clinical Innovation and the Mental Health Power Structure: A Social Case History" (Paper presented at the Meeting of the Eastern Psychological Association, Washington, D.C., April, 1968), p. 2.
2. William Ryan, ed., *Distress in the City: Essays on the Design and Administration of Urban Mental Health Services* (Cleveland: Press of Case Western Reserve University, 1969), p. 260.
3. Joan Doniger, "Talk for New York State Mental Health Association" (Buffalo, New York, April 14, 1964), p. 15.

INDEX

Abraham, A. S., 44
accountability, 115, 116, 117, 118
Action for Mental Health (Joint Commission Report), 16–17
aged mentally ill, 31*n*
Albee, George, on psychiatric hospitalization, 44
Albert Einstein College of Medicine, 175, 176
alcoholism, among auto workers, 193; in Washington, 150
AMA. *See* American Medical Association
Amarillo Community Mental Health Center, 33
American Medical Association (AMA), opposition of, to Community Mental Health Centers Act, 18, 20

American Psychiatric Association (APA), 8; on mental health coverage, 100
American Psychoanalytic Association, 60
APA. *See* American Psychiatric Association
"area," definition of, 72. *See also* catchment area
Area A Community Mental Health Center, Washington, D.C., 127*n*
Area B Community Mental Health Center, Washington, D.C., 113–114; appearance of, 135; catchment area of, 135–136; and the community, 140; deficiencies of, 138–144; foster homes in, 144; funding of, 136–138; and Howard University, 135, 136; limited

223